# SALALM in the Age of Multimedia: Technological Challenge and Social Change

Papers of the Forty-First Annual Meeting of the
SEMINAR ON THE ACQUISITION OF
LATIN AMERICAN LIBRARY MATERIALS

New York University
New York Public Library
NYU/Columbia Consortium for Latin American Studies
June 1-5, 1996

Peter A. Stern, Editor

SALALM Secretariat
Benson Latin American Collection
The General Libraries
The University of Texas at Austin

ISBN: 0–917617–58–4


Printed in the United States of America

# SALALM in the Age of Multimedia

SALALM Secretariat
Benson Latin American Collection
The General Libraries
The University of Texas at Austin

# Contents

## III. Media and Bibliography



## IV. Media and Conservation



## V. Media and Technical Services

## VI. Media and Education



## VI. Media in Latin America and the Caribbean

# Preface

The Forty-First Seminar on the Acquisition of Latin American Library Materials took place in a time of extraordinary excitement and uncertainty in the library world. The old, familiar "bi-polar" world of books and serials has given way to a complicated universe of multimedia resources, including the World Wide Web, compact disks, electronic databases (bibliographic and full-text), videos, graphic and text files, microforms, and so on. Along with the multiplication of media has come an accelerating trend toward the "virtual library," where resources are accessed from thousands of miles away and no longer need be physically present in the library building (along with equally remote library users!).

Along with swift technological change has come economic and social turmoil. The old "technology gap" between First and Third Worlds has narrowed to near-invisibility; Latin American societies have taken full advantage of new information technologies to leapfrog the old bottlenecks of time and space that separated the Northern from the Southern Hemispheres. But along with exciting technological developments have come doubt and confusion. Library budgets, which have long struggled to keep up with old-fashioned monograph and serial inflation, have been assaulted with new demands to accommodate emerging information technologies and formats. The economics of the new information age are far from certain; in an era of free-market economics, government "downsizing," and shrinking support for public education, the issue of free and equal access to information is very much in question.

Most of the essays in this volume are concerned with the new information environment which is coming into being as we near the next millennium. From the use of the Internet by the have-nots of society to the digitalization of deteriorating research materials, participants in SALALM XLI have struggled to conceptualize and frame answers to the complex questions which new technologies have engendered. The essays in this volume, however, do not capture the full range of activities from the sessions. José Soriano of the Red Científica Peruana described how his organization is bringing Internet access to ordinary people in Peru, who may not even own a telephone. There were panels on CDs and multimedia in Latin America, a demonstration by the Archivo General de Indias in Seville of developments in digitalization of the Archivo's extraordinary resources on colonial Latin America, a panel on ongoing digitalization projects of Caribbean newspapers and Brazilian documents, panels on effective bibliographic instruction in the age of multimedia, the "virtual library" in theory and practice, and many other topics.

What they all had in common was one overriding theme: that technology does not exist in a vacuum. It is always rooted in a social context, and its impact on our society will always bring unexpected benefits and problems. To close the "user-information gap," or more prosaically, to put a human face on the gadgetry, will increasingly be the challenge for librarians in the dawning age of multimedia.

Peter A. Stern

# Acknowledgments

I would first like to thank the Local Arrangements Committee, especially Angela Carreño and Denise Hibay, chair and assistant chair respectively, as well as Laurence Hallewell and Ramón Abad, who bore the brunt of the work in making sure that the forty-first meeting of SALALM in "the Big Apple" would be simulating, informative and, above all, fun. Mich Nelson, although only a library school student at the time, attended the planning meetings and pitched in tirelessly, as did Dror Faust, Judith Selakoff, Carmen Díaz, Laurie Yorr, Celia Cyrille, Bridget Wentworth, Ann Snoeyenbos, Lilia Vásquez, and a host of volunteers and student workers.

Our New York meeting was truly a consortial gathering, with New York University, Columbia University, and The New York Public Library working together to provide facilities for hosting the meeting. I am especially grateful to the Reed Foundation, Puvill Libros, and the Instituto Cervantes for their generous support for panels and receptions. Laura Gutiérrez-Witt, SALALM's Executive Secretary, was a constant source of advice and help on the difficulties of planning and executing a large and complex meeting.

Personally, I would like to take this opportunity to thank the people who helped proofread and format the papers, particularly Michael Foldy, Lori Mestre, Daphne Patai, and Stas Radosh, as well as Pat Graves and the students who helped retype especially recalcitrant papers. Of course, no SALALM papers would ever see the light of day without the hard work and patience of Barbara Valk, who has steered publications through many rocky reefs over the years and continues to demand (and get) the highest quality work from the Seminar's contributors.

# I. Media and Politics

# 1. The Internet, the Global Commercial Communication Revolution, and the Democratic Prospect

Robert W. McChesney

The current period is one of intense turmoil across the globe. On the one hand, capitalism reigns triumphant in a manner unknown for most of the century, if ever. This new era of capitalism is characterized by some as neoliberalism, referring to the acceptance of the market and profit maximization as the best regulators of human affairs. It is also characterized as globalization, referring to the manner by which the market economy is evolving from a national to a transnational foundation. There is no small amount of debate about the extent of globalization and its effects, but there is no question that many key firms and markets now operate globally or regionally rather than nationally. On the other hand, formal democracy now extends to a greater percentage of the human race than ever before. The key word, of course, is formal, because many of these democracies are quite corrupt and ineffectual. And even the purported guiding light of capitalist democracy, the United States, is a remarkably antidemocratic society, as its political process is typified by rampant depoliticization, minimal public awareness or debate, and open rule by powerful moneyed interests.

That capitalism and democracy are not synonymous should hardly be a surprise. Capitalism, even under the best of circumstances, is always a class society and democracy is most effective when there is limited class inequality. Democracy also works best when there exists a democratic spirit, a notion that an individual's welfare is directly and closely attached to the welfare of the community, however large community may be defined. Capitalism, with its incessant pressure to think only of number one regardless of the implications for the balance of the community, is hardly conducive to building a caring, democratic culture. In both of these areas capitalist societies have been made vastly more democratic and humane when labor movements have been able to organize significant economic and political power. The most striking examples in this regard are the social democracies of Scandinavia. But neoliberalism has earmarked organized labor a major foe to the successful operation of "free markets," and labor has been under severe political and economic attack for a generation. Accordingly, the caliber of democracy across much of the world has deteriorated as well.

But the present impasse of democracy is also magnified by an additional obstacle of considerable significance: the growing global commercial media system. All democratic theory is predicated upon the notion that the citizenry must have access to quality information and opinions in order to have meaningful self-government. The media have come to perform the lion's share of this function, and have done so with mixed results over the years. The results are increasingly less mixed. The current period is witnessing widespread corporate consolidation and concentration in both national and global markets, along with the marked decline in public service institutions and values. The global hyper-commercialized profit-driven media system is failing miserably at the task of providing the basis for an informed and participating citizenry. Related to this, in the global commercial media system the interests of labor and the working class are downplayed and marginalized, and at times repudiated. Conversely, the rule of business is accepted as the natural and democratic order of things.

Some argue that new digital communication networks, in particular the Internet, will override the antidemocratic implications of the global corporate media system. Although the Internet offers many exciting new possibilities, I believe its intrinsic democratic power has been exaggerated well beyond what can be realistically expected. The job of creating democratic media cannot be left to magical technologies; it requires political understanding and activity. In this paper I will explain why.

## The Emerging Global Commercial Media System

Until quite recently, when one considered media it was largely a national phenomenon. The most striking development in the 1990s has been the emergence of a global commercial media market, utilizing new technologies and the global trend toward deregulation. This global commercial media market is due to aggressive maneuvering by the dominant firms, new technologies that make global systems cost efficient, and neoliberal market policies encouraged by the World Bank, IMF, World Trade Organization, and the U.S. government to break down regulatory barriers to a global commercial media and telecommunication market. To the extent globalization is a viable concept, the global commercial media and telecommunication industries are at the forefront. These industries have rapidly reorganized along global lines. Indeed, their doing so is essential to the creation of a viable global market for goods and services.

A global oligopolistic market that covers the spectrum of media is now crystallizing with very high barriers to entry. National markets remain, and they are indispensable for understanding any particular national situation, but they are becoming secondary in importance. The global media market is dominated by a first tier of some ten enormous media conglomerates: Disney, Time Warner, Bertelsmann, Viacom, News Corporation, TCI, Sony, General Electric (owner of NBC), PolyGram (owned primarily by Philips, the Dutch electronics giant), and Seagram (owner of Universal). These firms have holdings in several media sectors and they operate in every corner of the world. Their annual sales in 1997 range from around $10 billion to $25 billion, placing most of them among the world's few hundred largest firms. Firms like Disney and Time Warner have seen their non–U.S. revenues climb from around 15 percent in 1990 to 30 percent in 1996. Early in the next decade both firms expect to earn a majority of their income outside of the United States. There is a second tier of another 40 or so media firms that round out the global media system. Most of these firms are from Western Europe or North America, but a handful are from Asia and Latin America. They tend to have strong regional and niche markets and have annual sales ranging from $1 billion to $5 billion.

This newly emerging global media market is obliterating some aspects of the old notions of media imperialism or cultural imperialism. National identities are quite unclear. Three of the biggest U.S.–based firms are owned by Australia's News Corporation, Japan's Sony, and the Canadian Seagram. The leading commercial media firms in the balance of the world, like Brazil's Globo or Mexico's Televisa, are all lining up with the global giants, hoping to establish joint ventures and strategic alliances of one sort or another. The overall logic is less one of the U.S.A. versus other nations as much as it is corporate commercialism versus all other values, or, dare I say it, of capitalism versus democracy.

A global commercial media system is not entirely new. For much of this century the export markets for motion pictures, television programs, music recordings, and books have been dominated by Western, usually U.S–based, firms. But the infrastructure of national media systems—radio, television, newspapers, periodicals—tended to remain nationally owned and controlled. The main development of the 1990s has been the rapid rise of a global commercial television system dominated almost exclusively by the world's 50 largest media firms. There has been a corresponding decline in public service broadcasting, which only a decade ago dominated most points in Europe and many points elsewhere. In Sweden and Germany, for example, the large public broadcasters have seen their audiences cut in half in the 1990s, and these are among the strongest public broadcasting systems in the world. Almost everywhere the traditional subsidies for noncommercial and nonprofit media are being cut. Even the venerable British Broadcasting Corporation (BBC) has acknowledged that its survival as a public service institution in Britain depends upon its becoming a significant commercial media force globally. It recently signed major joint venture agreements with the British Flextech and the U.S. Discovery Communications, both of which are either owned outright or significantly by the U.S. TCI.

What stimulates much of the creation of a global media market is the growth in commercial advertising worldwide, especially by transnational firms.

Advertising tends to be conducted by large firms operating in oligopolistic markets. With the increasing globalization of the world economy, advertising has come to play a crucial role for the few hundred firms that dominate it. In 1995, for example, the eight largest advertisers spent nearly $25 billion of the $300 billion or so spent on advertising globally. The spending on advertising per capita is increasing at a rate well above GDP growth rates almost everywhere in the world. From this vantage point it becomes clear, also, how closely linked the U.S. and global media systems are to the market economy. Moreover, the global advertising agency market has undergone a wave of consolidation every bit as striking as that in the media industry. In the late 1990s three enormous firms—WPP Group, Omnicom Group, and Interpublic—dominate the industry along with another half dozen or so agencies based mostly in New York, but also in London, Chicago, Paris, and Tokyo.

Why exactly do firms like Disney, Bertelsmann, and Time Warner feel the need to get so large? It is when the effects of sheer size, conglomeration, and globalization are combined that a sense of the profit potential emerges. When Disney produces a film, for example, it can also guarantee the film showings on pay cable television and commercial network television, it can produce and sell soundtracks based on the film, it can create spin-off television series, it can produce related amusement park rides, CD-ROMs, books, comics, and merchandise to be sold in Disney retail stores. Moreover, Disney can promote the film and related material incessantly across all its media properties. In this climate, even films that do poorly at the box office can become profitable. Disney's *The Hunchback of Notre Dame* (1996) generated a disappointing $200 million at the global box office. However, according to *Adweek* magazine, it is expected to generate $500 million in profit (not just revenues), after the other revenue streams are taken into account. And films that are hits can become spectacularly successful. Disney's *The Lion King* (1994) earned over $600 million at the global box office, yet generated over $1 billion in profit for Disney. Moreover, media conglomerates can and do use the full force of their various media holdings to promote their other holdings. They do so incessantly. In sum, the profit whole for the vertically integrated firm can be significantly greater than the profit potential of the individual parts in isolation. Firms without this cross-selling and cross-promotional potential are simply incapable of competing in the global marketplace.

In establishing new ventures, media firms are likely to employ joint ventures, whereby they link up—usually through shared ownership—with one or more other media firms on specific media projects. Joint ventures are attractive because they reduce the capital requirements and risk on individual firms and permit the firms to spread their resources more widely. The ten largest global media firms have, on average, joint ventures with six of the other nine giants.

They each also have even more ventures with smaller media firms. Beyond joint ventures, there is also overlapping direct ownership of these firms. Seagram, owner of Universal, for example, owns 15 percent of Time Warner and has other media equity holdings. TCI is a major shareholder in Time Warner and has holdings in numerous other media firms.

Even without joint ventures and cross ownership, competition in oligopolistic media markets is hardly "competitive" in the economic sense of the term. Reigning oligopolistic markets are dominated by a handful of firms that compete—often quite ferociously within the oligopolistic framework—on a non-price basis and are protected by severe barriers to entry. The "synergies" of recent mergers rest on and enhance monopoly power. No start-up studio, for example, has successfully joined the Hollywood oligopoly in 60 years. Rupert Murdoch of News Corporation poses the rational issue for an oligopolistic firm when pondering how to proceed in the media market: "We can join forces now, or we can kill each other and then join forces."

When one lays the map of joint ventures over the global media marketplace, even the traditional levels of competition associated with oligopolistic markets may be exaggerated. "Nobody can really afford to get mad with their competitors," says TCI chairman John Malone, "because they are partners in one area and competitors in another." The *Wall Street Journal* observes that media "competitors wind up switching between the roles of adversaries, prized customers and key partners." In this sense the U.S and global media and communication market exhibits tendencies not only of an oligopoly, but of a cartel or at least a "gentleman's club."

The global corporate media produce some excellent fare, and much that is good, especially in the production of entertainment material in commercially lucrative genres. But in view of the extraordinary resources the corporate media command, the quality is woeful. In the final analysis, this is a thoroughly commercial system with severe limitations for our politics and culture. As George Gerbner puts it, the media giants "have nothing to tell, but plenty to sell." The corporate media are carpet-bombing people with advertising and commercialism, whether they like it or not. Moreover, this is a market-driven system, one based upon one-dollar, one-vote rather than one-person, one-vote. In nations like Brazil or India, this means that a majority of the population will barely be franchised "citizens" in the new global media system.

Yet this will not be a global market where everyone in the world consumes identical media products; it will be more sophisticated than that. Disney, for example, has all of its characters assume local identities and speak local languages. As one executive put it, in an ironic twist on the environmentalist slogan, "the Disney strategy is to 'think global, act local'." But if the media products are differentiated by region, they nevertheless will be linked to global corporate concerns and determined by profitability. In short, the present course is one where much of the world's entertainment and journalism will be provided by a handful of enormous firms, each with distinct, invariably pro-profit and pro-global market, political positions on the central social issues of our times. Even allowing for the presence of the occasional dissenting voice, the implications for political democracy, by any rudimentary standard, are troubling.

## The Internet and the Digital Revolution

The rise of a global commercial media system is only one striking communication trend of the 1990s. The other is the rise of digital computer networks in general, and the Internet in particular. The logic of digital communication is that the traditional distinctions between telephony and all types of media are disappearing. Eventually, these industries will "converge," meaning firms active in one of them will by definition be capable of competing in the others. The present example of convergence is how cable and telephone companies can now offer each other's services. The Internet has opened up very important space for progressive and democratic communication, especially for activists hamstrung by traditional commercial media. This alone has made the Internet an extremely positive development. Some have argued that the Internet will eventually break up the vise-like grip of the global media monopoly and provide the basis for a golden age of free, uncensored, democratic communication. Yet whether one can extrapolate from activist use of the Internet to seeing the Internet become the democratic medium for society writ large is another matter. The notion that the Internet will permit humanity to leapfrog over capitalism and corporate communication is in sharp contrast to the present rapid commercialization of the Internet.

Moreover, it will be many years before the Internet can possibly stake a claim to replace television as the dominant medium in the United States, and much longer elsewhere. This is due to bandwidth limitations, the cost of computers and access, and numerous, often complex, technical problems, all of which will keep Internet usage restricted. Rupert Murdoch, whose News Corporation has been perhaps the most aggressive of the media giants to explore the possibilities of cyberspace, states that establishing an information highway "is going to take longer than people think." He projects that it will take until at least 2010 or 2015 for a broadband network to reach fruition in the United States and Western Europe, and until the middle of the twenty-first century for it to begin to dominate elsewhere. Even Bill Gates, whose Microsoft is spending $400 million annually to become an Internet content provider, acknowledges that the Internet as mass medium "is going to come very slowly." This is the clear consensus across the media and communications industries, and it explains the enormous investments in terrestrial broadcasting and digital satellite broadcasting that would be highly dubious if the broadband information highway was imminent. As MCA president Frank Biondi put it in 1996, media firms "don't even think of the Internet as competition."

It is also unclear how firms will be able to make money by providing Internet content—and in a market-driven system this is the all-important question. Even the rosiest see U.S. Internet advertising spending at only $5 billion by 2000, representing only 2 or 3 percent of projected U.S. advertising spending that year. The media giants have all established websites and have the product and deep pockets to wait it out and establish themselves as the dominant players in cyberspace. They can also use their existing media to constantly promote their online ventures and their relationships with major advertisers to bring them aboard their Internet ventures. In short, if the Internet becomes a viable commercial medium, there is a good chance that many of the media giants will be among the firms capable of capitalizing upon it. The other "winners" will probably be firms like Microsoft that have the resources to seize a portion of the market.

While the media firms do not face an immediate or direct threat from the Internet, such is not the case for computer software makers and telecommunication firms. The Internet is changing the basic nature of both their businesses, and both industries are turning their attention to incorporating the Internet into the heart of their activities. The eventual mergers and alliances that emerge will have tremendous impact upon global media as media firms are brought into the digital communication empires. This is speculative; it is also possible that the Internet itself will eventually be supplanted by a more commercially oriented digital communication network.

Owing to the privatization and commercialization that is the cornerstone of the global market economy, we are in the midst of a sweeping reconstruction of global telecommunication from the system of nonprofit national monopolies that dominated only 15 years ago. The process was formalized in 1997 when the World Trade Organization generated a landmark agreement for telecommunication deregulation signed by 68 firms (accounting for 90 percent of the global telecommunications market). It will open all markets to foreign competition and permit foreign ownership. In the late 1990s the world's largest telecommunication firms have raced to put together global alliances.

When British Telecommunication purchased MCI for some $20 billion in November 1996 to form Concert, it signaled that alliances may turn into formal mergers. AT&T has allied with Singapore Telecom and four major European national firms to form Uniworld or World Partners; Sprint, Deutsche Telekom, and France Telecom have formed Global One. The *Financial Times* predicts the endpoint may be "a handful of giants, straddling the world market." MCI president Gerald H. Taylor concluded in 1996 that "There's probably going to be only four to six global gangs emerge over the next five years as all this sorts out." Each of these global alliances strives to offer "one-stop shopping" of telephone, cellular, paging, and Internet access services to the lucrative global business market.

By the logic of the market and convergence, we should expect that the global media oligopoly will gradually evolve into a far broader global communication oligopoly over the next one or two decades. BT-MCI already owns 13.5 percent of News Corporation and U.S. West has a large stake in Time Warner. The media giants will link with the handful of telecommunication "global gangs," and they all will strike deals with the leading computer firms. As one writer puts it, the goal of all the "info-communication" firms is "to ensure they are among what will end up being a handful of communication monoliths controlling both product and distribution networks in the future. . . . The basic aim of future M&A [mergers and acquisitions] is to control the transmission of three basic telecommunication products—voice, data and video." In short, the Internet and digital communication networks will not undermine the development of a global communication oligopoly; rather, they will be an integral aspect of it. As a market-driven system, it will be built to satisfy the needs of businesses and affluent consumers. This is where the easiest profits are to be found.

Indeed, left to the market, the Internet will likely increase inequality between the advanced nations (and especially the United States) and the balance of the world. In 1996 only 4 percent of Internet usage was in the developing world, whereas nearly 75 percent of web users were in the United States. That discrepancy will probably lessen, but there is little reason to believe it will not remain a significant problem. On the one hand, English is, in effect, the official web language, thereby playing into the hands of U.S. firms and users. On the other hand, the Internet is being marketed in the developing world—as in the United States—as first and foremost a tool for business and the affluent. In this sense the Internet will probably increase inequality within nations as well as between them. Along these lines, when a Peruvian cooperative attempted to bring Internet access to a peasant community, the recently privatized Peruvian telecommunication service refused to provide the necessary equipment. It had plans to provide its own commercial Internet access service.

Long ago—back in the Internet's ancient history, like 1994 and 1995—some Internet enthusiasts were so captivated by the technology's powers that they regarded "cyberspace" as the end of corporate for-profit communication, because there people would be able to bypass the corporate sector and communicate globally with each other directly. That was then. Perhaps the most striking change in the late 1990s is how quickly the euphoria of those who saw the Internet as providing a qualitatively different and egalitarian type of journalism, politics, media, and culture has faded. The indications are that the substantive content of this commercial media in the Internet, or any subsequent digital communication system, will look much like what currently exists. Indeed, advertisers and commercialism arguably have more influence over Internet content than anywhere else. Advertisers and media firms both aspire to make the Internet look more and more like commercial television, as that is a proven winner commercially. In December 1996 Microsoft reconfigured its huge online Microsoft Network to resemble a television format. AT&T's director of Internet services says the Internet may become the ultimate advertising-driven medium: "If it's done well, you won't feel there's any tension between the consumerism and the entertainment." Frank Beacham, who in 1995 was enthused about the Internet as a public sphere outside corporate or governmental control, lamented one year later that the Internet was shifting "from being a participatory medium that serves the interests of the public to being a broadcast medium where corporations deliver consumer-oriented information. Interactivity would be reduced to little more than sales transactions and email."

# 2. Internetworking as a Tool for Advocacy and Research: The Case of Chiapas News, 1994-1996

Molly Molloy

The Internet provides a vehicle for human rights and development groups working directly with rural people in Chiapas and other areas of Mexico and Latin America to communicate with scholars and activists elsewhere in the world who need information from the field in order to act as informed advocates. Information can travel via computer networks directly to those most interested in the events. Eyewitness accounts of military actions in Chiapas in January 1994 and again in February 1995 reached the Internet community before wire service stories reached the news media. Even as the Mexican military barred journalists from the conflict zones, communiqués from Sub-Comandante Marcos, the leader of the Ejército Zapatista de Liberación Nacional (EZLN), were being read by subscribers to Peacenet conferences, Internet electronic mail lists, and Usenet newsgroups. Since February 1995, numerous Internet sites have been developed to provide coverage of events and archives of information.

This paper discusses the sociopolitical significance of Internet communications in relation to the conflict in Chiapas, as well as details of the process of providing archives of information for researchers.

> What governments should really fear is a communications expert.
> —Sub-Comandante Marcos
> Reported by *Newsweek* (Summer 1994)

## Current Awareness—Activism—"La guerra de los medios"

From the beginning of the Chiapas conflict in January 1994, the media (newspapers, television, and the Internet) played an important role, a role recognized and exploited by both the Mexican government and the rebels. National and international media provided intensive coverage of the earliest days of the conflict.[1] The Mexico City newspaper *La Jornada* provided and continues to provide the most detailed and distinguished coverage of the events in Chiapas. In contrast, Televisa the state-controlled and most powerful media entity in Mexico, has been criticized for giving only the official government point of view.[2]

As they entered Chiapas to confront the EZLN, the Mexican army barred both national and foreign journalists from the conflict areas. As early as January 1, 1994, however, scholars, activists, and some foreign tourists began to get the news out to friends in other parts of Mexico and the world using phones, fax machines, and electronic mail, providing rumors as well as factual observations of what was going on, at least in the cities of Chiapas. The government media crackdown had little effect on this networked approach to covering the events. The Zapatistas appropriated new media with enthusiasm and despite their military defeat (the fighting lasted only about 12 days) they have been able to "establish and maintain political connections throughout the world" and have continued their struggle through "words, images, imagination, and organization."[3]

Many people in Mexico, after reading the initial EZLN declaration of war (published in full in *La Jornada*), felt sympathy for the causes of the uprising and began to disseminate information about the EZLN and the uprising via computer networks. The most important early sources for this information were soc.culture.mexican andmisc.activism.progressive (Usenetnewsgroups), reg.mexico (Peacenet conference), activ-L (Internet email2listserv), and others. [4]

As the year wore on and the armed conflict subsided, the major news media also retreated to focus on other shocking events in Mexico, most notably the assassination of the PRI presidential candidate, Luis Donaldo Colosio, in April 1994. While traditional media lost interest in events in Chiapas, those sympathetic to the situation of indigenous campesinos there and in other Mexican regions continued to read, disseminate, discuss, and organize around the ideas expressed in the Zapatista communiqués authored by Sub-Comandante Marcos. Published in *La Jornada*, *Proceso,* and other printed sources, these communiqués often appeared several times per week and were widely circulated on the Internet.[5]

The Mexican government incursion into EZLN-held territory in Chiapas on February 9, 1995, sparked a new wave of interest and a flood of information on the Internet. According to reports in the mainstream press (*Newsweek*, *Washington Post,* and several wire services), protests from activists around the world who were concerned about the Chiapas events streamed into President Zedillo's office via fax. The Mexican government was portrayed as the aggressor and took a "public relations beating."

> . . . two weeks ago Mexican government troops lunged into the rain forests of Chiapas in renewed pursuit of the Zapatista rebels. When the federal soldiers reached an insurgent stronghold at Guadalupe Tepayac, the guerrillas melted into the jungle . . . taking with them their most valuable

> equipment—fax machines and laptop computers. In retreat, the Zapatistas faxed out a communiqué claiming that the army was "killing children, beating and raping women...and bombing us."

Soon the government was taking another public relations beating. It stopped the offensive and allowed reporters into the area. They found no sign of atrocities or bombing. But the government attack had been thwarted, and the rebels were free to fight on, with words as their best weapons.[6]

The media began to take an interest not only in the events in Chiapas, but also in the Internet coverage of the events. Those who actively circulated Chiapas information on the Internet earned a new label. In the words of Tod Robberson, *Washington Post* Foreign Service in Mexico City: "Within hours (of Zedillo's February 9 speech and army offensive) 'cyber-peaceniks' (emphasis not in original) and human rights activists here and elsewhere in Mexico had distributed the president's words verbatim via the Internet—along with a call for 'urgent action' to press Zedillo into reversing course."[7]

Robberson and others pointed to inaccuracies and exaggerations of government atrocities in some of the messages, calling into question the credibility of eyewitness and (usually) openly pro-EZLN accounts. In fact, many mainstream media stories discounted much of the Internet information as EZLN propaganda, implying that nongovernmental organizations (NGOs) in Mexico and Internet activists elsewhere were in a conscious alliance—even a conspiracy—to mislead the public and throw Mexico into chaos. [8]

One widely discussed incident on the Mexico news lists was a note that originated at the University of South Carolina reporting that San Cristóbal de las Casas had been surrounded by army troops and that casualties were flooding the hospitals. The posting originated on or around January 1, 1994, and was an attempt to gather more information after the poster received a distressing phone call from San Cristóbal. The details of the story were soon discounted and replaced with a flood of journalistic accounts of the actual events in Chiapas. Unfortunately, the original posting kept being re-posted months after the original request for information had been met.[9] After this incident (and some others reporting chemical weapons being used in Chiapas),[10] some Chiapas-L list participants, notably members of the Applied Anthropology Mexican Rural Development network (MRD), many of whom have worked in Chiapas, insisted on the accuracy and "verifiability" of information posted to the Internet and urged participants to seek verification before re-posting information from other sources. [11]

In fact, the volume and speed of Internet communications has actually contributed more to the verification of allegations than to the propagation of false information. One of the most interesting events revolved around the assertion that Wall Street had urged the Mexican government to take military action to "eliminate" the Zapatistas in order to assure intervention by the United States in the financial crisis that began in December 1994 with the peso devaluation. While this appeared at first to be an unsubstantiated claim by the National Committee for Democracy in Mexico (NCDM), the official EZLN representative in the United States, 12 subsequent questions on the Internet about the Wall Street-military connections in Mexico ferretted out an article by Ken Silverstein and Alex Cockburn in the newsletter *Counterpunch*. According to Harry Cleaver, professor of economics at University of Texas, Silverstein called to tell him about the internal Chase Manhattan report by Riordan Roett, professor in Latin American studies at the School of Advanced International Studies at Johns Hopkins University and consultant to Chase, which called for the "elimination" of the Zapatistas.[13]

A Chase employee had leaked the memo, titled "Mexico Political Update: Chase Manhattan Emerging Markets Group Memo, January 13, 1995," to Silverstein and Cockburn. Cleaver received a fax of the memo and the *Counterpunch* article and then retyped the information into a file that he uploaded to Chiapas-L. From that point, this version of the information began to explode into cyberspace, reaching many more readers than the relatively small circulation newsletter *Counterpunch*. Because of public outrage which pointed to the timing of the memo and Zedillo's decision to go after the EZLN, Chase is reported in an Associated Press story as attempting to distance itself from the memo.[14] Calls for protests and petitions to remove Roett from his position at Johns Hopkins circulated widely on the Internet.

Media attention to Internet activism became a hot topic on the Chiapas/Mexico channels on the Internet during February and March 1995. Some participants felt that we were inflating our importance, that, in reality, we were just "bourgeois professors" passing information around in our spare time. Others defended the activist role and pointed to the media attention as an acknowledgment that the EZLN voice was being heard, in part, because of what was happening on the Internet. Others took an even stronger stand, asserting that Internet activism had had a serious impact on the course of events and that intelligence services in Mexico and the United States were actively monitoring the activities.[15]

## "Netwar"—Estilo zapatista

Some information activists were contacted by local and national media to comment upon the situation. A RAND Corporation analyst, David Ronfeldt, who studies the information revolution and its effects on the present and future of military organization and strategy, introduced the concepts of "netwar" and "cyberwar" in a 1993 RAND report. Cyberwar is any kind of knowledge-related conflict and does not necessarily rely upon modern technology for its success. Netwar refers to societal struggles most often associated with low-intensity conflict by non-state actors: social activists, terrorists, or drug cartels. It is important to note that Ronfeldt considers social activists together with international terrorists, guerrilla insurgents, drug-smuggling cartels, low-intensity conflict that takes advantage of both the network structure and network communications.

> Most adversaries that the United States and its allies face in the realm of low-intensity conflict, such as international terrorists, guerrilla insurgents, drug smuggling cartels, ethnic factions, as well as racial and tribal gangs, are all organized like networks. . . . Perhaps a reason that the military (and police) institutions have difficulty engaging in low-intensity conflicts is because they are not meant to be fought by institutions. The lesson: institutions can be defeated by networks, and it may take networks to counter networks. The future may belong to whoever masters the network form.[16]

In a March 1995 interview by Pacific News Service reporter Joel Simon, Ronfeldt describes the current Mexican crisis as "social netwar" and warns that the astute use of technology by the EZLN rebels and their civic allies in Mexico and abroad may render the country "ungovernable." It is helpful to cite some examples of the EZLN's netwarfare, according to Rondfeldt. In August 1994, the National Democratic Convention brought together hundreds of diverse groups in the rebels' jungle stronghold to fashion a decentralized opposition. EZLN supporters around the world followed developments by reading Zapatista communiqués on the Internet. International NGOs operating in Mexico provide a "multiplier effect" for netwarriors: electronic communication allows Mexican groups to stay in touch with U.S. and Canadian organizations that share their goals and can coordinate an international response in the event of a government crackdown. Precisely because of their decentralization, the netwarriors do not have the ability to take national power, and their lack of any central political authority makes them less vulnerable to co-optation or repression. In February 1995 thousands marched in Mexico City to protest Zedillo's arrest warrant for Sub-Comandante Marcos, chanting: "Todos somos Marcos." "The country that produced the prototype social revolution of the 20th century may now be giving rise to the prototype social netwar of the 21st century." [17]

The group introspection, criticism, and praise that circulated in the first months of 1995 on the Internet resolves little but poses some interesting questions. How much effect do net-activists really have on the events in Chiapas? Can we hope to improve the situation for the indigenous communities in Chiapas by spreading their stories and exposing the government's action against them? Are we in danger of being co-opted by government security entities on the lookout for "netwarriors"? Can we actually endanger the workers in nongovernmental organizations, churches, and human rights organizations on the ground in Chiapas by overreacting to the government's actions, by spreading false accounts of government atrocities?

I do not have answers to many of these questions. In general it seems that the openness, the quantity, and the quality of discourse on the Internet concerning

Chiapas has helped the situation somewhat. The government did halt its offensive in March 1995 and called for new negotiations. Negotiations continued without much progress during 1995–1996, and the coverage of government and rebel actions continued on the Internet. The Zapatistas called for an international referendum on many of their demands during late 1995 and collected votes via the Internet. In April 1996, the "Encuentro Continental Americano por la Humanidad y contra el Neoliberalismo" held in La Realidad, Chiapas, brought together progressive NGO representatives from all over the Americas. Dialogue continues in the pages of Mexican newspapers between government spokesmen and the rebels. And some reporters have used the Internet to obtain leads on what is actually happening in the conflict zones. Journalists have used the Internet to contact scholars with a broad range and depth of knowledge about Chiapas and some of this knowledge may find its way into the mainstream media.[18] In a speech to a group of international businessmen at Mexico's World Trade Center on April 25, 1995, José Angel Gurría , head of the Secretaría de Relaciones Exteriores, acknowledged the role of words and computer networks in the Chiapas conflict. He stated that since the earliest days of January 1994, not one shot has been fired in Chiapas and that the war had been "a war of ink, of written words, and of the Internet."[19]

As far as being infiltrated or co-opted, I believe that the very openness of the Internet discourages its usefulness to the intelligence services. It is unlikely that anyone familiar with the Internet would post sensitive or damaging information about the activities of the EZLN or its many supporters in Mexico. However, there have been some reports of electronic mail in Mexico being confiscated or used as a pretext for government harassment. In late February 1995, Mexican legislator Carlota Botey declared that her electronic mail had been violated both from within Mexico and from the United States.[20] The Mexico City office of Equipo Pueblo has been broken into and its director, Carlos Heredia, reports being harassed because of the group's efforts to get Zapatista communiqués out onto the Internet.[21]

## Is Marcos Really on the Net?

The general assumption is that Marcos's elegant, though somewhat wordy, communiqués reach the Internet via a combination of high and low technologies especially suited to the situation—an example of a network being able to make good use of accessible technologies. Under an arrest warrant since February 9, 1995, Marcos spends most of his time in hiding in the Lacandon jungle. His communiqués are usually delivered to Mexican newspapers by hand and are neatly typed, apparently on a word processor. It is thought that the statements are composed on a laptop computer powered by a car battery. Messengers also deliver the documents to various church and development organizations located in Chiapas where they are sent via fax to Mexico City newspapers and to other outlets which then upload them to the Internet.

There is some speculation that Marcos may be able to transmit his messages directly to the Internet using a cellular telephone, a modem, and a satellite connection to the Internet, but I have no verification that this is true. I will add my own speculation, based on "gossip" from several sources somewhat familiar with this communications technology, but much less familiar with the on-the-ground situation in Chiapas. Here is the story—and this is only a story: The Associated Press (AP) and United Press International (UPI) are assigned an IP number (Internet address) to use in press transmissions from remote locations around the world. A reporter can uplink directly to a satellite with a small transmission disk like those used on press vans. The IP number assigned for use within a specified region allows the reporter to connect to the Internet through a satellite (the time is paid for by AP or UPI); the reporter can then send and receive text, images, sound, or video. If someone knew the IP number and had the transmission disk (apparently this technology is not very expensive) then that person could use the satellite (when it was not being used by AP or UPI) to "dump" information to the Internet. The person could also use the connection to Telnet to any machine on the Internet where he or she might have an account and receive messages or use other Internet services.[22]

Netwar, however, is not only high tech, but also relies on social networks. In some way, the direct connection to the Internet becomes less important for Marcos and the EZLN because of the decentralized character of the netwar being fought. The social networks needed to transmit the communications by hand simultaneously within Chiapas and across the country in Mexico City—and from there to the world through the Internet—indicate a wider degree of popular participation than if Marcos were simply posting to the Internet directly from the jungle.

## Archiving the Information for Research: "Mass Quantities" of Elusive Information

In addition to the valuable current awareness service provided by the Internet, many individuals and groups are participating in an "archiving" effort to ensure that these primary materials on the peasant rebellion in Chiapas (and on the other momentous events of recent months in Mexico) are available to researchers now and in the future.

In January 1994 I began collecting and transmitting information packets about Chiapas and other Mexican news on the Internet. I first sent the messages to the Applied Anthropology (ANTHAP) Mexican Rural Development (MRD) Network and a large list of other recipients who contacted me and asked to be placed on my distribution list. Jim Dow at Oakland University archived the stories on the Applied Anthropology Network gopher. These initial stories were edited and indexed as well. The files are still accessible via gopher or FTP (file transfer protocol) from the Applied Anthropology Network, although the format is problematic.[23] Since the files are a comprehensive record of events during the early days of the Chiapas conflict and the Internet activism associated with it, it is important to preserve them and make them more easily accessible. I still have these files on my own personal computer and plan to edit them into a web document in the near future.[24]

In August 1994 (before Mexico's presidential election) I again began collecting the stories and logging them on our own gopher server at New Mexico State University (which came online at about the same time). I posted information to the MRD net and to the rest of my original mailing list, as well as to other lists such as LASNET and Chiapas-L, and explained how to get to the news via gopher or the World Wide Web and how to make links to the archive. The work is ongoing. These files are arranged in rough chronological order, but I do not have the time to carefully edit or index the information. I view these files as a large and growing primary source of information about this turbulent period in Mexican history. I hope that researchers will be able to download the files and use the information for future analysis. Since September 1995, I have not been regularly archiving the news; however, beginning in February 1996, I did begin an archive of the Mexico 2000 list, as well as the MEXPAZ newsletters produced by Equipo Pueblo in Mexico City.[25]

In addition, by having access to my own Internet server, I am able to include links to other important resources and archives, such as *La Jornada*, the Chiapas 95 gopher maintained by Harry Cleaver at the University of Texas, and to news services and archives at UNAM and other Mexican universities.

The appearance of the independent Mexican newspaper *La Jornada* on the World Wide Web (one of the first Mexican newspapers to appear online) coincided almost perfectly with the outbreak of hostilities in early February 1995. This source provides same-day access to full-text articles and graphics of the newspaper and can be accessed by anyone with an Internet account and a web browser. I wrote to Justin Paulson at the email address listed for technical information on the *La Jornada* homepage and asked how this service came about. He responded:

> I was asked to collaborate with the newspaper on the project after some of their staff were impressed by the EZLN page that I maintain on the Web. Setting up the site was pretty easy—I just put it in my home directory on my account and changed the permissions to make it world-readable. Then with a little advertisement in the right places on the Internet, bingo—there's 8000 connections a week. I must get up early every morning to put the day's paper online, and I have to remove the older issues from time to time,

> but apart from that most of the maintenance involved is actually answering email. The appropriate parts of the paper are translated to HTML in the early morning via some software that a friend of mine at *La Jornada* wrote, and then the paper is sent to me in the form of a .tar.gz.uu bundle.[26]

As a librarian I find this account fascinating and also a bit troubling. While this service allows researchers an unprecedented, timely source for Mexico news (the paper subscription to *La Jornada* usually arrives about one week late to U.S. libraries), nothing guarantees its continued existence. What happens if Justin graduates or decides to work on a new project? His efforts are strictly voluntary as he explains on his EZLN page [http://www.ezln.org/about.html]. The archiving efforts of Harry Cleaver at the University of Texas, by myself at New Mexico State University, and others as well, are voluntary and receive no support other than the cooperation (or toleration) on the part of the computer systems people who provide the disk space. Another important voluntary effort is the "Mexnews" group, an informal collective that seeks out news from various Internet sources and re-posts the information to email lists such as Chiapas-L, Mexico 2000, and others.[27]

Most of the valuable, ongoing databases eventually require some kind of financial support to be maintained, to upgrade hardware and software, and to pay people for their work. Quality information sources are never really free. In general, the Internet provides exciting opportunities for scholars and librarians interested in preserving and making accessible information that may not be available in the mainstream press and commercial databases. The growing commercialization of the Internet is a real challenge (perhaps a threat?) to some of the independent, non-lucrative efforts to disseminate and preserve information by and about marginalized peoples and ideas.

"Zapatistas on the Internet" had their 15 minutes of fame in the mainstream media in 1995,[28] but the real story keeps happening in Mexico. Progressive organizations involved in indigenous issues, human rights, women's rights, peace, labor, environmental, and other causes have rallied around the actions and words of the Zapatistas to call for real reform of the Mexican political system. The move toward democratic change in Mexico is being led not by the major political parties, but by grassroots groups that have taken advantage of an international computer network originally built to maintain command and control in case of nuclear war.[29] As librarians, scholars, and (dare I say?) activists, we should look for ways to continue archiving the record of these struggles for researchers of the future.

## NOTES

The Internet Uniform Resource Locators (URLs) cited here are correct as of the time of the final revision of this paper (May 1997), but because of the mercurial nature of the Internet, their permanence cannot be guaranteed.

1. Pedro Reygadas, Iván Gómezcesar, and Esther Kravzov, eds., *La Guerra de Año Nuevo: Crónicas de Chiapas y México 1994* (Mexico: Editorial Praxis, 1994), p. 160.

2. The editors of *La Guerra de Año Nuevo* provide a "diccionario oficial" which translates official Televisa terms such as "profesionales de la violencia" into their commonly understood meaning, "Comandancia del EZLN." Ibid., p. 161.

3. Harry Cleaver, "The Zapatistas and the Electronic Fabric of Struggle," November 1995. [http://www.eco.utexas.edu:80/Homepages/Faculty/Cleaver/zaps.html], no pagination.

4. Harry Cleaver provides a very complete chronicle of these efforts, as well as an interesting analysis of the "cyberspace" struggle of the Zapatistas in his draft paper, available on his homepage and the Chiapas95 gopher, "The Zapatistas and the Electronic Fabric of Struggle." [http://www.eco.utexas.edu:80/Homepages/Faculty/Cleaver/zaps.html]

5. The most complete archive of EZLN communiqués to date is that on the YABASTA! EZLN page maintained by Justin Paulson. As of May 21, 1996, there were 113 communiqués in this archive. The current EZLN website arranges the communiqués chronologically from the years 1994–1997 and provides English and German translations of many of them [http://www.ezln.org/communiques.html].

6. "When Words Are the Best Weapon," *Newsweek,* February 27, 1995, p. 36.

7. Tod Robberson, "Mexican Rebels Using a High-Tech Weapon: Internet Helps Rally Support," *Washington Post,* February 20, 1995, A Section, p. A01.

8. See the article quoted below by Joel Simon for the Pacific News Service, "Netwar Could Make Mexico Ungovernable" (March 13,1995), posted to the Internet email list Chiapas-L on March 20, 1995. Simon quotes RAND Corporation researcher David Ronfeldt who had written previously on the concepts of "netwar" and "cyberwar." Ronfeldt's ideas became a hot discussion topic on the Internet in the context of the Chiapas situation in February–March 1995.

9. A Canadian Broadcasting Company (CBC) radio program, "Now the Details," focused on this incident on April 16, 1995. A transcript of the program was posted to Chiapas-L on April 24–25, 1995, by a participant in Canada, Claudia Guajardo-Yeo. The program' s host, Mary Lou Findley, untangles the incident as an example of how urban legends originate and travel, with added speed and urgency provided by the Internet. The program includes a phone interview with Professor Chuck Goodwin at the University of South Carolina who sent the original message. He justifies his intent—to be sure that indigenous people in Chiapas would not be attacked without the outside world being aware of it. He was concerned about continued propagation of the message, but stood by his original intent, which was not to perpetrate a hoax (as implied by the interviewer) but simply to draw attention to the situation.

10. While there was no evidence of chemical weapons in Chiapas, stories published in *La Jornada* and postings on the Internet by observers who visited abandoned Zapatista villages reoccupied by the Mexican army reported that stored food supplies had been ransacked and contaminated with animal wastes and that some wells were poisoned by insecticides and other chemicals. Discussed in a series of Chiapas-L messages in mid-April 1995.

11. Chiapas-L archives from February–April of 1995 are a source for following these events [gopher://profmexis.sar.net:70/11/foros/chiapas-L/anios]. However, as of May 1997, only archives for the current year (1997) are available at this URL. The Chiapas 95 Archive maintained by Harry Cleaver at the University of Texas also contains a digest of materials posted to several

different lists and newsgroups and maintains the archive back to 1994 [gopher://mundo.eco.utexas.edu:70/11/mailing/chiapas95.archive].

Another extensive archive of early 1994 events is maintained on the Applied Anthropologist's (ANTHAP) FTP site [ftp://vela.acs.oakland.edu/pub/anthap/Chiapas_ News_Archive/].

12. The National Commission for Democracy in Mexico (NCDM), located in El Paso, Texas, was designated as the official EZLN representative in the United States in a letter dated July 1994 from Sub-Comandante Marcos to Cecilia Rodríguez, the head of the Commission. I have a fax copy of the letter, signed by Marcos, sent to me by Cecilia Rodríguez in January 1995. For more information on the NCDM and its activities, see the homepage at [http://www.igc.apc.org/ncdm].

13. Harry Cleaver provides an archive of articles related to the Chase story and its coverage in the press and on the Internet [gopher://mundo.eco.utexas.edu:70/1m/mailing/chiapas95.archive/chase].

14. "Chase Bank Denies Urging Elimination of Mexican Rebels," Donald M. Rothberg, AP Diplomatic Writer (February 13, 1995). A copy of this story is available at [gopher://mundo.eco.utexas.edu:70/0R39397–42857-/mailing/chiapas95.archive/chase].

15. See the Chiapas-L archives for February–March 1995 or excerpts from these archives at the Chiapas95 site [gopher://mundo.eco.utexas.edu:70/11/mailing/chiapas95.archive].

16. John Arquilla and David Ronfeldt, "CyberWar Is Coming!," *Comparative Strategy* 12:2 (1993), 141–165. The text of this RAND report is posted on the Internet at [http://gopher.well.sf.ca.us:70/0/Military/cyberwar]. See also an earlier article by David Ronfeldt which discusses the role of information technology in governments and governing, "Cyberocracy Is Coming," *The Information Society* 8 (1992), 243–296. In this article Ronfeldt comments on the use of computer networks by activists: "Some of the heaviest users of the new communications networks and technologies are progressive, center-left, and socialist activists, through entities like the Association for Progressive Communications. Cyberspace is going to be occupied by all kinds of people, with all kinds of ideologies and agendas, from almost all areas of society" (p. 271).

17. Joel Simon, "Netwar Could Make Mexico Ungovernable," Pacific News Service, March 13, 1995, posted to the Internet email list Chiapas-L on March 20, 1995.

18. Jason Wehling, in his article " 'Netwars' and 'Activists' Power on the Internet" (April 10, 1995), further analyzes Ronfeldt's position and discusses other world events in which activists have been harassed because of their work on the networks. Wehling also quotes from a Marcos 90 communiqué in which he expresses his thanks to the global solidarity network for its support for the EZLN [http://snyside.sunnyside.com/cpsr/nii/cyber-rights/archive/OpEd-Articles/Wehling-NetWars].

19. "La de Chiapas, guerra de tintas y de Internet: Gurría," *La Jornada*, April 26, 1995, from the web version [http://serpiente.dgsca.unam.mx/jornada/1995/abr95/950426/gurria.html].

20. "Deputy Carlota Botey Denounces Interference in Her Internet," posted to Chiapas-L, February 23, 1995.

21. Sara Silver, "Mexican Rebels Get Ride on Information Highway," AP Wire, *Albuquerque Journal*, February 16, 1995, p. A-11.

22. This information was given to me in an email message from a friend who shall remain anonymous. It was accompanied by citations to several technical articles with details on the feasibility of this technology.

23. URLs: [ftp://vela.acs.oakland.edu/pub/anthap/Chiapas_News_Archive/] [gopher://gopher.acs.oakland.edu:70/1ftp%3avela.acs.oakland.edu%40/pub/anthap/].

24. The chronology of these events parallels my own activity on the Internet. In January 1994, I knew nothing about maintaining a gopher and had not even seen the graphical and hypertext

capabilities of the web. In the intervening time, I have helped to build and maintain a gopher and I am now in the process of "de-commissioning" that server and transferring all files to the web. See [gopher://lib.nmsu.edu:70/11/.subjects/.border/.news/.netnews].

25. There are links to these archives and to many other sources mentioned here at [http://lib.nmsu.edu/subject/bord/mxarch.html].

26. Justin Paulson, private email message, March 1, 1995, quoted with permission. *La Jornada* is now available at UNAM in Mexico and at several mirror sites in the U.S. and Canada:
[http://serpiente.dgsca.unam.mx/jornada/index.html]
[http://www.sccs.swarthmore.edu/~justin/jornada]
[http://csgrs6k2.uwaterloo.ca/jornada/index.html].
Justin Paulson maintains the Ya Basta EZLN page which contains a very complete set of Zapatista communiqués and other useful documentation
[http://www.peak.org/~justin/ezln/communiques.html].

27. For more information about the Mexnews collective, contact the coordinator, José Briones at [brioneja@ttown.apci.com].

28. See, for example, Martin Langfield, "Mexican Rebels Take Case to Cyberspace," Reuters, December 14, 1995; Jesús Ramírez, "Oliver Stone Praises Mexico's Zapatista Rebels," Reuters World Service, March 26, 1996.

29. Harry Cleaver deals with the international political implications of Internet activism in great detail in his draft article "The Zapatistas and the Electronic Fabric of Struggle," [http://www.eco.utexas.edu:80/Homepages/Faculty/Cleaver/zaps.html]. Molly Molloy, *Chiapas News*, May 1996 (revision May 1997) mexnet97.doc 1; Molly Molloy, *Chiapas News*, May 30, 1996.

# 3. Native Americans and Information Technology: Connection and Community

Michele M. Reid
Susan Shaw

This paper discusses the Native American World Wide Web sites in South Dakota and elsewhere that are being used at the South Dakota State Library to provide reference and research assistance to state government and users throughout the state. The listing (see Appendix) is not intended to be comprehensive, but a beginning guide to finding the most popular and useful sites that in turn provide gateways to other, more specialized, material. Note that we concentrate on Siouan resources, since Sioux tribes are the prominent Native American groups in South Dakota, but have also included sites containing material on other Plains Indians or of a more general nature.

South Dakota is known as the home of the Great Sioux Nation, made up of a loose confederation, called the Oceti Sakowin or Seven Council Fires, of three Siouan-speaking peoples who have retained their own unique dialects: the Lakota (Tetons) in the western part of the state, the Nakota (Yanktonai) in the southeast corner, and the Dakota (Santee) in the northeast. The Lakota are perhaps the most easily recognized of the three groups—their bold military tactics against white encroachment into their territories gained them a reputation in the last century of being one of the fiercest warrior societies of the Plains. Red Cloud, Spotted Tail, Sitting Bull, and Crazy Horse are a few of the most famous Lakota leaders. Notable historical sites in the state include Wounded Knee, the Sitting Bull memorial, and the unfinished sculpture of Crazy Horse near Mt. Rushmore.

Today, South Dakota has nine reservations totaling five million acres (Pine Ridge, Rosebud, Cheyenne River, Standing Rock, Lower Brule, Crow Creek, Sisseton, Yankton, and Flandreau) and five tribal colleges (Sinte Gleska University, Oglala Lakota College, Oglala Sioux Community College, Cheyenne River Community College, and Sisseton-Wahpeton Community College). Oglala Lakota College and Sisseton-Wahpeton College Libraries are dial access members, while Sinte Gleska University Library recently became a full member, with catalogued holdings, of the South Dakota Library Network (SDLN), a statewide automated system that, since 1988, has provided access to the online catalogs of major libraries in the state, and, in recent years, access to periodical and local newspaper indexes and to library collections in North Dakota and Minnesota. Last year SDLN added Telnet access, and this summer, through a Title III Higher Education Grant, will provide full-text of academic and business journal and general periodical and newspaper articles through Information Access Corporation.[1]

The rural nature of South Dakota has led to an early emphasis on long-distance communication and distance learning, with the state recently completing a conversion of its analog backbone to all fiber optic lines to support increasing Internet traffic and an expanding system of teleconferencing sites used for online demonstrations, conference feeds, and remote college and university classes. Currently, in addition to eighteen two-way video and audio sites, the state's Rural Telecommunications Network provides one-way satellite communications capability to over forty other smaller sites, all of which can also be connected with any other national or worldwide video network. Over the last two years, the state's interactive system has been used to deliver over 140 college-level courses to over 1,900 students.[2]

Oglala Lakota College and Sinte Gleska University Libraries are participants in the ALA/Microsoft Libraries Online! project grant awarded to the South Dakota State Library to enhance Internet access to rural areas and disadvantaged communities, including Native American reservations. The project will expand the state's server network and upgrade computer equipment to allow these tribal libraries full World Wide Web connectivity for the first time. It is hoped that all the tribal libraries will be active web users in the near future. Two tribal colleges, Sisseton-Wahpeton College and Sinte Gleska University, currently maintain an active presence on the web, with Sisseton-Wahpeton College also responsible for the Dakota Language homepage. Sinte Gleska's site is still under construction by the Computer Science faculty and is now using the IndianNet server, but will soon move to the university's own server. Oglala Lakota College is now in the process of developing its own site, which should be available soon as well.

The listing gives an idea of what is currently available on the World Wide Web relating to Native Americans in general and the Sioux in particular. Some sites offer scholarly material, such as Stanford, LeMoyne College, and other academic pages, but most information is tourist-related or of more popular interest. There is a need for more material from academic and research institutions, particularly in the upper plains states. For example, the South Dakota State Archives and the Center for Western Studies at Augustana College, Sioux Falls, both with fairly large manuscript collections, have yet to mount sites on the World Wide Web.

# APPENDIX

Selected Native American World Wide Web Sites
Compiled by Michele M. Reid

## I. South Dakota Sites

**American Indian Home Page**
http://www.state.sd.us/state/executive/tourism/indian.htm
Deals almost exclusively with Dakota/Lakota sites

**Dakota Language Home Page**
http://swcc.cc.sd.us/daklang3.htm
Part of the *24 Hours in Cyberspace* project; includes several interactive lessons

**Guide to the Great Sioux Nation**
http://www.state.sd.us/state/executive/tourism/sioux/sioux.htm
Maintained by the Department of Tourism; features powwows, art, points of interest; links to South Dakota tribal pages

**RapidNet**
http://www.rapidnet.com/
Commercial provider in western South Dakota with links to Native American pages

**Sinte Gleska University Home Page**
http://sinte.hills.net/
New page under development by the Computer Science Department and currently using the INDIANnet server; scheduled to move to the University's own server

**Sisseton-Wahpeton Sioux Tribe Home Page**
http://swcc.cc.sd.us/homepage.htm
Tribal information maintained by Sisseton-Wahpeton Community College

**South Dakota Arts Council**
http://www.state.sd.us/state/executive/deca/sdarts
Directory of regional arts festivals and powwows; information on native artists

**South Dakota Department of Education and Cultural Affairs**
http://www.state.sd.us/deca/
Links to South Dakota universities and colleges as well as K-12 statistics

**South Dakota State Library**
http://www.state.sd.us/state/executive/deca/st_lib/st_lib.htm
Features Telnet access to the South Dakota Library Network online catalog of the holdings of all major libraries in the state, including Sinte Gleska University

**State of South Dakota**
http://www.state.sd.us
Links to the state Department of Tourism and Office of Indian Affairs

## II. Dakota/Lakota Sites

**Lakota Information Home Page**
http://maple.lemoyne.edu/~bucko/lakota.html
Joint project of Martin Broken Leg at Augustana College (SD) and Raymond Bucko at Le Moyne College (NY); includes an extensive bibliography of scholarly works relating to Dakota and Lakota religion; links to electronic texts, legal documents, and treaties

**Yamada Language Center Lakota Home Page**
http://babel.uoregon.edu/yamada/guides/lakota.html
University of Oregon language guide site

## III. General

**Bill Henderson's Links to Aboriginal Resources**
http://www.bloorstreet.com/300block/aborl.htm
Canadian barrister's links to full-text treaties, native listservs, journals, and newsletters

**Circumpolar & Aboriginal North America Resources**
http://www.nunanet.com/~nic/WWWVL-ANA.html
A Virtual Library project, updated weekly, developed by the Canadian Nunavut Implementation Commission (NIC) in conjunction with the Australian National University (http://coombs.anu.edu.au/WWWVL-Aboriginal.html)

**Elenco delle Maggiori Risorse sui Nativi d'America Presenti sull'Internet**
http://www.studionet.it/lakota.htm
Italian site with links to University of Massachusetts and South Dakota sources as well as electronic texts

**Fourth World Documentation Project**
http://www.halcyon.com/FWDP/fwdp.html
Online electronic library from the Center for World Indigenous Studies

**Humboldt State University Native American Studies Page**
http://sorrel.humboldt.edu/~nasp/
Native American news, events, and announcements

**Index of Native American Resources on the Internet**
http://hanksville.phast.umass.edu/misc/NAresources.html
Excellent, extensive gateway to cultural, historical, educational, and governmental resources as well as museums, commercial sites, and electronic texts

**National Indian Policy Center**
http://www.gwu.edu/~nipc/
New site, under construction, at George Washington University; reservation maps, links to their gopher server

**Native American Net Server**
gopher://alpha1.csd.uwm.edu/11/UWM%20Information/
Native%20American%20Net%20Server
Older gopher server at the University of Wisconsin-Milwaukee containing book reviews, case law articles, and BBB information

**Native Americans and the Environment**
http://pantheon.cis.yale.edu/~lisamc/
Current issues, regional listings, bibliographies

**Native Cybertrade**
http://www.atiin.com/cybertrade/Resources.html
Lists links to businesses, nonprofit organizations, tribal and U.S. government agencies, K-12 schools and colleges

**Other Native American Information (Native Americans at Princeton)**
http://www.princeton.edu/~naap/links.html
Gophers, ftp servers, newsgroups, academic pages, native organizations at other schools and colleges

**Stanford's Native American Studies Home Page**
http://www-sul.stanford.edu/depts/ssrg/native/indian.html
Bibliographies of Stanford University's extensive holdings

**Tribal Voice**
http://www.tribal.com
Colorado site with graphics, list of resources, chat software

**Yahoo Native American Directory Listing**
http://www.yahoo.com/Society_and_Culture/Cultures/Native_American/
Latest web pages

## IV. Organizations and Government Agencies

**American Indian Higher Education Consortium (AIHEC)**
http://www.fdl.cc.mn.us/aihec/aihec.html
AIHEC and American Indian College Fund mission statements, description of *Tribal College Journal*, and a membership map

**Bureau of Indian Affairs**
http://info.er.usgs.gov/doi/bureau-indian-affairs.html
BIA press releases and general information

**Canadian Indian**
http://www.inac.gc.ca/pubs/indian/
Canadian government page that includes historical and cultural information on Plains Indians; a directory of Indian and related organizations

**CodeTalk**
http://www.codetalk.fed.us/
Federal agencies that operate Native American programs provide news and links to related sources

## V. Literature and Publishing

**Indigenous People's Literature**
http://www.indians.org/welker/natlit1.htm
Includes famous quotes, prayers, music, and poetry as well as a list of writers and speakers

**Native Book Centre**
http://www.9to5.com/9to5/NBC/index.html
Catalog of more than 1,100 titles relating to Native Americans

**Redhawk Publishing**
http://www.tiac.net/users/redhawk/
Native American publishing company specializing in traditional culture and religion, especially Lakota; includes links to Sioux sites

**University of South Dakota Press**
http://www.usd.edu/~usdpress/
Specializes in Native American and western history

## VI. Art and Cultural Sites

**National Museum of the American Indian**
http://www.si.edu/organiza/museums/amerind/
Includes current exhibit descriptions, hours, research opportunities

**Native American Art Resources on the Internet**
http://hoek.lib.uoknor.edu/slis/resources/native/NAart.html
List of galleries and museums

**Native American Resources at the Smithsonian**
http://www.si.edu/perspect/amind/
Links to appropriate Smithsonian museums and galleries

**Native Events Calendar**
http://www.dorsai.org/~smc/native/all.html
Events calendar for Canada and the United States, including arts festivals and powwows

**Powersource**
http://www.powersource.com/gallery/
Links to various cultural sites; listing of Native American artists

## VII. Electronic Mailing Lists and Networks

**Aboriginal Super Information Hwy.**
http://www.abinfohwy.ca/
Canadian information network

**INDIANnet**
http://indiannet.hills.net/
First national computer network owned and operated by Native Americans

**Michael Wilson's American Indian Web Page**
http://www.uwm.edu/~mwilson/
NativeLit-L and Native History-L archives

**Native American Information Resource Server Mailing Lists**
http://www/afn.org/~native/mlists.htm
Extensive list of discussion groups and listservs, including directions on how to subscribe to each; links to tribal homepages and other sites found at www.afn.org/~native

**NativeNet**
http://www.fdl.cc.mn.us/natnet/
Homepage of Native-L listserv; contains references to other websites; server located at Fond du Lac Tribal College in Minnesota

**NativeWeb**
http://web.maxwell.syr.edu/nativeweb
Gateway to worldwide resources concerning native peoples

## NOTES

1. *Factbook '95* (Brookings: South Dakota Library Network, 1996), p. 20.

2. *State and Local Strategies for Connecting Communities: A Snapshot of the Fifty States, Prerelease Draft* (Benton Foundation and Center for Policy Alternatives, March 1996), p. 98.

# 4. Providing Instruction on the Research Use of the Internet for Political Science and Human Rights Studies

Sarah Landeryou

This paper discusses the use of World Wide Web resources for research in political science and human rights. I would like to make the disclaimer, however, that by no means do I wish to exclude print resources and indexes. The paper merely focuses on the possibilities of using the web as a supplemental tool for research in these fields.

Web and other electronic sources are especially valuable for libraries without the budget, time, staff, or space to acquire publications from the many intergovernmental organizations and grassroots organizations devoted to international causes. The fact that many mainstream international and especially non-mainstream groups are placing their documents on the web allows students and researchers convenient access to electronic versions of the documents.

At the University of Denver we inform students about the availability of web resources through bibliographic instruction, in the form general sessions, sessions specific to a single resource, and subject-specific sessions. The latter is perhaps the most important; in this case, the librarian makes a presentation to the class, in the library, explaining the available resources to support research in a particular field. I have found that students are interested in the web and, in fact, expect a class in using library resources to have a web component. They realize that the web may be a tremendous resource, but seek guidance in using it effectively as tool for their research and writing.

Studies have shown that the academic community comprises a large segment of web users. Unfortunately, however, many abandon their searches quite unsatisfied—probably because of the vast amount of material available, and the potential to become sidetracked by the multitude of items of personal interest, as well as lack of indexing, cataloging, or control.

Thus the responsibility falls on librarians to try to make some sense of it all and to assist users in finding the information they seek. This often involves finding information not available in the library collection, as in the case of materials from intergovernmental organizations, grassroots groups, and advocacy groups which make their publications available on the web.

In providing one-on-one or group instruction, I provide the web address of sites that represent the best attempts to organize materials. These sites are good places to begin web searches because they are faster than using a search engine, such as Alta Vista. These sites facilitate browsing in a subject area because, by the nature of the site, a certain degree of selection has already taken place.

Finding or creating a good website of this kind for a specific subject is difficult and time consuming, however, and the responsibility for such a project falls on the subject specialist, whose time is most likely one of the scarcest resources in the library.

For the purpose of this discussion, I have selected sites that constitute good starting points for using the web in human rights and political science research. How did I evaluate the sites, and how do you teach others to do so? Keep in mind that evaluating and comparing websites is difficult because of the lack of standardization and coherence. In general, good websites of this kind have the following characteristics:

Includes a mission statement or statement of purpose from the creator or institution affiliated with the page

Is well organized and authoritative

Provides a framework for the organization of material on the web

Is comprehensive, but selective.

## Project Diana

A good example of a site that exhibits these qualities is Project Diana, a collaboration of Yale University, the University of Cincinnati, and the University of Minnesota. The project's goal is "to bring together full-text human rights documents to become the most comprehensive global resource on human rights available electronically."

The site is easily accessible and organized and is properly maintained. It provides access and links to treaties, conventions, charter documents, and proceedings of human rights groups, as well as legal briefs and secondary materials such as bibliographies. Among the organizations represented are the OAS, the United Nations, the European Court of Human Rights, the Inter-American Commission on Human Rights, and the U.S. State Department. Also included are links to organizations like Human Rights Watch, Amnesty International, and smaller groups like the Grandmothers of the Plaza de Mayo, Global Democracy Network, Derechos, the Freedom Forum, and Attorneys without Borders. All of these organizations are listed on one page, thus providing quick access to current information, full-text reports, press releases, official reports, and other documents. Materials from little-known organizations are also brought to the attention of researchers. While not all of the organizations represented on the site are activist or grassroots groups, many of the documents provided are important for activists themselves in understanding the issues involved in human rights.

## Political Science Resources/University of Keele

Political science is a broader topic than human rights, and it is therefore more difficult to locate the information one is looking for on the web. A website that assembles, in one place, a listing of resources in this field requires more links and maintenance. One that has handled the task very well is the University of Keele. The site includes an introduction, which defines its scope, a mission statement, and a guide to the content of the pages. It incorporates links to international organizations, official national, regional, and local government pages, elections data (quite nice when broken down by province!), and political parties, groups, and movements. This is a suitable place to begin because it facilitates browsing and increases the user's awareness of what is available. The content is international, serving to broaden the scope of any library collection.

But more important than each of these sites, individually, is our responsibility to integrate such resources into bibliographic instruction and collection development and show users how to find, evaluate, and use web resources. We need to treat such materials as items in the collection (on a par with maps, treaties, constitutions, etc.) by including them in new book lists and bibliographies, and by advertising their existence in newsletters and other communication with our users.

These are the challenges for librarians as we attempt to assist users in integrating the use of web documents in their research:

Explain the vulnerability of the web and that it is merely a supplement to other library resources

Take the time to find and identify resources

Work with students and researchers who may find it difficult to adapt to the research methods particular to the web

Work to maintain connections and an understanding of the web without the interference of commercial indexers or institutions so that the diversity is not sacrificed.

## APPENDIX

Useful Websites for Human Rights and
International Studies Research

**Project Diana: University of Cincinnati, Yale University, University of Minnesota**

http://www.law.uc.edu/Diana/
http://elsinore.cis.yale.edu/dianaweb/dyale.htm
http://www.umn.edu/humanrts/

A consortium devoted to bringing together research materials relevant to the study of human rights; includes treaties, conventions, declarations, and links to human rights organizations.

**Political Science Resources/University of Keele.**
http://www.keele.ac.uk/depts/po/psr.htm

Site editor Richard Kimber has created a simple presentation of sites relevant to political science, either in teaching or research with excellent international emphasis. The site includes links and documents related to official government sources, constitutions, treaties and declarations, election statistics and electoral systems, political parties, political theory and thought, area studies and international relations, collections of social and economic data, and journals and magazines.

**Foreign Government Resources on the Web/University of Michigan**
http://www.lib.umich.edu/libhome/Documents.center/foreign.html

This page incorporates extensive use of graphics to organize its links. The organization is similar to the University of Keele site, but is less comprehensive.

## REFERENCES


Balas, Janet. "The Internet and Reference Services." *Computers in Libraries* 15:6 (June 1995), 39–41.

Bane, Adele F., and William D. Milheim. "Internet Insights: How Academics Are Using the Internet." *Computers in Librarie*, 15:2 (February 1995), 32–36.

Basu, Geetali. "Using Internet for Reference: Myths vs. Realities." *Computers in Libraries* 15:2 (February 1995), 38–40.

Collins, Boyd. "Beyond Cruising: Reviewing." *Library Journal* 121 (February 1996), 122–124.

Doran, Kirk. "The Internot: Helping Library Patrons Understand What the Internet Is Not Yet." *Computers in Libraries* 15:6 (June 1995), 22.

Perry, Clifford. "Travelers on the Internet: A Survey of Internet Users." *Online* 19:2 (March/April 1995), 29–34.

Perry, Stephen. "Using the Internet for International Research." *American Studies International* 33:1 (April 1995), 86–98

Tillotson, Joy, Joan Cherry, and Marshall Clinton. "Internet Use through the University of Toronto Library: Demographics, Destinations and Users' Reactions." *Information Technology and Libraries* (September 1995), 190–198.

*Training Kit: Human Rights*. American Association of Law Libraries Research Instruction, 1995.

# II. Media and the Arts

# 5. Collective Memory of a Continent: The Theater of Latin America

Louis A. Rachow

The International Theatre Institute, chartered by Unesco in 1948, is a worldwide communications network serving the professional needs of theater practitioners and theatrical institutions. The United States Center (ITI/US) is one of 96 national centers established to promote and facilitate the international exchange of people, practices, and information in the performing arts. To make the resources of this network available to the American theater, ITI/US pays annual dues for this country's participation in the worldwide organization; serves on the executive committee on playwrights, new theater, dance, communications, music theater, training, cultural identity, and development; and, in addition, sponsors an American delegation to the biennial congress so that the voice of American theater can be heard. Using this communications network as a base, ITI/US has designed a program of services beneficial to American artists, producers, and managers. These include the Visitors Service, International Exchange Program, Consultation Service, and the Library and Information Service.

Recognizing a need for the systematic collection and dissemination of information on contemporary theater abroad, ITI/US established a permanent library focusing on international theater since World War II. The collection emphasizes the acquisition of materials that are not readily available in this country, but which flow steadily to the U.S. Center from the 96 national centers, other worldwide contacts, and a variety of international exchanges. Opened to the public by appointment in 1970, the theater of 146 countries on five continents is documented not only by books, periodicals, programs, and plays, but also by directories, newsletters, house organs, press releases, monographs, pamphlets, production schedules, yearbooks, brochures, reviews, and clippings. Although the ITI/US collection is used by universities, foundations, corporations, publishers, service organizations, and government agencies, its primary users are professional theater practitioners: the artists, managers, and producers of performing arts companies engaged in some form of international work.

In 1987, the Americas Society (formerly the Center for Inter-American Relations) donated the Theatre of Latin America (TOLA) Collection to the ITI/US library—2,650 items documenting modern theater in twenty Latin American countries and the Caribbean. This material, acquired and collected by Joanne Pottlitzer, founder and artistic director of the New York–based Theatre of Latin

America, Inc. from 1966 to 1980, was continuously augmented and housed at the America Society's headquarters until its transfer to ITI/US. Although the collection included a few items from Spain and Portugal, its main focus was on the theater of Argentina, Bolivia, Brazil, Chile, Colombia, Costa Rica, Cuba, Dominican Republic, Ecuador, El Salvador, Guatemala, Jamaica, Mexico, Nicaragua, Panama, Paraguay, Peru, Puerto Rico, Uruguay, and Venezuela.

With a grant from the Ford Foundation, ITI/US engaged Joanne Pottlitzer to work with library director Elizabeth Burdick on cataloging the TOLA holdings—none of which had ever been cataloged or even made accessible to researchers, scholars, and lay people. Pottlitzer's fluency in Spanish and Portuguese, her firsthand knowledge of theater practice in Latin America, and her obvious familiarity with, and interest in, the materials she herself had collected were essential assets to the project. Burdick's experience in establishing the ITI/US library, in organizing materials from foreign countries, and in developing an information system for theater practitioners made it possible to incorporate the TOLA Collection into the library's holdings under the existing catalog scheme.

The contents of twenty-two cartons containing the TOLA Collection were sorted into two sections: (1) materials relative to theater practice in each country represented, and (2) the 1,277 play scripts from each country. Each play, whether in manuscript form, in a periodical, in a published anthology, collection or single-title edition, was cataloged by author and title in one alphabetical index, and by country of origin and by author in a second index. All three entries include bibliographical data for each play. The plays, except for those in periodicals, are housed by country in the international play section of the library.

Elizabeth Burdick, after consultation with Pottlitzer, cataloged the 1,373 books, periodicals, playbills/programs, photographs, clippings, and monographs. These items, cataloged and shelved by country of origin in the theater-of-nations section, were fed into existing holdings under such classifications as theory, criticism, history, dramaturgy, production, technology, cultural policy, festivals, and theatrical forms. For each country, there is also a division on performing arts companies—brochures, programs, press releases, photographs, reviews, and clippings providing information on their respective productions.

Although the countries of Central and South America and the Caribbean have always been, and continue to be, represented in the ITI/US library, Latin America had been the weak link in its holdings. This circumstance, certainly not intended, was the result of political, social, and economic problems in some Latin American nations, making acquisition and information exchanges difficult if not impossible. The TOLA Collection, therefore, was a most welcome gift, and its inheritance has rounded out the library. The material is valuable. Many of the volumes and manuscripts are one of a kind. Some are no longer in print or available in the country of origin or publication. Most are not available anywhere in the United States.

Originally the ITI/US library housed 497 plays from Latin America and the Caribbean. The TOLA Collection added 1,277 plays, almost quadrupling the holdings, bringing the present total to nearly 1,900 plays from thirty countries. Joanne Pottlitzer stated that the primary reason for placing the Americas Society Collection with ITI/US is that the library's international play service makes scripts available to American theater groups, assists in locating translations, and helps in tracing the rights to foreign plays.

The 153 issues of a variety of periodicals from the Society filled numerous gaps in the library's holdings. For instance, *Conjunto*, a theater publication from Cuba, covers all of Latin America. The library owned complete issues from 1967 to the present, but not from 1964 through 1966. The TOLA Collection provided the early issues, thus filling out the run. The periodicals *Talia* (Argentina), *Dionysos* (Brazil), *Apuntes* (Chile), and others were similarly augmented and the gaps closed. In all periodicals, the plays and key articles are cataloged under their respective subject headings.

In addition, the TOLA Collection includes programs brochures, reviews, and illustrations describing the work of theaters and performing arts companies. These materials, added to the ITI/US holdings, form mini-archives on approximately 300 performing arts companies in the countries represented. Such information is extremely helpful to American managers and festival producers interested in bringing Latin American theater to the United States.

The books, histories of theater, biographies, critical studies of playwrights, and volumes dealing with particular forms—folk drama, puppets, circus, children's theater, popular entertainment—illuminate the theatrical scene for American scholars, researchers, and artists alike.

The TOLA Collection has enhanced the international status of the ITI/US library. It allows the staff to provide enlightened information and more substantial resources to a growing number of theater practitioners who are interested in Hispanic theater, who desire to investigate the artists and companies of Latin America, who are looking for Hispanic dramas to produce, who wish to engage Latin American artists to work with their own companies, and who wish to import Hispanic companies to appear in theaters and at festivals throughout this country.

In essence, the TOLA Collection is a unique archival and collective memory of theater South of the Border—fragments of which are not accessible, or even available, on that continent— all of which is an invaluable historical and contemporary record generated by the working theater of Latin America.

# 6. The Boom Wasn't Just Novels: Audiovisual Archives and Modern Latin American Culture

Jerry W. Carlson

In Latin American Studies these days it is always safe to begin with a quotation from Gabriel García Márquez. "Years later, as he stood before the firing squad, Colonel Aureliano Buendía was to remember that distant afternoon when his father took him to discover . . . the movies."

Please excuse my modest change. We all know his father took him to discover ice. However, García Márquez, who has founded a film school with the profits of his literary activities, would probably agree that a Latin American child raised after World War II would be far more likely to discover the icy beauty of Dolores del Río than the mundane transformation of water into its solid state.

My playful beginning points to a key fact of Latin American society. In the past fifty years it has been transformed—in different ways at different velocities in different places—from a dominantly agrarian continent to the site of massive urban concentrations. This transformation has strong implications for how we study the narratives produced by these cultures. It is not merely that many modern novels—for example, *Pedro Páramo* or *Chronicle of a Death Foretold*—have been turned into films. More profoundly, the literature itself has been produced under the complex influence of the motion pictures.

Let me cite a familiar list: Adolfo Bioy Casares, Jorge Luis Borges, Guillermo Cabrera Infante, Alejo Carpentier, Carlos Fuentes, Gabriel García Márquez, Juan Carlos Onetti, Manuel Puig, Augusto Roa Bastos, and Mario Vargas Llosa. Apart from greatness, what links all of these writers is the fact that they have all worked in, written for, or written about film. There is a full academic career in studying the relations to film of each one.

Here let me substitute some simple anecdotal evidence of this overwhelming cultural phenomenon rather than begin one of those academic careers. Consider how *The Death of Artemio Cruz* is a re-writing of *Citizen Kane*. Or how *Chronicle of a Death Foretold* has the quality of a documentary newsreel edited out of sequence. Or how the aesthetic and ethical success of *Kiss of the Spiderwoman* depends upon a compelling recreation of Hollywood films of the 1940s.

If what I am asserting is true, what implications does it have for the archiving of Latin American materials? Many. Let me divide my remarks into three areas: problems of recognition, problems of retrieval and storage, and problems for the future.

## Recognition

What do we need to recognize and why has it taken us so long to do so? Let me take the second part first. Institutional traditions have impeded vision in several ways. Because literacy has remained an issue in much of Latin America, the development, preservation, and promotion of print culture has been a burden not felt in the same way in Europe and North America. In circumstances when it is difficult to acquire books themselves for libraries or archives, one is unlikely to look for other problems to solve. Moreover, in those places where significant institutions exist—for example, in Mexico City or Buenos Aires—the division of labor has frequently created competing bureaucracies with little contact with each other. There is no easy prescription to remedy these problems.

Still, I can outline what we need to recognize so that we can begin seeking focused solutions. I begin with the assertion that the print and audiovisual cultures of Latin America are intertwined in obvious but complex ways that only highly specialized intellectuals could fail to see.

First, we must recognize that by aesthetic transformation the audiovisual materials dwell within many of the important books. To read *The Death of Artemio Cruz* is to re-screen *Citizen Kane*. To read *Chroncle of a Death Foretold* is to watch a new form of newsreel. And to read *Kiss of the Spiderwoman* is to go to a Saturday matinee but, of course, one in a prison.

Second, we need to recognize what the Latin American artists have always known: that Latin America produced great films as it was producing great fiction and that these were narratives related to the novels by bonds of aesthetic affiliation, professional organization, and personal relations. The films of Luis Buñuel and Arturo Ripstein in Mexico should be placed by the novels of Carlos Fuentes and Juan Rulfo; the films of Tomás Gutiérrez Alea and Julio García Espinosa in Cuba by the novels of Alejo Carpentier and Guillermo Cabrera Infante; and the films of Leopoldo Torre Nilsson and Fernando Solanas in Argentina by the stories of Jorge Luis Borges and Juan Carlos Onetti. All of these artists—and they are a brief set of examples—partake of narrative traditions that are not bounded by institutionally defined notions of print and audiovisual media. While we should read Juan Rulfo to understand Arturo Ripstein, we should see Luis Buñuel to know Carlos Fuentes.

Last, we need to recognize that these artists—writers and filmmakers alike—partake of international audiovisual culture. We know the importance of William Faulkner to Borges and García Márquez. We need to also consider the relevance of, say, Italian neorealism to the creation of the Latin American testimonial novel or of American film noir to the urban landscapes of Onetti.

Future researchers who claim to study Latin American novels in their fullest context must, I clearly believe, come to terms with Latin American and other international audiovisual materials. If archives and libraries recognize this fact, what problems of retrieval and storage do they face?

## Retrieval and Storage

Let me begin with something obvious but crucial. In the 1960s when the Boom novels began to appear, one could soon find them in paperback. Thus a suitcase and an airline ticket could send a writer or one of his friends to another country with enough copies of a work to get it into the hands of important gatekeepers of literary opinion and culture. Such was not the case with 35mm feature films. Bulky, weighty, and expensive, they do not travel well. Moreover, once they arrive they require an intermediary technology—a projector—to decode the materials for spectators. When one finished reading a Boom novel it went on the shelf or into the hands of a friend. When one finished seeing *The Exterminating Angel* at the theater, the lights came up and the image disappeared until a booking at a revival house or on a university campus.

Although we now live in the age of videocassettes and laser discs, this issue of accessibility has been further complicated by economics and politics. Private and public monies have limited the flow of Latin American audiovisual materials into the hands of others. Many of the finest Latin American films have been made by small entrepreneurial producers. The pattern has been repeated many times: gathering funds, making the film, sending it to festivals, selling it to foreign buyers, and moving to the next project as the film plays out its commercial destiny. What the pattern lacks is a safe place for the film to rest after its initial exploitation. Major films—I only wish I were jesting—are put in closets. Small businesses fail; assets are seized; and films are lost.

The antidote to this ill would seem to be state-funded promotion and archiving of films. In an ideal world it might be the cure; however, in Latin America it has frequently been another disease. The economic resources of state agencies have all too frequently been misused.

Let me give a Kafkaesque example from my personal files. In 1990 I went to a nameless Southern Cone country bordered by Chile and Uruguay and not known for its humility. I contacted, or tried to contact, its National Film Institute in order to secure some films for screening on the educational cable channel for which I program materials. Here are some of the things I found out. I could not get through on the telephone for two days. Once I did, I was routed to the "international affairs" department where no one spoke French or English in addition to Spanish. I could not arrange screenings of films. They had no rights to the films that they possessed, and they could not supply me with the names and addresses of the producers who did own the rights. All of this service was given to me by an institute that at that moment had several hundred employees. Officially, the institute was well funded and staffed. The problems I encountered all stemmed from a bureaucratic culture committed to long afternoons in cafes complaining about how nothing works.

Such economic difficulties have always been made more severe by political issues. Many filmmakers have lost access to their work as a consequence of censorship and exile. The Pinochet dictatorship, for instance, drove Chile's best filmmakers into exile when it did not manage to kill them. It would hardly archive and promote the works of such people. Jesús Díaz and Sergio Giral, two of Cuba's best filmmakers, are now living abroad while several recent films such as *Alice in Wondertown* and *Queen & King* have been held back from distribution in Cuba. Indeed, Cuba's great archives are now threatened by its economic and political isolation. Film archives need air conditioning, something in short supply these days in Cuba.

## The Future

So where does this leave us for the future? Not without hope, I might surprise you by saying. Despite the difficulties that I have outlined, much has survived. For that we can thank many archivists, filmmakers, and their friends. Two developments—one social, the other technological—give us room for modest hope. First, the stage of recognizing the importance of these materials seems well under way. Witness the panel that solicited this essay. A number of film festivals—Toronto, Chicago, Havana, Cartagena, and, most recently, Mar del Plata—continue to focus attention on the issues. Curricula in universities are rapidly adding audiovisual materials to their syllabi in order to address an educational audience that would never question their worth. Cassettes now stand alongside books in most homes. One is unlikely to preserve something before one acknowledges the need to do so.

At the same time the falling costs of video technology and the emergence of more stable digital technologies suggest how archives can be created and multiplied using more modest economic resources. Let me return to my earlier Kafkaesque anecdote. To conduct certain forms of research I need not now, only six years later, return to a certain city fabled for the tango. I can stroll from my office to a relatively new site where my integrated interests in prose fiction and film can be served: the Instituto Cervantes of New York.

Their new library is not only dedicated to all Spanish-speaking cultures, but also houses audiovisual materials. What is more, their World Wide Web site allows me to do certain forms of research from my own computer. For instance, I can begin to assemble a list of Jesús Díaz's narrative activities, as a novelist, screenwriter, and director. I can then go to the Instituto where I can find the books and cassettes for my research.

Clearly, not all places will be able to gather and maintain materials on the scale that has already been accomplished by the Instituto Cervantes. What is more important is adopting an inclusive, integrative model of collecting such as they have done.

Before I conclude let me make some observations about what I have omitted by emphasizing film as an aesthetic object. These remarks pertain to certain implications that arise from print culture once film is recognized as important and to the states of audiovisual media other than film.

My discussion has emphasized film as an aesthetic object comparable to the novel. We know, however, that archival activity does not limit itself to the objects alone: the materials generated by modes of production, distribution, and reception are also key to our understanding of how the objects are interpreted and used by their audiences.

Let me put this more concretely. If we assume that the success of the Boom novels depends in some measure upon the activities of publishers and agents as well as upon the inherent artistic value of the novels, then it follows that documents from the office of the agent Carmen Balcells and from the editorial house of Seix-Barral deserve archival preservation. By analogy, if we assume that the value of the New Latin American cinema has been created in part by the activities of film festivals, then it follows that documents from the Toronto and Havana festivals, among others, equally merit archival preservation. Thus the inclusion of film in archival activity brings with it new aspects of acquiring materials from print culture.

Let me now also admit that my emphasis upon film, which I believe is historically and strategically justifiable, has led me to neglect other audiovisual media: music, video, and television. Music, which has reached a new level of archival stability in CDs, is the simplest case. The intellectual and historical arguments I have offered for film hold equally for music. We need to know the tango culture of the 1920s and 1930s to understand Borges just as we need to know a range of musical styles to understand the narrative and referential structure of works by Carpentier. Equally important, where could we possibly draw the line between contemporary lyric poetry and the songs of Silvio Rodríguez and Rubén Blades?

Video, by contrast, is a very recent phenomenon. Mobile and inexpensive, video is an alternative to film that offers enormous flexibility and accessibility. As such, its very freedom creates problems for archives. Much is of value and will be of value. However, the key questions of where these objects are and how they are to be acquired remain open.

In the case of television, there is no question about where it is: it is *everywhere*. This pervasiveness creates problems of selection from massive quantity. It is an issue that advanced industrial societies themselves are beginning only now to address.

Let me conclude as I began: anecdotally. I may still toss in bed thinking about the fate of the films of Sergio Giral, the most important Latin American director of African descent; but I will fall asleep knowing that because the Instituto Cervantes and other libraries have new models of collecting I will always be able to stroll through Havana with the characters of the novel *Three Trapped Tigers* and the film *Memories of Underdevelopment*.

# 7. Latin American Cinema Resources on the Internet

Gayle Ann Williams

Within the broad scope of Latin American studies, film has developed as a discipline from an early interest in using films from and about Latin America in the classroom to gain a direct look at its peoples and cultures to a research-oriented focus in which scholars examine the actual films as a reflection of both local and universal themes, the growth and development of national industries, and the medium's appeal within the realm of popular culture. In the introduction of Volume 52 of the *Handbook of Latin American Studies*, the editor noted that the decision to discontinue the appearance of the chapter "Latin American Film" in alternative volumes of the Humanities volume was due to the metamorphosis from an "emerging area of study" to a field that has come into its own.[1]

Despite this confidence in the undeniable increase of monographs and journal articles, Latin American cinema also remains a field in which documentation of the primary materials or sources is still scattered and elusive. As a point of contrast, a scholar involved in the study of literature can generally find the particular novel or collection of poems of the individual author on whom research efforts center. An array of archives and manuscript collections in Latin America and throughout the world continue to make historical research a reality for many topics. How then does a researcher in Latin American cinema determine the whereabouts or actual existence of a particular film or video in order to focus on the total work of a particular director? When preparing a study on how native peoples are portrayed in documentaries, do adequate filmographies exist for a particular country or region that disclose a variety of titles?

The offerings in the local video rental store are bound to be the few though familiar titles of popular films released in the United States such as *Bye, Bye Brasil*. The array of general reference materials on film available in video ape this distribution pattern and rarely attest to the actual universe of international cinema offerings. Though filmographies for particular countries have been published, their appearance is often irregular or inconsistent. Randal Johnson's observation in 1990 that "A need exists for veritable archaeological research to establish definitive filmographies for most Latin American countries" unfortunately still rings true today.[2] Johnson notes the budgetary limitations of Latin American film archives that have prevented irregular or nonexistent preparation of filmographies. Added to this as a factor is the scale of film production from country to country. While Mexico, Brazil, and Argentina have historically enjoyed a long and prolific record of production, they have slowly been followed up by other Latin American nations whose feature film output has only started to emerge though still at a much reduced scale. It can actually be easier to determine the number of Mexican feature films in a given year than the few (if any) made in Uruguay in the same period.

The ongoing development of the Internet brings with it the intriguing sense of what sources will be developed or available on it that support a particular topic or area of study. So far in this regard Latin American film is an area where Internet sources follow models of organization seen in the print medium. The general movie/movie review databases tend to overlook Latin American films just as do many English-language general reference books on film. As seen in the concluding list of Internet sources, some online library catalogs do provide access to their collections of film and video. Naturally, items with an exclusive focus on Latin American film exist. Film festival and seminar announcements, screenings of local film societies, and the homepage on the website of an Argentine cinema journal are examples of items that appear on a regular basis.

The Internet may eventually provide a solution for the national *cinematecas* who want to use it to promote their activities and documentation. Early promise of this is seen with the website of the Fundación Cinemateca Nacional de Venezuela's Centro de Investigación y Documentación. Its agenda to provide an array of documentation (both online and in CD-ROM format) is coupled with its intent to coordinate the activities of other Latin American film archives in the same vein under the cooperative banner of the Red Latinoamericana de Información de Archivos de Imágenes en Movimiento.[4] At least one *cine club* is also going beyond mere scheduling of its programs to include filmographies for Peru.[5] Other film societies could consider providing a cooperative basis for support and equipment for the film archive of their country as a strategy in dealing with limited financial or technological resources.

In addition to the Internet, other new technological developments need to be taken into account. The Venezuelan Cinemateca Nacional's mention of producing CD-ROM products may or may not be influenced by the recent appearance of the *Cine argentino 1933-1995* CD-ROM issued by the Fundación Cinemateca Argentina. It is noted to be "...el primer CD-ROM dedicado al cine en toda Iberoamérica. . . ."[6] It stands to reason that the CD-ROM format would be ideal for compiling filmographies of countries with larger film/video production. Interestingly, the CD-ROM's appearance is close to that of the monograph *Un diccionario de films argentinos* by Raúl Manrúpe (Buenos Aires: Corregidor, 1995) which also leads us to believe that traditional print technology will continue to support the study of Latin American film.

## INTERNET SOURCES

### Library Catalogs on the Internet

Biblioteca Nacional, Venezuela (address: biblio.iabn.ve or 150.189.3.2, login: biblio, choose luin; opening screen may appear without it; to exit, enter the command sali or press CTRL-D twice).

> This collective online library catalog includes bibliographic records for films and videos primarily collected by the Biblioteca Nacional's Divisi6n de Cine. An author (for director) or title search can be used for the search command for individual films/videos. Records contain technical credits in varying degrees of completeness. Though the primary focus is on Venezuelan productions, other countries are also available. To see lists of holdings, use the subject search m (materia) as in, m=cine—venezuela—videograbaciones or m=cine—venezuela—películas or the keyword search k=videograbaciones.su. and country.su. (in a keyword search the field begins and ends with a period, ex., k=bibliografía.su.). When a film is in both reel and videocassette tape format, there is an individual record for each format. The videotape format's record usually contains the technical credits. If a film is only in the collection in reel format, fewer technical credits will appear on the bibliographic record.

Dedalus, Universidade de São Paulo (address: bee08.cce.usp.br or 143.107.28 or server.usp.br, login: dedalus, press enter, then enter BUSCA on the opening page; to exit, CTRL-Q).

> The online library catalog for the Universidade de São Paulo (USP) uses a guided command field screen to determine what file is being searched and what terms are used. Under Transação Corrente< Busca, enter Módulo with U to search Univídeo, the video database. Use C (completo) for Formato de saída. Search terms are then entered in the author, title, subject (autor, título, assunto) fields. Press enter after filling in all search terms. Use the tab key or arrow keys to move the cursor from field to field. Most videos found here are student films made in the USP Escola de Comunicações e Artes but Univídeo also contains videos of some popular Brazilian feature films. There appear to be few if any other videos of Latin American films. Technical credits are included in varying degrees of completeness.

UCLA Film and Television Archive catalog, Orion Information System, University of California, Los Angeles (address: mvs.oac.ucla.edu; Note: an ORION account is required for non-UCLA users to receive a logon ID and password. Enter "menu" and press enter to select; choose 9 to enter the archive catalog; to exit, type logoff).

The online catalog of the UCLA Film and Television Archive includes films (on video) from and about Mexico as a result of its Mexican Cinema Project. The archive appears to have almost nothing else from Latin America. Use the command FSU films, mexican for a complete listing. Individual directors' names and film titles can also be searched. Most technical credits are fairly complete and a summary of the film's plot is also provided.

**Filmographies on the World Wide Web**

Corbett, Bob. "A List of Files [sic] about Haiti and Some Comments on Them." [http://neal.ctstateu.edu/history/world_history/archives/haiti/haiti022.html]. March 1996

Substitute the word "Films" for "Files" in the title and you have the correct emphasis. This annotated filmography (in title alphabetical order) describes both feature (fiction) and documentary films from and about Haiti. Unfortunately, while a variety of Hollywood feature films and U.S. documentaries dealing with Haiti and/or voodoo (ex., *I Walked with a Zombie*, and *Bitter Cane*) are listed, Corbett includes almost none of the Haitian film directors who have been working since the 1960s because this list concentrates on films of which he owns copies. Only minimal technical credits are included.

"Cortometrajes peruanos (35 y 16mm)." [http://antara.rcp.net.pe/cine-lub/page/corto.html]. 1995?

This filmography of Peruvian short-length films (feature and documentary) is arranged alphabetically by name of film director with the titles. Only year of production and DOC or FIC are included with film titles. It is one of three filmographies included in the Cine-Club Miraflores site.

"Filmes disponíveis = Available Films." [http://www.ibase.org.br/~cinemabrazil/indfilmm.htm]. 1996?

The Cinema Brazil website first appeared to solicit funds for production of a Brazilian film. Recently it has also inaugurated the first "cyber-catalog" of Brazilian films with "Filmes disponíveis" organized under the sponsorship of the Departamento de Cinema of the Universidade Federal Fluminense. This online database can be browsed by alphabetical order or searched with separate search strings. It uses the Alta Vista search engine. Other searching requires Netscape 2.0 and other Java compatible browsers. Technical credits for some titles are presently missing though their completion is anticipated.

"Films." In University of Florida Center for Latin American Studies home page. [http://www.latam.ufl.edu/filmlibrary.htm]. 1995?

This is an extensive annotated filmography of films (in video and film formats) from and about Latin America (feature and documentary) held in various locations at the University of Florida campus in Gainesville. Only minimal technical credits are included.

"Películas peruanas (largometrajes 35mm)."[http://antara.rcp.net.pe/cine-club/page/peru.html]. 1995?

This title list of Peruvian feature films is arranged chronologically by year of production. Technical credits are complete with the exception of cast lists. This is another of the three filmographies included in the Cine-Club Miraflores website.

"Videos peruanos (NSTC)." [http://antara.rcp.net.pe/cine-club/page/video.html]. 1995?

This title list of Peruvian films available on video is not arranged in any particular order and contains minimal technical credits. It is one of the three filmographies included in the Cine-Club Miraflores site.

## NOTES

1. Dolores Moyano Martin, *Handbook of Latin American Studies, vol. 52, Humanities* (Austin: University of Texas Press, 1992), p. xxii.

2. Randal Johnson, "Film," in Paula H. Covington, ed., *Latin America and the Caribbean: A Critical Guide to Research Sources* (New York: Greenwood Press, 1992), p. 558.

3. "Festival Internacional de Curtas Metragens de São Paulo," [http://www.puc-rio.br/mis/]; "Cine club Las Américas," [http://www.adlap.mx.udla/eventos/cine/cineclub_homepage.html]; "The Panorama of Mexican Cinema: An International Seminar at the University of Guadalajara," [http://www.sucp.com/~cmora/mexcine.html]; "*El amante*," [http://www.apriweb.com/amante/index.html].

4. "Fundación Cinemateca Nacional de Venezuela, Centro de Investigación y Documentación," [http://www.mysite.com/cidven/cid.htm]. 1995?

5. The Cine-Club Miraflores of Miraflores, Peru, has provided this service. [http://antara.rcp.net.pe/cine-club/page]. 1995?

6. Martin García Cambeiro[cambeiro@cnea.edu.ar], "CD-ROM cine," in LALA-L, [lala-l@uga.cc.uga.edu], March 27, 1996.

# 8. Making Connections: A Centralized, Online Resource of Latin American and Latino Film and Video

Karen Ranucci

We have a dream—an obsession really. And it is not far from being realized. The treasure trove of Latin American cinema and video is for the most part inaccessible in the United States. Just to locate information about Latin American cinema and video is often time-consuming, costly, and fruitless.

For the past ten years the Latin American Video Archives (LAVA) has been making connections between Latin American film and video makers and U.S. audiences. We have organized video festivals, curated traveling exhibitions of Latin American popular video, published a directory of Latin American film and video production groups, and are about to release a directory of 440 Latin American titles with descriptions (including suggestions for classroom use) written by more than 300 U.S. educators. Our ever-expanding video archive now includes 1,500 titles and is available for viewing by the public at our center.

Throughout the years we have been maintaining a database of Latin American and U.S. Latino film and video which includes basic production information, synopses, and contact information for both the filmmakers and their U.S. distributors (if applicable). Our goal is to centralize information about the field of Latin American cinema and video in order to facilitate access to these materials.

Before LAVA, to find a film or tape users had to search many sources for information. If they were successful in locating the item, obtaining a copy meant contacting the makers directly, which in most cases proved to be very expensive or impossible. Now, filmmakers leave a VHS preview copy on deposit in our archive. If after viewing it, someone is interested in purchasing a copy of the tape, we act as a go-between with the filmmakers and in this way serve as a distribution company.

Our information service receives about twenty requests a week. This frequency proves to us that there is a large interest among U.S. educators in locating authentic, Latin American-made materials. Because our database is physically located in our office and is presently not online, we do the search ourselves and provide the interested party with a printout. This is a very time-consuming activity.

Now the dream part—an international resource that listed film/video title, director, country, subject, and complete contact information. With the Internet, this dream can be realized.

We are in the process of preparing our database to go online. Even though we have more than 4,000 titles listed, in many ways this is just a drop in the bucket. Thoughout Latin America and the United States, key sources such as cinematecas and film/video production festivals have information about film/video production computerized; some even have their information online. Even though there are many different sources, one must still surf the net to find them. All have their information organized in different ways and almost none list contact information for the sources. A cooperative effort must be undertaken to conform these various sources into a worldwide system.

Such a resource would need to be constantly updated as new productions are made and contact information changes. The system needs to be interactive. Filmmakers and distributors can have their work listed by filling out an online form that can be automatically integrated into the database.

We are now looking for funding to pay for the computer programming necessary to conform the various film/video information resources into a centralized database. LAVA is dedicated to making it happen. But in order to make this a cooperative international resource, we can use all the help we can get. The Bobst Library at New York University has offered us space for a website on its server. Any programming advice or technical assistance would be extremely welcome.

There is no question that such a service would be heavily utilized. The sky is the limit and, by working together, we can make it happen.

LAVA: Latin American Video Archives
A project of the International Media Resources Exchange
124 Washington Place
New York, NY 10014
(212) 463-0108 (212) 243-2007 (fax)
Email: imre@igc.apc.org

# III. Media and Bibliography

# 9. The Orthodox Method of Creating the Gabriel García Márquez Bibliography

Nelly S. González

A striking example of the difference between compiling a bibliography according to the old-fashioned, or what I will call the orthodox, method and the electronic method can be expressed by noting that in the orthodox manner you "earn it" while the electronic way involves a little less blood, sweat, and tears. The purpose of this paper is to show in a guided manner the step-by-step process of producing a bibliography when one does not have access to a computer or does not want to use one. It is not my intention to present a comprehensive guide to bibliographic compilation and organization, but simply to share my own methods and experience in the hope that they may be interesting or helpful. By following these basic steps, one may develop a bibliography without having to refer to a complicated and potentially confusing array of sources and manuals.

James Harner, in *On Compiling an Annotated Bibliography,*[1] says that bibliographies should be "intelligent, accurate, thorough, efficiently organized works that foster scholarship by guiding readers through accumulated studies as well as implicitly or explicitly isolating dominant scholarly concerns, identifying topics that have been overworked, and suggesting needed research." Librarians, publishers, bookdealers, academicians, and scholars alike have a significant role in promoting greater access to, and appreciation of, the wealth and variety of human knowledge, and the primary vehicle for providing this access is the annotated bibliography. Here lies the importance of bibliographies.

The most important question a compiler needs to ask is what area to begin working in. Usually this question can be answered according to the knowledge, interest, and background of the compiler. It is important to consider, in addition, whether there is scholarly interest and demand in your chosen area, for your hard work will have value only if it is published and used by researchers. The subject for my bibliography is Gabriel García Márquez and his literary work, and my experience in compiling it resembles that of other researchers dealing with Latin American literature; thus the sources consulted and the manner of collecting material are similarly applicable.

A fortuitous chain of events led to my choice of subject. The period from 1956 to 1994 witnessed a dramatic explosion in both the volume and variety of literature generated in the Americas. Several distinct, creative styles developed and flourished in the nourishing environment before, during, and after the "boom." The most apparent fruits of this literary activity are the Nobel Prizes for Literature won by Miguel Angel Asturias (Guatemala, 1967), Pablo Neruda (Chile, 1971), Gabriel García Márquez (Colombia, 1982), Octavio Paz (Mexico, 1990), and Derek Walcott (West Indies, 1992). The tremendous contribution of these great writers was complemented by that of many other Latin American authors, and together they expanded the breadth and vision of the literature of the period.

At the same time, the rising tide of the feminist movement contributed to the emergence of Latin American female writers. Isabel Allende is perhaps the best known of these women; her tremendous commercial, as well as critical, success paved the way for others such as Laura Esquivel and Elena Poniatowska.

This literary explosion led to the proliferation of bibliographies, some annotated, some not. Those that merely listed sources proved to be of little use. In contrast, an annotated bibliography provides a means of selecting and evaluating sources more readily. Thus, as I embarked on my project, an annotated bibliography seemed the natural format in which to present the diverse works of García Márquez.

Having chosen a subject, the next step is to do some homework to determine whether a bibliography on the subject already exists. Of course, the final ingredient is "luck." If you choose the right subject, your work will be rewarding and the finished product in high demand. In my case, a colleague of mine, Margaret Eustella Fau, had worked on an annotated bibliography of Gabriel García Márquez for the period 1947–1979. In 1980 she recruited me to work with her to update the second volume which covered the years 1979–1985. With the publication of *Cien años de soledad* and its subsequent translation into English in 1970, García Márquez skyrocketed into prominence in the literary world. In 1982 came the ultimate reward, the announcement that García Márquez had won the Nobel Prize for Literature. This sparked an increased academic interest in his work, as well as in Latin American literature in general. The "García Márquez hype" was impressive. Suddenly everyone was reading, interpreting, and criticizing his works. The robust body of work published after his Nobel Prize provided us a rich crop of new material for our work. Fortunately for us, the subject of our bibliography had become not only a prominent literary figure, but also a multifaceted writer involved with the social and political struggles of the Latin American peoples and anyone or anything in need of support. To date, he is the most written-about Latin American author.

In 1986, our 182-page *Bibliographic Guide to Gabriel García Márquez, 1979–1985* was published by Greenwood Press. The volume that followed

(456 pp.), covering the period 1986–1992, was my "solo" experience in compiling a bibliography. It updates the second volume and also includes citations that had previously been omitted because of difficulties in acquiring the works or simply because they were unknown to us at the time. Lon Pearson of the University of Nebraska at Kearney states, ". . . this is a key work and I have been impressed because of its scope and thoroughness. It should be in every university library. Moreover, serious researchers and teachers of the 'Boom' period will want to ensure that they have a copy." The first volume won the prestigious "Choice" award. The next two volumes won the "José Toribio Medina Award" for their outstanding contribution to Latin American scholarship.

## Methodology

Planning your research is imperative for producing a good bibliography. One must be thorough, accurate, consistent, and well organized. A good book begins with a well-written and well-prepared manuscript. Choose a standard style manual, such as *The Chicago Manual of Style*[2] or the *MLA Style Manual.*[3] It is better to adopt a format presented in these well-known manuals than to try to modify the style to fit your preferences. As the bibliography progresses, one encounters a myriad of problems related to the citation format. So, in the beginning if one adheres to and follows the manual, life is more bearable and problems are solved by consulting the manual. One must be strict in this respect, in order to avoid future problems. This kind of work does not require creativity; one simply needs to apply the rules to each citation in a consistent manner.

Appendix B lists the indexes and sources upon which I rely in searching for material, as they generally yield articles on Latin American literature.

## Implementation

The following organizational tools are essential:

1. Index cards (3" x 5") to record the citations
2. Card file boxes with index card guides
3. Folders

The index cards serve to record all the information needed. The annotation must be accurate and without errors. Any doubt at the time of compiling the data, regarding the author's name, publisher, place of publication, and so on should be resolved immediately to avoid having to deal with the problem when one is ready to type the final manuscript. Record any potentially useful information at this time, while you have the item that you are examining in your hand. On the left bottom side of the card, type the correct entry of the name, the way it should appear in the index. This is important because when compiling the index, there may be doubts about the name and surname in many cases. Type all the citations exactly in the manner that your chosen manual of style requires. Copy the entries completely and accurately. For your own reference, note the source where the citation was found, including year, volume, page, call number, and entry number. This will prove very useful if for any reason there is need to revise the information later. On the right side of the card, select the location of the citation in your work, in accordance with the method of division (like that shown in Appendix A). At this point, you are ready to write the annotation of the work. The annotation consists of an abstract of two to five sentences, where you highlight the main points of the work. Your purpose is to present to the reader an accurate, concise, illustrative description of the work, avoiding any criticism or interpretation of your own. Harner states, "Whether paraphrase or commentary, good annotations accurately and incisively—but not cryptically—distill the essence of works."[4] The bibliographer skillfully and knowledgeably provides the information, even for an entire book-length study, in a few sentences. It is advisable to double-space the abstract to make editing easier because corrections can be inserted between the lines. If one encounters certain authors whose writing styles make it difficult to summarize their work, it is good to quote statements from the authors themselves which serve to clarify their purpose and the ideas they express. Such quotes may sometimes illuminate the very heart of the author's message.

Having completed the citation card, make two copies of it. The original is filed in Card File Box 1 in alphabetical order. Copy 1 is filed in Card File Box 2, in the appropriate section, in alphabetical order within the section, following the division listed in Appendix 1. Copy 2 is attached to the article when appropriate and saved in a file that holds all the material collected and divided according to the division shown in Appendix A. All this material is filed in alphabetical order also within the folder or category. For my work, fourteen file folders were needed, corresponding to the fourteen sections into which the bibliography was divided. Each article to be saved, with Copy 2 of the abstract attached, should be stored in the appropriate folder. Additional folders may contain: lists of titles already done, lists of sources that should be checked regularly (e.g., MLA), titles in process of searching, lists that should be checked (e.g, lists of titles from a vendor), titles that should be searched, titles that were requested through interlibrary loan, and titles that turned out to have nothing to do with your subject.

## Layout

A typical bibliography may consist of the following sections:

Preface: Here the bibliographer states the purpose of the work and describes the format. One should also explain the scope, limitations, and organization of the bibliography, clearly specifying what is included and excluded. Remember that the reviewers are without mercy and sometimes mean. They go to extremes to find errors and omissions, and even take sentences out of context to produce criticism that is not always fair or accurate.

Acknowledgments: A bibliography is a "work of love" but also a cooperative venture. Your support comes from various sources. Academic institutions often provide research grants or other types of help. Additional sources of support may include fellow scholars, librarians, translators, research assistants, editors, friends, keyboarders, and so on. In this section one pauses to remember all the help and cooperation received and to recognize those individuals who generously contributed to the work.

Chronology: This is an important feature. Here one provides a year-by-year record of the main events and circumstances of the subject's life, including the years of publication of his or her works, as well as the dates of greatest accomplishments and major recognitions received.

Introduction: Here one presents an overview of the writer's career, emphasizing certain biographical data. This include highlights of the writer's life and works as well as some references to similar works. Such an overview should be concisely presented and restricted to the most salient facts, since most if not all of the information is probably contained in biographies of the subject by experts in the field. The bibliographer may also explain the purpose in compiling the work; for example, to make a contribution to the literary community by gathering the information and presenting it in an orderly manner.

The organization of the main body of a bibliography will of course depend to some extent on the nature of the material. As shown in Appendix A, the *Bibliographic Guide to García Márquez* is divided as follows: Part One comprises primary sources which include the author's narrative works; nonfiction articles and books; audiovisual materials, including video, voice recordings, plays, and cartoons by and about García Márquez, as well as articles and reviews about those works; anthologies of his short stories; and translations of his works into various languages. Part Two consists of bibliographies; books; theses (doctoral, master's and bachelor's) on García Márquez and his works; critical articles from scholarly journals and periodicals; interviews; biographical articles and others that deal with García Márquez in his multifaceted activities; and a section called Miscellanea, into which I have placed all the materials that do not fit into the categories listed above, but have been included because they briefly refer to García Márquez or his literary influence, and therefore may be of some use to scholars in their research. The last two sections comprise, respectively, reviews of the laureate's work and reviews of books written about García Márquez. The citations are numbered consecutively, beginning with the first entry of Primary Sources and continuing through the last entry of Secondary Sources. The indexes cite the item number.

Indexing is the final step in preparing the bibliography and should be done with extreme care to ensure accuracy and avoid omissions or repetitions. This is particularly important because many reviewers consider the index a reliable indicator of the bibliography's value as a reference work. My bibliography provides both an Index of Names, which lists all persons whose works are included in the citations or annotations, and an Index of Titles. My reason for including the latter is briefly explained in the Preface: "I . . . find that this index is necessary as an access point because some users remember only the title of the work, but not the author or the compiler."[5] It is further explained that this index does not represent the full title of a work, but only serves as a guide to the entry (see Appendix A).

## Conclusion

While we are witnessing an extraordinary revolution in the information world, involving heretofore undreamed-of ways of harnessing information, the basic need for more and better bibliographies remains. Our task now is to determine how we may employ evolving technology to better serve this need—to complement, rather than to abandon, the classic foundations upon which a good bibliography is built. This point may be illustrated by considering the valid complaint that bibliographies often become out-of-date almost as soon as they are published. Today, such a problem can be resolved by constant updating through online computer indexing services. Thus, the printed bibliography constitutes a core which may be enlarged by many other available services, providing researchers, students, and teachers of Latin American literature with an ever-increasing wealth of the most up-to-date information.

## APPENDIX A

*Bibliographic Guide to Gabriel García Márquez, 1986–1992*

Contents

# APPENDIX B

## Selected List of Sources that Contain Literary Publications by and about Gabriel García Márquez

*HAPI (Hispanic American Periodicals Index).* Los Angeles, CA: UCLA Latin American Center.

*MLA (International Bibliography of Books and Articles on the Modern Languages and Literature).* New York: Modern Language Association.

Covington, Paula H. *Indexed Journals: A Guide to Latin American Serials.* Madison, WI: SALALM, 1983.

González, Nelly S. *Periodicals from and about Latin America and the Caribbean held by the University of Illinois Library that are included in the MLA directory of periodicals.* Urbana: University of Illinois Library, 1991.

**Other Indexes**

*Arts and Humanities Citation Index (and Current Contents).* Philadelphia: Institute for Scientific Information.

*British Humanities Index.* London.

*Bulletin Bibliographique Amérique Latine.* No. 1 (1981)–. Paris: Editions Recherche sur les Civilisations, 1982–.

*Dissertation Abstracts International.* Ann Arbor, MI: University Microfilms International.

*Humanities Index.* New York: H. W. Wilson Co.

*Index to Theses with Abstracts Accepted for Higher Degrees by the Universities of Great Britain and Ireland and the Council for National Academic Awards.* London: Aslib, 1986–.

*Internationale Bibliographie der Zeitschriftenliteratur.* Osnabruck: F. Dietrich 1984–.

*Reader's Guide to Periodical Literature.* New York: H. W. Wilson Co.

**Other Sources (Not included in above indexes)**

*ABC.* Asunción, Paraguay.

*Acta Litteraria Academiae Scientarum Hungarica.* Budapest, Hungary.

*Amaru.* Lima, Peru.

*Araucaria de Chile.* Pamplona, Spain.

*Atenea.* Concepción, Chile.

*Avanti.* Milan, Italy.

*Baleares.* Palma de Mallorca, Spain.

*Boletín Cultural y Bibliográfico.* Bogotá, Colombia: Biblioteca Luis-Angel Arango, 1958–.

*Carlino Sera.* Bologna, Italy.

*Clarín.* Buenos Aires, Argentina.

*Corriere della Sera*. Rome, Italy.
*Council on National Literatures*. Whitestone, NY: Griffon House for Council on National Literatures, 1987–.
*Crítica*. Bogotá, Colombia.
*Cromos*. Bogotá, Colombia.
*Crónica*. Bogotá, Colombia.
*Duquesne Hispanic Review*. Pittsburgh, PA.
*Encuentro Liberal*. Bogotá, Colombia.
*Ercilla*. Santiago, Chile: Sociedad Editora Revista "Ercilla".
*Escarbajo de Oro*. Buenos Aires, Argentina.
*Estudios Latinoamericanos*. Mexico City, Mexico.
*L'Espresso*. Rome, Italy.
*L'Express*. Paris, France.
*Fiera Letteraria*. Milan, Italy.
*Gallo Ilustrado*. La Plata, Argentina.
*Hispanic Literatures*. Indiana University, Bloomington, IN.
*Indice*. Buenos Aires, Argentina.
*Insula*. Madrid, Spain.
*Journal of Latin American Studies*. London.
*Kentucky Romance Quarterly*. Lexington, KY.
*Latinoamericana*. Buenos Aires, Argentina.
*Latinoamericana*. Stockholm, Sweden.
*Letras Nacionales*. Bogotá, Colombia.
*Library Literature*. Chicago, IL.
*Marcha*. Montevideo, Uruguay.
*Mapocho*. Santiago, Chile.
*Mito*. Bogotá, Colombia.
*Nueva Narrativa Hispanoamericana*. Garden City, NY.
*Oiga*. Lima, Peru.
*Papeles*. Caracas, Venezuela.
*Pease Sera*. Rome, Italy.
*Pensamiento Crítico*. Lima, Peru.
*Razón y Fábula*. Bogotá, Colombia.
*Revue des Langues Vivantes*. Brussels, Belgium.
*Siculorum Gymnasium*. Catania, Italy.
*Siempre*. Mexico City, Mexico.
*Stampa*. Milan, Italy.
*Stampa Sera*. Turin, Italy.
*Tabla Redonda*. Caracas, Venezuela.
*Year's Work in Modern Language Studies*. London.
*World Press Review*. New York.

**Newspapers**

*El Día*. Mexico City, Mexico.
*Diario*. Madrid, Spain.
*El Espectador*. Bogotá, Colombia.
*Jornal do Brasil*. Rio de Janeiro, Brazil.
*Le Monde*. Paris, France.
*El Mundo*. Bogotá, Colombia.
*El Nacional*. Caracas, Venezuela.
*Nazioni*. Florence, Italy.
*Tiempo*. Bogotá, Colombia.

## NOTES

1. James L. Harner, *On Compiling an Annotated Bibliography* (New York: The Modern Language Association of America, 1991), p. 1

2. *The Chicago Manual of Style*, 13th ed. (Chicago: The University of Chicago Press, 1982).

3. Joseph Gibaldi, *MLA Handbook for Writers of Research Papers* (New York: Modern Language Association of America, 1995).

4. Ibid., p. 26.

5. Nelly S. González, *Bibliographic Guide to Gabriel García Márquez, 1986–1992* (Westport, CT: Greenwood Press, 1994), p. xiv.

# 10. La preparación de bibliografías electrónicas

Luis M. Villar

Durante la reunión de SALALM en Athens, Georgia, Nelly González, mediante una sencilla pregunta presentó un gran desafío técnico tanto para mí como para los administradores del catálogo electrónico de Dartmouth College. La pregunta fue, "¿Luis, tú crees que se puede preparar una versión electrónica de mi bibliografía de y sobre la obra de Gabriel García Márquez?" Le contesté inmediatamente que sí, pues ya estaba trabajando en el prototipo para una bibliografía comprensiva sobre Sor Juana Inés de la Cruz, siguiendo las normas que presenta el *Guidelines for Electronic Text Encoding and Interchange*.[1] Después de un año de trabajo, por fin, el prototipo de la bibliografía de la compatriota de Micaela Chávez Villa está listo. Hoy tendremos la oportunidad de ver cómo se codifica un corpus bibliográfico y cómo se despliegan las entradas del prototipo de la bibliografía de Sor Juana en el ordenador.

## La iniciativa para la codificación de textos electrónicos

La iniciativa para la codificación de textos electrónicos (TEI) tiene como objetivo la codificación sistemática de textos en una forma estándard. La *Guía* utiliza el Standard Generalized Markup Language (SGML) para la codificación de textos en prosa, poesía, teatro y referencias bibliográficas. La adopción de SGML tiene grandes ventajas ya que exhibe varias características que le rinden universalidad al texto: (a) es un estándard internacional;[2] (b) se puede usar en cualquier sistema; (c) es un lenguaje enteramente descriptivo; (d) los documentos son transferibles de un componente físico (hardware) o programas (software) a otro sin pérdida de información.

La unidad textual fundamental de SGML, en tanto que componente estructural, es el *elemento*. Este es un nombre lógico diseñado para identificar cada parte significativa de un documento. Normalmente, está en las manos del creador de un texto electrónico escoger los nombres de los elementos que ellos identifican y documentar su uso en la codificación. La *Guía*, sin embargo, presenta un conjunto de marcas y modelos adecuados para la codificación de bibliografías y de diversas estructuras literarias. Aunque los modelos de TEI son adecuados, el codificador tiene la oportunidad de crear una serie de marcas para complementarlos.[3]

Los modelos bibliográficos que se presentan en la *Guía*, exhiben una serie de marcas o etiquetas para codificar los elementos estructurales característicos de una entrada bibliográfica. Las marcas se componen de una etiqueta inicial o "start-tag" y otra final o "end-tag". El par de marcas delimita las estructuras en una forma similar a los signos auxiliares « ... » de la ortografía tradicional. En informática, la etiqueta o marca se construye con los ángulos-paréntesis < y >, entre los cuales se incluye un identificador genérico o nombre lógico del elemento. Por ejemplo, los elementos correspondientes al autor y título de una entrada bibliográfica tradicional serían representados de la siguiente forma:

| Etiqueta inicial | Etiqueta final |
|---|---|
| <author> | </author> |
| <title> | </title> |

es decir,

<author> García Márquez, Gabriel</author>
<title>El otoño del patriarca</title>.

Puede observarse en el ejemplo que la etiqueta final es idéntica a la etiqueta inicial, aunque contiene una barra oblicua "/" tras el primer paréntesis angular, </. Como regla general, cada elemento está delimitado por una etiqueta inicial y otra final. Sin embargo, las reglas de minimización de SGML permiten reducir la etiqueta final a la siguiente notación: </>, omitiendo el nombre del elemento. Para efecto de la bibliografía, se utilizan ambas etiquetas sólo con el propósito de ser consistentes en la codificación integral del documento. Así, en cada entrada utilizamos la etiqueta inicial, <biblStructure>; y final, </biblStructure>, para identificar el principio y fin de una entrada bibliográfica.

Los elementos, además, pueden ir acompañados de atributos. Estos complementan los elementos de la misma forma en que un adjetivo complementa a un sustantivo. Los más comunes en la bibliografía son: tipo (**type**), nivel (**level**) y valor (**value**). Por ejemplo:

**<note type=subjects>**

Obsérvese que el atributo se incluye dentro de los paréntesis angulares.

## Referencias bibliográficas

La codificación de bibliografías en forma electrónica requiere una estructura sistemática y lógica. La organización rigurosa es esencial para producir documentos útiles, para facilitar la recuperación de datos; y, para distinguir, sin dificultad alguna, los diferentes elementos que componen un registro bibliográfico cuando éste se despliega en la pantalla del ordenador. Las características que se describen a continuación corresponden, hasta cierto punto, con las prácticas de preparación de bibliografías tradicionales y con las reglas de catalogación.

## Elementos de referencias bibliográficas

La *Guía* presenta cuatro posibles elementos para marcar referencias bibliográficas en un documento ya sea como unidades individuales o como grupo:

| | |
|---|---|
| <bibl>: | contiene una cita bibliográfica en la cual sus partes constitutivas pueden o no estar marcadas; |
| <biblStruct>: | contiene una cita bibliográfica enteramente estructurada. Esta estructura exhibe sólo elementos bibliográficos; y, en un orden específico;[4] |
| <biblFull>: | contiene una estructura bibliográfica íntegra similar en contenido al registro MARC; |
| <listBibl>: | contiene una lista de referencias bibliográficas ya sea <bibl>, <biblStruct> o <biblFull>. |

El elemento **<bibl>** es la forma más sencilla y, normalmente, aparece dentro de un pasaje en prosa. Por ejemplo:

<p>El autor de <bibl><title>Cien años de soledad,</title> Gabriel García Márquez, **</bibl>** obtuvo el premio Nóbel de literatura en 1982.</p>[5]

De entre otros elementos para registrar referencias bibliográficas la estructura bibliográfica, <biblStruct>, por su organización rigurosa, es la forma más adecuada para organizar el ensayo bibliográfico de y sobre la obra de Gabriel García Márquez. Con este propósito en mente, hemos tomado cuatro entradas de la bibliografía compilada por Nelly González para ilustrar el modelo. Estas ejemplifican los tipos de entrada más comunes en la bibliografía impresa: monografías, artículos en revistas literarias, reseñas y traducciones.

## Monografías

Entre las entradas para libros en la bibliografía impresa se encuentra la siguiente:

García Márquez, Gabriel. *El amor en los tiempos del cólera.* Bogotá, Colombia: Editorial Oveja Negra, 1st ed., c1985, 1985, 473 p.[6]

*Versión electrónica:*

```
<biblStruct id=GAR85>
        <monogr>
```

```
            <author>García Márquez, Gabriel</author>
            <title level=m lang=es>El amor en los tiempos del cólera</title>
            <edition>1 ed.</edition>
            <imprint>
                <pubPlace>Bogotá, Colombia:</pubPlace>
                <publisher>Editorial Oveja Negra,</publisher>
                <pubDate value='1985'>1985.</pubDate>
            </imprint>
        </monogr>
        <extent>473 p.</extent>
        <idno type=ISBN>9580600007</idno>
        <notesStmt>
            <note type=materialType>Book</note>
            <note type=subjects>
                <list type=simple>
                    <item>Fiction</item>
                    <item>Ficción</item>
                    <item>Novel</item>
                    <item>Novela</item>
                </list>
            </note>
        </notesStmt>
    </biblStruct>
```

## Análisis

Como se ha señalado, las etiquetas que marcan las partes lógicas de un documento en SGML están limitadas por los paréntesis angulares **<** y **>.** Dentro de los paréntesis aparece el nombre del elemento que se está codificando y, por ende, definiendo. Así, la etiqueta inicial de la entrada bibliográfica, **<biblStruct id=GAR85>**, exhibe varios niveles de significado:

(1) marca el principio de una entrada bibliográfica electrónica
(2) define la entrada como una estructura bibliográfica la cual, según la norma de TEI, contiene una cita bibliográfica cuyos elementos aparecen en un orden consistente a través del corpus bibliográfico
(3) incluye una notación identificadora.

El atributo ***id*** funciona como unidad identificadora. El código es útil en aquellos casos en que se desee hacer referencia a la entrada en otros lugares de la bibliografía. Las mayúsculas del código corresponden a las tres primeras letras del apellido del autor, **GAR**cía, seguido de dos dígitos los cuales corresponden a los últimos dos números de la fecha de publicación de la monografía, 19**89**.

El elemento **<monogr>** (monografía) contiene elementos bibliográficos que describen el libro en tanto que objeto publicado como entidad única. Dentro de **<monogr>** aparecen los sub-elementos:

**<author>** ... **</author>**
**<title>** ... **</title>**
**<imprint>** ... **</imprint>**.

El elemento **<author>** delimita el nombre de la persona responsable del contenido intelectual de la monografía.[7] El elemento **<title>** marca el título de la obra y posee dos atributos: ***level*** (nivel) y ***lang*** (idioma). El nivel tiene el valor "**m**" para señalar que se trata de una monografía. El atributo ***lang*** identifica el idioma principal de la monografía, cuyo valor, "**es**", representa el código según la International Organization for Standardization (ISO).[8]

Si la monografía tuviese un subtítulo, el codificador tendría la opción de marcarlo. En este caso, el título se marcaría con los atributos ***main*** para identificar el título principal; y, ***subordinate*** para el título secundario o subtítulo. Por ejemplo:

**<title type=main>**Hacia "El otoño del patriarca":**</title>**
**<title type=subordinate>**La novela del dictador en Hispanoamérica**</title>**[9]

El elemento **<edition>** (edición) describe las particularidades de la edición del texto. El elemento **<imprint>** (impresión) agrupa la información relativa a la publicación o distribución de la monografía. Este tiene tres sub-elementos: **<pubPlace>** (lugar de publicación),[10] **<publisher>** (casa editora o impresor), **<date>** (fecha de publicación):[11]

```
<imprint>
        <pubPlace>Bogotá, Colombia:</pubPlace>
        <publisher>Editorial Oveja Negra,</publisher>
        <pubDate value= '1985'>1985.</pubDate>
</imprint>
```

Puede observarse que la fecha de publicación tiene el atributo **<value>** (valor), 1985, encerrado entre comillas. Este atributo es optativo como son también los signos de puntuación. Algunos sistemas insertan la puntuación automáticamente. Si se incluye puntuación, ésta debe incluirse dentro de las etiquetas.

La etiqueta final, **</monogr>**, cierra y delimita los elementos esenciales del ítem bibliográfico.

Los próximos elementos —**<extent>**, **<idno>**, **<series>**, **<notesStmt>**— proveen información complementaria sobre la monografía y son, creemos, recomendables en la creación electrónica de bibliografías en tanto que expanden el punto de acceso a la entrada bibliográfica.

El elemento **<extent>** (extensión) registra el tamaño o extensión aproximada de la monografía:

**<extent>**473 p.**</extent>**

El elemento **<idno>**, o número de identificación, añade un número estándard o no estándard al ítem bibliográfico e incluye el atributo ***type*** (tipo). La monografía puede ser distinguida por dos tipos básicos de signaturas: el Library of Congress Control Number (LCCN)[12] y el International Standard Book Number (ISBN):

**<idno type=ISBN>**9580600007**</idno>**

Si *El amor en los tiempos del cólera* hubiese sido publicada en una serie monográfica, la entrada llevaría los siguientes elementos para marcar la serie y el número:

```
<seriesStmt>
        <title level=s> ... </title>
        <biblScope>   ... </biblScope>
</seriesStmt>
```

La "**s**" del atributo ***level*** significa que se está codificando el título de una serie. Si la serie es numerada, se incluye el sub-elemento **<biblScope>** para definirla.

El elemento **<notesStmt>** aparece, normalmente, en la estructura de la bibliografía completa o <biblFull> y se utiliza para agrupar cualquier número o tipo de notas que provean información sobre la monografía en adición a la información registrada en otras partes de la descripción bibliográfica. Este elemento tiene uno o más sub-elementos los cuales se codifican con las etiquetas **<note>** ... **</note>.** Cada nota puede estar acompañada del atributo ***type*** para describir un tipo específico y único. Las más comunes en una entrada bibliográfica son:

**<materialType>**
**<contents>**
**<subjects>**
**<perName>**

El elemento **<materialType>** (tipo de material) puede ser definido como artículo, libro, microfilm, manuscrito o cualquier otra clase de material que defina con precisión la naturaleza del objeto bibliográfico. **<Contents>** incluye normalmente el índice de la monografía. **<Subjects>** marca los temas principales de que trata la obra. El usuario de bibliografías electrónicas tiende a ejecutar búsquedas por temas con el propósito de recuperar la mayor cantidad de entradas relativas a un asunto. Por ello, las notas deben ser precisas y consistentes en la totalidad del corpus bibliográfico. Con el interés de hacer el banco de datos accesibles al mayor número de usuarios, la entrada registra los temas en inglés y español. La etiqueta **<perName>** marca los nombres personales en forma inversa. Esto facilita, posteriormente, la preparación de un índice onomástico.

## Artículos en revistas

La entrada para una revista, por su naturaleza, tiene una estructura y elementos característicos que la definen. A continuación se presenta el modelo tradicional seguido de la versión para ser procesada por un ordenador:

Flores Olea, Víctor. "*El amor en los tiempos del cólera*: El libro de una educación sentimental." México: *Cuadernos Americanos*, v. 264, no. 1, (January/ February, 1986), pp. 202–208. García Márquez, in writing *Love in the Time of Cholera*, uses his narrative linear style in producing a work that flows easily, presenting all the ingredients of love.[13]

*Versión electrónica:*

```
<biblStruct id=FLO86>
    <analytic>
        <author>Flores Olea, Víctor</author>
        <title level=a lang=es><hi rend=underline>El amor en los
tiempos del cólera</hi>: El libro de una educación sentimental</title>
</analytic>
<!— in —>
<monogr>
    <title level=j>Cuadernos Americanos</title>
        <imprint>
            <biblScope type=volume>264, </biblScope>
                <biblScope type=issue>1,</biblScope>
                <pubDatevalue= '1986–'>(January/February,
                1986):</pubDate>
                <biblScope type=pages>202–208.
                </biblScope>
        </imprint>
    </monogr>
    <idno type=LCCN>451784//r82</idno>
    <idno type=ISSN>0185-156X</idno>
```

```
                    <notesStmt>
                              <note type=materialType>Article</note>
                              <note>García Márquez, in writing <hi
rend=underline>Love in the Time of Cholera</hi>, uses his narrative linear style in
producing a work that flows easily, presenting all the ingredients of love.</note>
                              <note type=subjects>
                                        <list type=simple>
                                                  <item>Criticism and interpretation</item>
                                                  <item>Crítica e interpretación</item>
                                                  <item>Love story</item>
                                                  <item>Historia de amor</item>
                                                  <item>One Hundred Years of
                                                  Solitude</item>
                                                  <item>Cien años de soledad</item>
                                                  <item>Sentimental education</item>
                                                  <item>Educación sentimental</item>
                                                  <item>Style</item>
                                                  <item>Estilo</item>
                                        </list>
                              </note>
                    </notesStmt>
          </biblStruct>
```

La diferencia entre la entrada para una monografía y la entrada para un artículo reside en un punto distintivo: la entrada para un artículo exhibe un elemento analítico, **<analytic>**, bajo el cual aparecen los sub-elementos **<author>** y **<title>**. El sub-elemento **<title>** tiene dos atributos: ***level*** (nivel) acompañado del valor "**a**" para designar el nivel analítico. El atributo **lang** es el mismo que el de la monografía. Las etiquetas **<hi rend=underline> ...</hi>** marcan el título o cualquier partícula(s) textual(es) como gráficamente diferente al texto circundante.

Es preciso enfatizar que según TEI, la codificación bibliográfica de un artículo publicado en una revista requiere dos niveles de información: el nivel analítico y el nivel monográfico. El nivel analítico registra el nombre del autor y el título del artículo. El nivel monográfico contiene los elementos particulares de la revista misma. Por tanto, después de la instrucción **<!— in —>**[14] se incluye el elemento **<monogr>** bajo el cual aparecen los sub-elementos **<title>** e **<imprint>**. En la etiqueta para marcar el título de la revista,

**<title level=j>** ... **</title>**

el atributo ***level*** (nivel) posee el valor "**j**" (journal) para señalar, con precisión, que se trata de una revista y no de una monografía.

El elemento **<imprint>** (impresión) contiene dos sub-elementos: **<biblScope>** y **<pubDate>**. El primero define la extensión de la referencia bibliográfica y es complementado por el atributo ***type*** (tipo) cuyos valores son:

> ***volume*** (volumen): para indicar que el elemento contiene el número del volumen en que se publicó el artículo
> ***issue*** (número): el elemento contiene el número de la revista
> ***pages*** (páginas): el elemento contiene el número de página(s)

Si consideramos que las bibliografías comprensivas tienen un carácter internacional, la fecha de publicación de un artículo puede aparecer en una variedad de formas. Para ser consistente, y si se desea conservar las peculiaridades culturales del idioma original del artículo, se puede transcribir la fecha tal y como aparece en la revista. El atributo de la fecha, **value** (valor) sigue uno de los modelos que se ofrecen en el ISO 8601.[15]

Al igual que la monografía, la etiqueta final, **</monogr>**, cierra la descripción de los elementos identificadores de la entrada. Los elementos que siguen, aunque optativos, son recomendables, pues, ofrecen otros puntos de acceso a la entrada bibliográfica.

El elemento **idno** (número de identificación) seguido del atributo ***type*** registra el Library of Congress Control Number (LCCN) y el International Standard Serials Number (ISSN).

La información que se incluye bajo el elemento **<notesStmt>** puede ser similar a las notas que se registran en las monografías, salvo una excepción. La nota que identifica el tipo de material, **<note type=materialType>**, define la entrada como la de un artículo y, en el proceso, lo diferencia de la monografía. Esta diferenciación es importante ya que el usuario, al hacer búsquedas en el banco de datos, puede limitar el resultado a artículos o libros.

## Reseñas

La entrada de una reseña según la bibliografía impresa reza:

> Butt, John. "The Liberator in Defeat." London, England: *TLS, Times Literary Supplement*, no. 4502, (July 14–20, 1989), p. 781. John Butt reviews García Márquez's novel *El general en su laberinto* and talks briefly about the historical figure of the Latin American Liberator, Simón Bolívar, who he says has become a controversial character in García Márquez's hands, and therefore García Márquez "has managed to offend all sides."[16]

La codificación de la entrada bibliográfica para las reseñas es similar a la entrada para un artículo en una revista. Los puntos de diferencia residen en el elemento **<title>** el cual se complementa con la frase "[book review]" después del título; y, en el elemento **<note type=materialType>** que identifica la entrada como una reseña. La entrada se podría codificar como sigue:

```
<biblStruct id=BUT89>
        <analytic>
                <author>Butt, John</author>
                <title level=a lang=en>The Liberator in Defeat
                [book review].</title>
        </analytic>
        <monogr>
                <!— In —>
                <title level=j>TLS, Times Literary Supplement</title>
                <imprint>
                        <biblScope type=issue>4502</biblScope>
                        <pubDate value='1989–07'>(July 14–20, 1989):</pubDate>
                        <biblScope type=pages>781.</biblScope>
                </imprint>
                <idno type=ISSN>0307–661X</idno>
                <idno type=LCCN>8939064</idno>
        </monogr>
        <notesStmt>
                <note type=materialType>Review</note>
                <note>John Butt reviews García Márquez's novel <hi
                rend=underline>El general en su laberinto</hi> and talks briefly about
                the historical figure of the Latin American Liberator, Simón Bolívar,
                who he says has become a controversial character in García Márquez's
                hands, and therefore García Márquez "has managed to offend all
                sides."</note>
        </notesStmt>
</biblStruct>
```

## Traducción de un cuento en una antología

La traducción de la obra de Gabriel García Márquez al inglés ha sido muy popular desde la aparición de la publicación de *Cien años de soledad.* El siguiente modelo presenta la entrada bibliográfica para el registro de la traducción de un cuento publicado en una antología según la bibliografía tradicional y su posible versión electrónica:

García Márquez, Gabriel. "Tuesday Siesta." J. S. Bernstein, tr. In *Collected Stories.* New York, NY: Harper and Row, 1984, pp. 99–106.[17]

*Versión electrónica*:

```
<biblStruct id=GAR84>
    <analytic>
        <author>García Márquez, Gabriel</author>
        <title level=a lang=en>Tuesday Siesta</title>
        <title level=a type=parallel lang=es>La siesta del martes</title>
        <respStmt><resp>Translated by</resp>
            <name>J. S. Bernstein</name>
        </respStmt>
    </analytic>
    <monogr>
        <!— In —>
        <title level=m lang=en>Collected Stories</title>
        <imprint>
            <pubPlace>New York, N.Y.:</pubPlace>
            <publisher>Harper and Row,</publisher>
            <pubDate value= '1984'>1984.</pubDate>
        </imprint>
        <biblScope type=pages>99–106.</biblScope>
    </monogr>
    <idno type=LCCN>84–47826</idno>
    <idno type=ISBN>0060153644</idno>
    <notesStmt>
        <note type=materialType>Short story</note>
        <note type=subjects>
            <list type=simple>
                <item>Translation of short stories into
                    English</item>
                <item>Traducción de cuentos al inglés</item>
                <item>Short stories</item>
                <item>Cuentos</item>
            </list>
        </note>
        <note type=nameInv>
            <list type=simple>
                <item>Bernstein, J. S.</item>
            </list>
        </note>
    </notesStmt>
</biblStruct>
```

## Análisis

La entrada tiene cuatro elementos distintivos: título paralelo, traductor, editor, nombre inverso.

Para efecto de la bibliografía, denominamos título paralelo al título del original. La inclusión del original es útil porque si se toma el título como punto de acceso, se puede recuperar el original y las traducciones a menos que se limite la búsqueda por idioma. Si se opta por este método, se codifica primero el título según aparece en la fuente primaria:

**<title level=a lang=en>**Tuesday Siesta**</title>**

Luego, se codifica el título original con la siguiente notación:

**<title level=a type=parallel lang=es>**La siesta del martes**</title>.**

Para registar el nombre de la persona responsable de la traducción, se puede utilizar el elemento **<respStmt>**, seguido del sub-elemento **<resp>** para marcar el tipo de responsabilidad. El elemento **<name>** delimita el nombre del traductor según éste aparece en la fuente original. Así tenemos,

**<respStmt><resp>**Translated by**</resp>**<br>
    **<name>**J. S. Bernstein**</name>**<br>
**</respStmt>**

Si la antología tuviese un editor, éste se incluiría inmediatamente después del título de la siguiente forma:

**<respStmt><resp>**Edited by**</resp>**<br>
    **<name>**Joe R. Smith**</name>**<br>
**</respStmt>**

Finalmente, el codificador tiene la opción de incluir una nota para codificar los nombres incluidos en la entrada en forma inversa. Esta nota facilitará la preparación de un índice onomástico. Los elementos se pueden codificar como sigue:

```
<note type=nameInv>
        <list type=simple>
                <item>Bernstein, J. S.</item>
        </list>
</note>
```

Esperamos que estos modelos ayuden a abrir el camino hacia la preparación de bibliografías electrónicas.

# NOTAS

1. *Guidelines for Electronic Text Encoding and Interchange*, ed. C. M. Sperberg McQueen y Lou Burnard (Chicago: Text Encoding Initiative, 1994). En adelante la *Guía*.

2. SGML. Véase ISO 8879 en: http://www.sgmlsource.com/8879rev/.

3. Véase en la *Guía*, las secciones 28 y 29 de la 5ta. parte.

4. Según la *Guía*, entre los programas consultados para diseñar la estructura bibliográfica, (<biblStruct>), fueron ProCite, BibTex y Scribe.

5. Es necesario enfatizar que las etiquetas que marcan las diversas partes del documento no aparecen en el producto final, ya sea una copia impresa del documento o en la pantalla del ordenador.

6. Nelly Sfeir de González, *Bibliographic Guide to Gabriel García Márquez, 1986–1992* (Westport, CT: Greenwood Press, 1994), p. 1.

7. El autor puede ser una o más personas, una asociación u organización. En caso de que las entradas tengan más de un autor, se incluirán tantas etiquetas para los nombres como sean necesarias. Por ejemplo, la entrada número 757 de la página 91 de la bibliografía sería:

<author>Cordero S., Gloria </author>

<author>Savoini O, Virginia</author>

8. Para consultar las abreviaturas de los idiomas según el International Organization for Standardization, véase: http://www.de.relator.research.ec.org/mlhtml/ISO-lg-codes.mlhtml.

9. González, p. 105.

10. Obsérvese que el elemento condensa el nombre en una palabra transformándolo en un código único. Así, la frase "place of publication" pasa a ser "pubPlace".

11. La *Guía* utiliza el elemento <date>, pero lo hemos modificado y utilizado en su lugar el elemento <pubDate> con el propósito de poder utilizar el elemento <date> para identificar otras fechas importantes en las entradas bibliográficas.

12. Hemos consultado dos registros de la edición de *El amor en los tiempos del cólera* de la Editorial Oveja Negra en OCLC. Ninguno tiene el número de control de la Biblioteca del Congreso. Si lo tuviese, éste iría antes del ISBN y marcado de la siguiente forma:

<idno type=LCCN>85-34980</idno>.

13. González, p. 218.

14. La expresión <!— in —> es un comentario en SGML; no se considera parte del texto.

15. Seguimos el modelo de ISO 8601, *'año-mes-día'*, donde año es un número positivo, mes es un número entre 1 y 12, y día es un número entre 1 y 31. La construcción *'mes/día/año'*, es posible. También *'mes/día'*, donde se omite el año. El nombre de los meses puede ser escrito en su integridad o abreviarse, utilizando las tres primeras letras de cada mes, posiblemente seguidas de un punto para cerrar la abreviatura. También es posible abreviar *'September'* como *'Sept'*.

16. González, p. 352.

17. Ibid., p. 77.

# IV. Media and Conservation

# 11. Ochenta años de historia en imágenes: la digitalización del periódico *El Mundo*

Víctor F. Torres-Ortiz

El periódico *El Mundo* es el rotativo más importante del periodismo puertorriqueño del siglo XX. Fundado en 1919 por Romualdo Real, quien junto a su hermano Cristóbal era propietario de la revista *Puerto Rico Ilustrado*, el primer número circuló el 17 de febrero. En pocos años *El Mundo* se convirtió en el periódico de más solvencia del país y uno de los más importantes de América Latina (Pedreira 1982:345–346). El periódico disfrutó de la preferencia indiscutible del pueblo puertorriqueño: a la altura de 1976, su circulación era mayor que la de los 4 periódicos rivales (Ayala 1986:7). Ya en la década del ochenta, perdió terreno frente a sus competidores, sobre todo *El Nuevo Día* que para 1986 lo sobrepasaba en la venta de anuncios y circulación (Rivera 1991:85–86). En el 1985 cambió a un formato tabloide, pero nunca llegó a recuperar su popularidad. Una huelga prolongada, seguida de un cambio de administración en 1987, contribuyó a su caída que culminó con su cierre definitivo el 7 de diciembre de 1990.

En julio de 1991, el Recinto de Río Piedras de la Universidad de Puerto Rico adquirió en subasta pública, mediante una orden ejecutiva que creó un fondo interagencial de más de $300,000, la colección del periódico *El Mundo*. La misma incluía fotografías, caricaturas, la colección completa, encuadernada, del periódico y de la revista *Puerto Rico Ilustrado*, 18 títulos de revistas, 12 títulos de periódicos microfilmados o encuadernados, 1,595 obras generales de referencia y el mobiliario de la biblioteca que poseía el periódico (Ordóñez [1992]:3). Luego de la compra, se creó una unidad bajo la Oficina del Director del Sistema de Bibliotecas de la Universidad de Puerto Rico, Recinto de Río Piedras, con el nombre de Proyecto de Digitalización del Periódico *El Mundo*. Este proyecto, coordinado en la actualidad por la Profesora Myra Torres Alamo, cuenta con un catalogador a tiempo completo, un catalogador a tiempo parcial, una secretaria, una bibliotecaria auxiliar y una docena de estudiantes asistentes. Su objetivo principal es "digitalizar y preservar la colección de fotografías del periódico *El Mundo* con el fin de ofrecerla al público a través de medios electrónicos" (Torres Alamo 1996:1).

## El proyecto

Debido a la magnitud del proyecto, el mismo se ha dividido en dos etapas. La primera, ya en curso, consta de tres componentes. Primero, la transferencia de 100,000 fotografías y negativos al medio electrónico (digitalización). Hasta la fecha se han digitalizado 10,000 fotografías (positivo) en blanco y negro. El segundo componente consiste en entrar las fotos a un programa interactivo; el programa empleado es el XEROX Photograph Management System (XPHOTO), un sistema que permite la recuperación de fotos a través de diversas categorías tales como: nombre de personas en la foto, lugar, acontecimiento, nombre del fotógrafo, texto al calce de la foto y fecha. Se han entrado en la base de datos 5,000 fotos. Finalmente, está la catalogación de las fotos y la entrada de los registros al catálogo en línea de la Universidad de Puerto Rico. Los registros también se pueden localizar en la base de datos OCLC.

La segunda etapa del proyecto es ciertamente la más ambiciosa: nos referimos al diseño e implantación del sistema de acceso electrónico. Se contempla un sistema que permita realizar búsquedas en línea y en tiempo real de las imágenes desde cualquier parte del mundo y a su vez que le permita al usuario obtener copia de las fotos ya sea a través de una impresora láser o grabando la imagen en un disquette. Se contempla, además, ofrecer cierta flexibilidad de manera que el usuario pueda manipular la imagen y ejecutar las siguientes opciones: controlar tono y contraste de la foto, agrandar o reducir la imagen, invertir la imagen (si es positivo, ponerla en negativo o viceversa). Esta manipulación no deberá afectar la imagen original en el sistema ("Request" 1994: 55–56).

El proyecto cuenta con el siguiente equipo: una red Novell de cuatro estaciones, un servidor, un "jukebox" y un impresor láser. La digitalización se realiza con el programa Desk Scan II, integrado a Adobe Photoshop, versión 3.05.

## La colección

La colección de fotos suma 1.2 millones y se distribuye de la siguiente manera:

569,480 fotos en positivo
448,489 negativos
16,945 diapositivas
94,555 misceláneas (incluye láminas, mapas, caricaturas)

A pesar del deterioro de gran parte de la misma, especialmente de los negativos anteriores a la década del 50, se estima que una vez finalice el proyecto de digitalización, la colección sobrepase la colección de imágenes digitalizadas de la Biblioteca del Congreso y la del Smithsonian (Torres Alamo 1996:4).

La riqueza de la colección no es sólo numérica; su alcance temático es de un valor incalculable ya que documenta en imágenes la trayectoria del pueblo puertorriqueño durante el siglo XX así como los acontecimientos más relevantes a nivel mundial. De hecho, la colección incluye fotos anteriores al 1919[1] y su valor se acentúa con la existencia de numerosas fotos que nunca se publicaron.

Sin ánimo de ser exhaustivo, y limitándonos al ámbito puertorriqueño, podemos señalar algunas de las áreas o temas mejor representadas en la colección:

**Nacionalismo.**—Los hechos históricos que marcaron profundamente al pueblo puertorriqueño en el siglo XX como son los acontecimientos protagonizados por el nacionalismo. La primera foto pertenece a la Masacre de Ponce, evento acaecido el 21 de marzo de 1937 en el que la marcha de los Cadetes de la República del Partido Nacionalista fue interrumpida por un tiroteo que dejó un saldo de 19 muertos y casi 100 heridos. La foto capta el cadáver de Eusebio Sánchez, uno de los dos policías que perdió la vida en el incidente.

Trece años más tarde, en octubre de 1950, se produce la Revolución Nacionalista que incluyó el ataque a los cuarteles de la policía en Ponce, Arecibo y Peñuelas, el ataque a la Fortaleza y la toma del pueblo de Jayuya. Esta foto pertenece a los sucesos que acontecieron en Jayuya una vez se aplacó la revuelta con la intervención de la Guardia Nacional. Aunque no existe un texto, podemos inferir que la foto capta el arrastro de uno de los vecinos de Jayuya, específicamente del Barrio Coabey, de donde partieron los nacionalistas. Según un informe del periódico *El Imparcial*, la Guardia Nacional realizó una redada general en dicho barrio apresando a numerosos vecinos (Scarano 1993:731).

**Partido Popular.**—Uno de los aspectos mejor representados de la colección es el de los partidos políticos, entre ellos el Partido Popular Democrático, y sus dirigentes. La colección recoge el desarrollo de todos los partidos desde el Partido Nacionalista, fundado en 1922, hasta el Partido Renovación Puertorriqueña de la década del 80. Esta foto en particular pertenece a los comienzos del Partido Popular y aunque la misma no lleva fecha se puede ubicar antes de 1951 por la presencia de Vicente Géigel Polanco quien desertó las filas de ese partido para ingresar al Partido Independentista en esa fecha. Aparte de Muñoz Marín, al centro de la foto, aparecen otros fundadores del partido como Ernesto Juan Fonfrías, Ernesto Ramos Antonini y Felisa Rincón.

**Huelgas.**—Las diferentes huelgas ocurridas en el país, en especial las realizadas por obreros y por los estudiantes del Recinto de Río Piedras de la Universidad de Puerto Rico. Esta foto representa un instante de la famosa huelga de estudiantes del 1948 y capta una reunión del claustro de la Universidad de Puerto Rico, reunidos en el Teatro de la Universidad bajo la tutela del entonces rector, licenciado Jaime Benítez. Entre los profesores podemos distinguir a la Dra. Margot Arce.

**Virgen del Pozo.**—La foto es especial por dos razones. Primero, nos muestra una instantánea del tren, empresa que dejó de funcionar en 1957. Además, según el calce de la foto, del 26 de mayo de 1954, no se trata de simples pasajeros, sino de algunos de los peregrinos que viajaron al pueblo de Sabana Grande donde apareció una virgen conocida como la Virgen del Pozo que captó la atención de todo el país y suscitó el desplazamiento de miles de puertorriqueños al sudoeste del país. La colección incluye cientos de fotografías que captan el lugar, los visitantes y los acontecimientos del mes de mayo de 1954.

**Televisión.**—La televisión se inició en Puerto Rico en marzo de 1954 cuando WKAQ-TV, empresa fundada por el también propietario del periódico *El Mundo*, Angel Ramos, comenzó su transmisión. La foto recoge el primer programa en vivo que se produjo en la televisión de Puerto Rico, *Mapy y Papi*, estelarizado por los actores puertorriqueños Mapy y Fernando Cortés. El programa salió al aire el 28 de marzo en el espacio de las 7:30 de la noche. En la foto aparece Mapy Cortés junto a Alicia Moreda. Cabe señalar que las fotos de la televisión, en particular de los programas transmitidos por el canal 2, tales como novelas, noticieros y programas musicales, constituyen una de las fortalezas de la colección.

**Arte.**—La colección recoge el desarrollo de las artes en Puerto Rico así como sus exponentes. La colección incluye fotos de representaciones teatrales, el cine hecho en Puerto Rico, pintores, actores, cantantes y músicos, tanto del país como los visitantes o de aquellos residentes permanentes como el distinguido cellista Pablo Casals. Casals se radicó en Puerto Rico en 1956 y un año después fundó el Festival Casals. La foto pertenece a un concierto del festival de 1959 cuando los mismos se llevaban a cabo en el teatro de la Universidad de Puerto Rico.

**Elecciones.**—Se encuentran asimismo fotos que captan los candidatos, la votación y las campañas de todas las elecciones celebradas desde el 1922 hasta el 1988. En esta foto tenemos una escena del plebiscito realizado en 1967 con los resultados finales obtenidos por las tres ideologías representadas.

**Deportes.**—Otro aspecto que cubre la colección es el deporte en la Isla así como la participación de los atletas borucas en eventos a nivel mundial como las Olimpiadas y los Juegos Centroamericanos y Panamericanos. En la foto aparece uno de los deportistas más destacados de todos los tiempos, Roberto Clemente, cuando dirigió a los Senadores de San Juan en la temporada de 1970–1971. La foto, tomada en el Estadio Hiram Bithorn, se publicó el 23 de enero de 1971 y muestra a Clemente discutiendo con el árbitro Germán Pizarro.

**Personalidades.**—Las fotos de las personalidades destacadas del país son numerosas. Aparte de retratos, la colección incluye momentos dramáticos en las vidas de las figuras puertorriqueñas del siglo XX. Ejemplos de estos son:

La visita de Pedro Albizu Campos a la Catedral de San Juan luego de su regreso a la Isla en diciembre de 1947 tras diez años de prisión en Atlanta.

El recibimiento que le ofreció el pueblo a Marisol Malaret, primera puertorriqueña en obtener el título de Miss Universo, en 1970. En la foto, la caravana hace su entrada al Viejo San Juan por la calle San Francisco.

El sepelio de Luis Muñoz Marín el 31 de abril de 1980 en el pueblo de Barranquitas. En la foto vemos como lucía el pueblo para recibir la comitiva fúnebre que viajó de San Juan.

El alcance y la riqueza de la colección permanecen por descubrir ya que hasta ahora se han manejado exclusivamente las fotos. A medida que se organice y se comience a trabajar con los negativos, tendremos un cuadro más amplio del contenido. Ciertamente, una vez finalice el proyecto, la colección aportará una fuente de material único para el estudio de la sociedad puertorriqueña durante el siglo XX.

## NOTA

1. Hemos tomado esto en cuenta para titular nuestro trabajo "Ochenta años de historia en imágenes".

## BIBLIOGRAFIA

Ayala, Elena. 1986. "El periódico *El Mundo* ante la puertorriqueñidad:análisis del discurso editorial". Tesis de maestría. Escuela de Comunicación Pública, Universidad de Puerto Rico.

Ordóñez, María Elisa. [1992.] "Documento de trabajo para la organización, conservación y acceso a la información de la biblioteca de *El Mundo*". S.l.: s.n.

Pedreira, Antonio S. 1982. *El periodismo en Puerto Rico.* Río Piedras, P.R.: Edil.

"Request for the Proposal of *El Mundo* Newspaper Integrated Imaging System". 1994. Río Piedras: University of Puerto Rico.

Rivera Rivera, Nayda L. 1991. *Análisis histórico cronológico de las causas que condicionaron el cierre y venta del periódico* El Mundo *en agosto de 1987.* Tesis de maestría. Escuela de Comunicación Pública, Universidad de Puerto Rico.

Scarano, Francisco. 1993. *Puerto Rico: Cinco siglos de historia.* San Juan: McGraw-Hill.

Torres Alamo, Myra. 1996. "El proyecto de digitalización de las imágenes de la colección de fotos del periódico *El Mundo*". Río Piedras: Sistema de Bibliotecas, Universidad de Puerto Rico.

# 12. Project Open Book and Preservation in the Digital World

Paul Conway

To define the overarching concept of the "virtual library" is a fruitless task in today's evolving technology environment. One person's virtual library is another person's database. To some, the World Wide Web is the ultimate virtual library; to others, a true virtual library has yet to be built and the whole idea remains very poorly conceived. This paper focuses, instead, on the key preservation constructs that must be central driving forces behind any collection of digital resources, if that collection is to endure beyond the life-span of the technology systems upon which it is built.[1]

My perspective is that of an archivist, a preservation librarian, and a student of the history of technology who sees wild opportunity and serious danger coexisting amidst the headlong rush into the digital future. This paper (1) describes three uses of the term "preservation" in connection with digital technologies; (2) outlines five priority areas for preservation action in the digital environment; and (3) briefly describes how Yale University's Project Open Book [http://www.library.yale.edu/preservation/presyale.htm] and other initiatives at the university fit into this preservation action scenario.

## Preservation in the Digital World

The concept of preservation is at the heart of the virtual library just as it is at the heart of a traditional research library or archival repository. To affirm that this is so, we can ask this rhetorical question: "Can any institution—library, archives, historical society, or museum—afford to squander its investment in digital technologies when moving from pilot project to operational system?" The risk of catastrophic loss is real without a serious effort to ensure long-term access to today's digital image files.

As librarians and archivists have experimented with the capabilities of digital imaging technologies, the concept of preservation has acquired three different meanings. It is important to distinguish among them in building a comprehensive definition of "preservation" in the digital world.

**Protect Original Items.**—Digital image technology can be used to create a high-quality copy of an original item. By limiting direct physical access to valuable documents, digital imaging becomes a "preservation application," distinct from an "access application." The original order of the collection or book is "frozen," much like microfilm sets images in a linear sequence. Sophisticated indexing schemes facilitate browsing and minimize the potential for damage or disruption to a collection caused by "fishing expeditions" through the published or unpublished record. Preservation via digital copying has been the most compelling force in motivating archives and libraries to experiment with hardware and software capabilities.

**Make Use Possible.**—For a small subset of valuable but deteriorated documents, digital imaging technology is a viable, and possibly the only, cost-effective mechanism for facilitating research use. A recent experiment involving digitizing oversize color maps demonstrated that the only way to really use the maps, which have faded badly and are very brittle, is to view them on a large color monitor after they have been digitized and enhanced.[2] Similarly, the managers of the Andrew Wyeth estate have found that reproductions of the artist's work are accurate in digital form.[3]

**Maintain Digital Objects.**— Once digital conversion of the original document has been completed, the challenge to protect the digits from corruption or destruction becomes the focus. This phase, "digital preservation," focuses on the choice of interim storage media, the life expectancy of a digital imaging system, and the concern for migrating the digital files to future systems as a way of ensuring future access.[4] A workable framework for preservation in the digital world should take into account the use of digital imaging technology for reproducing research materials, the choice of appropriate technologies, and the protection of the digital information as long as that information has value to the institution and its patrons.

Digital imaging technology is more than just another reformatting option. Imaging involves transforming the very concept of format, not simply creating an accurate picture of a book, document, photograph, or map in a different medium. The power of digital enhancement, the possibilities for structured indexes, and the mathematics of compression and communication together alter the concept of preservation. The digital world transforms traditional preservation concepts from protecting the physical integrity of the object to specifying the creation and maintenance of the object whose intellectual integrity is its primary characteristic.

## Preservation Priorities for Action

The principles of preservation in the digital world are the same as those in the analog world: longevity, choice, quality, integrity, and access.

**Longevity.**—Preservation in the digital world has little concern for the longevity of optical disks, magnetic tape, and newer, more fragile storage media. The viability of the virtual library is much more dependent on the life expectancy of document management systems—a chain only as strong as its weakest component. Today's digital media should be handled with care, but most likely will far outlast the capability of systems to retrieve and interpret the data stored on them. Since we can never know for certain when a system has become obsolete, libraries must be prepared to migrate valuable image data, indexes, and software to future generations of the technology.

**Choice.**—Selection for preservation in digital form is not a one-time choice made near the end of an item's life cycle, but rather an ongoing process intimately connected to the active use of the digital files. The value judgments applied when making a decision to convert documents from paper or film to digital image are valid only within the context of the original system. With the need to migrate data to another storage and access system comes the mandate to revisit the wisdom of the initial choice. It is a rare collection of digital files, indeed, that can justify the cost of a comprehensive migration strategy without factoring in the larger intellectual context of related digital files stored elsewhere and their combined uses for research and scholarship.

**Quality.**—Quality in the digital world is conditioned by the limitations of capture and display technology. Digital conversion places less emphasis on obtaining a faithful reproduction of the original in favor of finding the best representation of the original in digital form. Mechanisms and techniques for judging quality of digital reproductions are different and more sophisticated than those for assessing microfilm or photocopy reproductions. Additionally, the primary goal of preservation quality is to capture as much intellectual and visual content as is technically possible and then to display that content to viewers in ways most appropriate to their needs.

**Integrity.**—As with traditional preservation, the concept of integrity of the virtual library has at least two facets: physical and intellectual. A commitment to the physical integrity of a digital image file has far less to do with the media upon which the data are stored than with the loss of information that occurs when a file is created originally and then compressed mathematically for storage or transmission across a network. In the domain of intellectual integrity, index information is not independent of the content of the item but rather is an integral part of the digital file. Structural indexes and data descriptions traditionally published with an item as tables of contents or prepared as discrete finding aids or bibliographic records must be preserved—as metadata—along with the digital image files themselves. The preservation of intellectual integrity also involves authentication procedures—like audit trails—to make sure files are not altered intentionally or accidentally.

**Access.**—In the digital world, the concept of access is transformed from a convenient byproduct of the preservation process to its central motif. The content, structure, and integrity of the information object assume center stage; the ability of a machine to transport and display this information object becomes an assumed end result of preservation action rather than its primary goal. Preservation in the digital world is not simply the act of preserving access but also includes a description of the "thing" to be preserved. In the context of the virtual library, the object of preservation is a high-quality, high-value, well-protected, and fully integrated version of an original source document.

Decisions about long-term storage and access cannot be deferred in the hope that technological solutions will emerge like a medieval knight in shining armor. An appraisal of the present value of a book, a manuscript collection, or a series of photographs in its original format is the necessary point of departure for making a judgment about preservation of the digital image version. The mere potential for increased access to a digitized collection does not add value to an underutilized collection. Similarly, the powerful capabilities of a relational index cannot compensate for a collection of documents whose structure, relationships, and intellectual content are poorly understood. Digital image conversion in an operational environment requires a firm, long-standing institutional commitment to preservation, the full integration of the technology into information management procedures and processes, and strong leadership in developing appropriate definitions and standards for digital preservation.

## Project Open Book and Preservation at Yale University Library

Project Open Book is a multifaceted, multiphase research and development program at Yale University Library. Its purpose is to explore the feasibility of large-scale conversion of preservation microfilm to digital imagery by modeling the process in an in-house laboratory. The project has three goals: (1) create a large-volume digital image library and, in doing so, evaluate issues of selection, quality, and cost; (2) enhance intellectual access to the image files by creating structured indexes; and (3) enhance physical access to digital materials by providing distributed access over the Yale University campus network.[5]

Since 1991, Project Open Book has unfolded in a sequence of phases, designed in part to allow the project to evolve as the digital imaging marketplace changed. In the first phase—the organizational phase—Yale conducted a formal bid process and selected the Xerox Corporation to serve as its principal partner in the project.[6] During the second phase—the setup phase—Yale acquired a single integrated conversion workstation, including microfilm scanning hardware and associated conversion and enhancement software; tested and evaluated this workstation; and made the transition to a fully engineered production system.[7] The Commission on Preservation and Access provided partial funding for the setup phase. In the third phase—the production conversion phase—Yale built a multi-workstation conversion system, hired technical staff, converted

2,000 volumes from microfilm, indexed the volumes, stored the results, and tested a prototype World Wide Web access tool developed by Xerox.[8]

Preservation in the digital world places fairly stringent criteria on a digital imaging system in a given library. How does Project Open Book measure up to these criteria? The answer is a mixed bag. Let us look briefly at the criteria.

**Longevity.**—The storage media chosen, 5.25 magneto-optical disks at the base of a hierarchical storage concept, is the most standard and most rugged available. The project uses well-established technology standards for creating, tagging, and compressing the digital images. Indexing and database tools are proprietary Xerox products that do not conform to present open technology standards. The options for migrating to future systems are limited without additional, and possibly expensive, investment.

**Choice.**—Significant effort went into identifying the 2,000 items to be sure of their value and potential usefulness for scholarly research. It is outside the scope of this brief essay to explain the selection process in detail. The central issue is not the value or usefulness of the individual items, but the intellectual cohesiveness of the whole. Without a well-conceived and well-implemented evaluation of the content of Project Open Book, the question of long-term value remains open.

**Quality.**—Given the natural limitations of bitonal scanning from microfilm, the quality of the digital images in Project Open Book is superb. Bitonal scanning at 600 dpi produces an extraordinarily clear and crisp representation of text and many kinds of illustrations. A judicious mix of bitonal and grayscale scanning would increase image quality even further.

**Integrity.**—Project Open Book meets most of the complex criteria pertaining to the preservation of physical and intellectual integrity of the original book when converted to a digital image. The system uses lossless compression routines and well-documented image file headers. The indexing procedures for each digital "book" retain the intellectual and physical structures of the original item. The security of the digital data is assured by limiting access to the original item.

**Access.**—Because of the proprietary nature of the Project Open Book system software, the entire corpus of materials converted from microfilm is not yet available for consultation. More important, it remains to be seen whether the image and index database can be "exported" to an open technology standards platform in the near future.

On balance, I would give Project Open Book a grade of "B" if I were to score it according to the five criteria, although this is really not fair because, as with most pilot projects in libraries and archives, Project Open Book was never intended to meet preservation criteria standards that were barely conceived of when the project began.

## Next Steps

The next steps, now in the planning stages, that Yale University Library will be taking to move ahead on its "virtual library" initiatives are the following:

1. Associate University Librarian Don Waters chaired a joint CPA/RLG Task Force on Archiving the Digital Record. The conclusions of the report, which has just been published, will no doubt be influential in the development of the library's organizational infrastructure.
2. The Commission on Preservation and Access will be awarding a grant to Yale to model and test an archiving strategy for social and political polling data stored in the library.
3. The library will be migrating the image and index data in Project Open Book from its proprietary system to one that utilizes open technology standards.
4. Full patron access to all 2,000 volumes will be possible through links from a new World Wide Web gateway to the library's online catalog.

### NOTES

1. Paul Conway, *Preservation in the Digital World* (Washington, DC: Commission on Preservation and Access, March 1996).

2. Janet Gertz et al., *Oversize Color Images Project, 1994–1995: Final Report of Phase I* (Washington, DC: Commission on Preservation and Access, 1995).

3. Fred Mintzer and John D. McFall, "Organization of a System for Managing the Text and Images That Describe an Art Collection," *SPIE Image Handling and Reproduction Systems Integration* 1460 (1991): 38–49.

4. Task Force on Archiving of Digital Information, *Preserving Digital Information: Final Report and Recommendations* (Washington, DC: Commission on Preservation and Access, May 1996). [http://www.rlg.org/ArchTF/]

5. Donald J. Waters, *From Microfilm to Digital Imagery* (Washington, DC: Commission on Preservation and Access, June 1991).

6. Donald J. Waters and Shari Weaver, *The Organizational Phase of Project Open Book* (Washington, DC: Commission on Preservation and Access, September, 1992).

7. Paul Conway and Shari Weaver, *The Setup Phase of Project Open Book* (Washington, DC: Commission on Preservation and Access, June 1994).

8. More information on Project Open Book is available at http://www.library.yale.edu/preservation/presyale.htm.

# 13. Sight and Sound: Hispanic Audiovisual Archives in the Cybernetic Age

Georgette M. Dorn

Peruvian poet Antonio Cisneros recorded selections from his work at the Library of Congress on May 10, 1996, heeding the words of Gabriela Mistral, the first Latin American Nobel laureate in literature, who said that "Poetry hushed and inert in books fades away and dies . . . the air not the printed word is its natural home. Recordings serve it well."[1] Thus Cisneros became the 640th writer to add his voice to those preserved at the Library of Congress in the Archive of Hispanic Literature on Tape, a collection which contains not only poetry, but also recordings of prose fiction, theater, essays, and interviews with authors, nine of them on videotape.

To date 31 countries are represented in this unique and diverse audiovisual archive. In addition to Spanish, the collection features readings in Catalan, Portuguese, French, Creole, Náhuatl, Quechua, Zapotec, Aymara, Papiamento, and English by the writers themselves. Among the authors recorded to date are eight Nobel laureates. Three are from Spain: Juan Ramón Jiménez, Vicente Aleixandre, and Camilo José Cela; five are from Latin America: Mistral, Miguel Angel Asturias, Pablo Neruda, Gabriel García Márquez, and Octavio Paz. Other world-renowned figures in the archive include Jorge Luis Borges, Mario Vargas Llosa, Julio Cortázar, Jorge Amado, Nélida Piñón, Carlos Fuentes, and Isabel Allende. About 6 percent of the readings or interviews are by political figures, essayists, and historians, such as Leopoldo Zea, Angel María Garibay, Juan José Arévalo, José Honório Rodrigues, Manuel Moreno Fraginals, Austregésilo de Athayde, Vianna Moog, and Alberto Miramón. Notable interviews, many on videotape, are with Vargas Llosa, Cortázar, Borges, José Donoso, Abel Posse, Nélida Piñón, Ernesto Sábato, and Guillermo Cabrera Infante, among others.[2] The archive offers unique research strategies because the spoken word provides a new dimension in the relationship between the writer and the text. Many authors preface their reading with introductory remarks, or offer commentaries between selections. A number of authors have recorded more than once (Borges, Juan Liscano, Donoso, Sophia Andresen). Harvey Johnson, University of Houston, and John Fein of Duke University said that by choosing both well-known authors and those just beginning their careers, the Library has compiled "the best in Hispanic literature."[3]

Curated by Francisco Aguilera from 1942 to 1971, and since that date by the author of this paper, the development of the Archive of Hispanic Literature on Tape can be divided into two phases. During the first or formative phase, guidelines were established by Aguilera and an informal board of advisors, and 232 figures were recorded for the archive, at a time when tape-recordings were still comparatively rare. To date, 408 writers have been added to the collection during the second phase (1971–1996). In the 1970s, the Hispanic Division expanded the archive's scope by including figures from the non-Hispanic Caribbean, as well as U.S. Hispanic writers.

## History of the Archive, 1942–1971

The collection of Hispanic recordings was begun when the Uruguayan poet Emilio Oribe passed through Washington in 1942 and recorded his poem titled "Oda al cielo de la Nueva Atlántida" dedicated to Archibald MacLeish, the poet who was then Librarian of Congress. He was followed by the Venezuelan poet Andrés Eloy Blanco in 1943. As in 1942 the Library had set out to formulate a program to record North American poets, the Hispanic Division decided to assemble a similar archive of recorded poetry in Spanish. Francisco Aguilera concluded "that a project with a defined scope would be desirable." By 1953, the materials accumulated since 1942 were acknowledged to be "unique and of the highest quality. . . . Scholars, creative writers, librarians, educators, publishers, and other users of the Library's materials were unequivocal in their high regard for the developing collection and its possibilities."[4] It was decided to develop a collection of oral literature in a systematic fashion. Criteria for inclusion in the archive were to be based on recognition of a writer by critics, professors, award committees, the media, and the public.

Many major poets had recorded by the end of the archive's first decade. Spanish poet Pedro Salinas came to the Library to tape "El Contemplado," a poem inspired by the sea near Puerto Rico where he had lived. In 1950 the Library issued a long-playing (LP) record of this poem.[5] Jiménez's recording of *El platero y yo* for the archive was converted into a "talking book" by the National Library Service for the Blind and Physically Handicapped. According to Prof. Graciela Palau de Nemes from the University of Maryland, this publication fulfilled the Nobel Prize Committee's requirement of a publication by the candidate the year that the prize was awarded.[6] Mistral's recording for the Library in 1956 is her only extant one; it was issued as an LP record in 1971.[7]

Not all the writers the Library wanted to record could come to Washington; therefore Aguilera began a carefully crafted program to commission specific authors to record in other countries, either at U.S. embassies or at radio stations, a practice still followed today. Thus, in Madrid the Library was able to record almost all of the major Spanish poets who developed under the tutelage of Jiménez. Ten Catalan poets read for the archive at Radio Catalunya in Barcelona. Recordings in Portuguese were added in 1951–1953 when poets

Sophia de Mello Breyner Andresen, Júlio Dantas, and others read in Lisbon. Manoel Bandeira, Ascenso Ferreira, Jorge de Lima, and Augusto Schmidt recorded before the microphones of the United States Information Service in Rio de Janeiro. Five Haitian poets read selections from their work in Port-au-Prince.[8]

By 1958 the Hispanic Division decided to further develop its collection of oral literature by adding prose fiction, theater, and essay selections. Curator Aguilera, with grants from the Rockefeller Foundation, undertook three major acquisition trips to Latin America to record a representative selection of writers in order to form a well-integrated archive. During the first trip (1958) he recorded a total of 68 writers in Lima, Santiago, Buenos Aires, and Montevideo. Aguilera brought back recordings by 48 authors from his second acquisitions trip in 1960 to Panama, Guatemala, and Mexico. Aguilera's third journey, sponsored by Rockefeller in search of voices, took him to Ecuador, Colombia, and Venezuela and he was able to record 42 authors.[9]

Writers also continued recording at the studios of the Library. In 1961 Paz read selections of poetry and essays for ninety minutes. Neruda visited the Library in 1966 to participate in meetings of the International P.E.N. Clubs and recorded for the archive his famed poem "Alturas de Macchu Picchu." Among other major figures added during the 1960s and early 1970s were the aforementioned Cela, Ana María Matute, Homero Aridjis, Gustavo Sainz, Ernesto Cardenal, and Rómulo Gallegos. We recorded the Chilean poet Nicanor Parra, the Ecuadoran Jorge Carrera Andrade, and the Haitian poet Philippe Thoby-Marcelin, all of whom attended the International Poetry Festival at the Library of Congress, April 13–15, 1970. The first 232 authors and their respective selections are listed in *The Archive of Hispanic Literature on Tape: A Descriptive Guide*, compiled by Aguilera and edited by the author of this paper.

## The Second Phase, 1971–1996

The 1970s witnessed the peak of the "Boom" in Latin American literature and these were also boom years for the archive. We were able to add the great narrative writers of our times. Fuentes, who was writing *Terra nostra* at the Woodrow Wilson Center for Scholars in Washington, taped large portions of his novel in progress. Juan Goytisolo recorded readings and commentary for the Library just after Franco's death. Novelists Vargas Llosa and Cortázar[10] read and were interviewed by José Miguel Oviedo and me, respectively. García Márquez visited Washington in October of 1977, accompanying President Omar Torrijos, who came to sign the Panama Canal Treaties, and recorded the last chapter from *El otoño del patriarca.* Soon after leaving Cuba, Reinaldo Arenas stopped at the Library where he recorded for the archive. Other Cubans added in the late 1970s and early 1980s include Antonio Benítez Rojo, Severo Sarduy (in Paris), Lourdes Casal, Cabrera Infante (on audio and videotape), and Heberto Padilla. Donoso recorded in 1977 and 1981, was interviewed on video in 1987 at the Library while he was a fellow at the Woodrow Wilson Center, and again in 1993. Many other authors were recorded at the Library during this period, such as Ernesto Sábato (on audio and videotape), Luisa Valenzuela, Osvaldo Bayer, Enrique Anderson Imbert, Marta Traba, Ivan Angelo, Carmen Laforet, Jorge Edwards, Gonzalo Rojas, Juan Gustavo Cobo Borda, Rei Berroa (who also played the guitar), and Elvira Orphée. A very interesting videotape was made with Alastair Reid interviewing Borges in 1984. Other renowned intellectuals added were Jaime Benítez, Arturo Morales Carrión, and Fernando Belaúnde Terry.

Only five Brazilian writers had recorded by 1972. In order to add more Portuguese-speaking authors, the Hispanic Division asked the Library's Field Office in Rio de Janeiro to systematically record specific Brazilian writers. In Rio I recorded Jorge Amado, as well as José Cândido de Carvalho. To date 91 more Brazilians have been added to the archive, most of them recorded in Rio. Brazilian writers in the archive include, among others, Cabral de Melo Neto, Carlos Drummond de Andrade, Rachel de Queiroz, Henriqueta Lisboa, Raul Bopp, Affonso Romano Sant'Anna, José Sarney, José Mindlin, and Moacyr Scliar. At the U.S. Embassy in Lisbon, I recorded Vergilio Ferreira and Pedro Tamen in 1978 and Ana Hatherly, Nuño Judice, Olga Gonçalves, and others in 1992, and at the Library of Congress Alberto Lacerda, Helder Macedo, and Natalia Correa.

With the help of U.S. cultural affairs officers and the United States Information Service (USIS) and their recording laboratories, we were able to tape a great many authors in Madrid, Mexico, Port-au-Prince, Montevideo, Caracas, and Buenos Aires. The collection was further enriched with recordings by Alvaro Mutis, Elena Poniatowska, Carlos Augusto León, Marie Thérèse Colimon-Hall, Miguel Delibes, Ernestina Champourcin, and Demetrio Aguilera Malta, among others.

U.S. and Canadian university faculty members traveling abroad often assist the Hispanic Division in actually recording literary figures for the archive, often with the assistance of USIS. In this manner Angela Dellepiane of CUNY taped Angélica Gorodischer and Vlady Kociancich in Buenos Aires in 1995. Rosa Garrido of Trent University, Ontario, taped Soledad Puértolas, Rosa, and others in Spain in 1994. Catalina Case recorded Paraguayan writers Josefina Plá, José Luis Appleyard, and José M. Sanjurjo in Asunción in 1980. Juan Bruce-Novoa recorded Chicano writer Luis Leal, as well as writers in Mexico, such as Manuel Felguerez and Jaime Labastida. Margaret Crahan, Hunter College, was able to record Miguel Barnet, Edmundo Desnoes, Nancy Morejón, and others during a trip to Cuba in 1977. The Center of Inter-American Relations in New York also lent its support to the recording program by taping Jorge Arbeleche, José Bianco, and Manuel Puig in 1977–1980. The University of Puerto Rico recorded 14 of the island's major writers, such as Nilita Vientós,

Juan Antonio Corretjer, Abelardo Díaz Alfaro, Pedro Juan Soto, and Violeta López Suria. While participating in a conference in Puerto Rico, I was able to record Cuban playwright José Triana and the Puerto Rican novelist Luis Rafael Sánchez. At the Library, we recorded well-known Puerto Ricans Rosario Ferré, Enrique Laguerre, Jaime Benítez, and Arturo Morales Carrión.

Over the years, members of the Hispanic Division, supported with a bequest from Archer Huntington, have traveled to participate in conferences as well as to record writers. I taped Cortázar in 1975 at the University of Oklahoma, where he was honored at the Fifth Oklahoma Conference on Writers of the Hispanic World, and in 1977 I recorded Vargas Llosa, who was the honoree at the sixth conference of that name. Vargas Llosa was videotaped reading from his book *El pez en el agua* at a 1994 event sponsored by the Library's Poetry and Literature Center. I recorded authors in Caracas (Raúl Gustavo Aguirre, Gloria Stolk, and Antonia Palacios, 1977), in Ottawa at the Third Inter-American Conference of Women Writers (Carmen Conde, Mercedes Levinson, Marta Lynch, Hilda Perera, etc., 1978), in San Juan, Puerto Rico (Gustavo Agrait, etc., 1982), in Paris (Severo Sarduy, Julio Ramón Ribeyro, Fernando Ainsa, 1983), in Barcelona (Joan Brossa, Père Calders, Père Gimferrer, Salvador Espriù, 1984), in San Diego (Olga Orozco, Margo Glantz, 1985), and in Albuquerque (Rudolfo Anaya, Sabine Ulibarri, etc., 1985). Former Hispanic Division chief William E. Carter taped an interview in Miami with famed Cuban anthropologist Lydia Cabrera in 1981. In 1983, Dolores Martin, editor of the *Handbook of Latin American Studies*, recorded noted Nicaraguan poets Mariana Sansón and Beltrán Morales while attending SALALM in Managua. She also recorded Dominican poets Pedro Mir and Freddy Gatón Arce during a 1989 trip to Santo Domingo.[11]

In 1979 Juan Bruce-Novoa became the first Chicano author to record for the archive. In 1985, while attending the Latin American Studies Association meeting in Albuquerque, at the University of New Mexico I was able to tape Sabine Ulibarri, Rudolfo Anaya, Carlos Morton, Tony Mares, and Cecilio García Camarillo. Other Hispanic American authors included since then were Denise Chaves, Ana Castillo, and Dagoberto Gilb.[12] Kamau Brathwaite from Barbados was the first Anglophone Caribbean author represented in the archive. He was followed by Jamaican John Hearne, Zee Edgell from Belize, David Edgecombe from Monserrat, and in 1995 by Trinidanian Lynn Joseph. The French Caribbean is represented with the voice of Leon Damas and the Dutch area by Surinam's Shrinivasi [pseud.]. The more recent authors recorded at the Library, in addition to those already mentioned, are Arturo Bryce Echenique, Gloria Alfaro, and Eraclio Zepeda.

Of the 640 authors represented in the archive, 60 percent recorded abroad and 40 percent did so at the Library of Congress. An informal advisory board chaired by this writer periodically evaluates the authors recorded, offering advice on new names and alerting the Hispanic Division about emerging trends in Luso-Hispanic and Caribbean literature. The archive is considered by scholars as a major research tool for the study of literary generations and for textual comparisons with voice recordings. Researchers can explore the rich gamut of ethnic expressions in what is also an Indo-Afro-Iberian resource by listening to Nicolás Guillén's "Songoro cosongo," or "Canción del bongó," or to Costa Rican Eulalia Bernard's selections in English, Spanish, and Creole. The archive is used by linguists, historians, anthropologists, and sociologists who can listen to Jorge Icaza, Octavio Paz, Gilberto Freyre, Manuel Moreno Fraginals, or Daniel Cosío Villegas.

## The Archive of Hispanic Literature on Tape and Automated Technologies

With the exception of the four published offerings on cassette/LP, currently the recordings of the Archive of Hispanic Literature on Tape are only accessible to researchers in the Library's Hispanic Reading Room.[13] Several years ago the Hispanic Division concluded that it is important to broaden the universe of potential users by making part or all of the archive's collection available electronically. We are planning to digitize the list of authors, the titles of the works read, and relevant bibliographies. Eventually we want to add a selection of the authors' voices and some of the accompanying still photographs and video footage, as well as the full text of selected writings. The digitized database would be mounted on the Internet and/or published on a CD-ROM.

At present, each recording in the archive has a separate MARC record in the Library's online catalog; these MARC entries are accessible from any Library of Congress terminal and on the Internet.[14] As a first step toward providing wider access to the information contained in the archive, we plan to extract and mount these records on the Hispanic Division's World Wide Web site. Ideally, these records would form their own small database in MARC format and would be searchable using Inquery or some other Internet search tool to allow for fielded searching. However, if we see that designing such a database will take too much time, we will create a simple ASCII database, searchable only through each browser's own search tool(s), while we explore options that will provide fielded searching of this data.

We are also exploring options for converting to electronic format *The Archive of Hispanic Literature on Tape: A Descriptive Guide*, an alphabetical guide to the first 232 authors who recorded for the archive up to 1971. For each author, this book contains a list of selections read, bio-bibliographic information, and critical assessments. It also features a list of the authors by country. Digitizing this book will probably be accomplished by scanning the print edition, performing optical character recognition (OCR), followed by careful manual proofreading of the scanned text.

As for the 347 authors recorded since the publication of the aforementioned guide, a succession of academic interns and fellows at the Hispanic Division have prepared notebooks for each author which include typewritten lists of the titles recorded, photocopied or transcribed texts of the selections read, and, in some cases, transcriptions of recorded interviews. The data pertaining to most of the more recent authors are already available in electronic format, in WordPerfect files. The remainder of the information will need to be scanned from the typewritten pages. The project may be complicated somewhat by the fact that the photocopied texts and the typewritten pages in the notebooks have different formats, layouts, and fonts. In some cases we may need to resort to rekeying information, since the quality of some of the typewritten pages will not permit clean scanning.

We hope eventually to enhance the electronic archive by adding at least one scanned photograph of each author (if available), thereby bringing the authors' likenesses to the user. We also want to explore the feasibility and cost of adding a selection of the recorded voices as well as moving images from the videotapes. In addition, we hope to include portions of the full text of selected writings recorded for the archive; it is most likely that these texts will be converted as scanned image files rather than text files.

Although we can begin immediately to list the authors and the titles recorded for the archive either on the Internet or CD-ROM, in order to add full text, images, and/or voices, the Hispanic Division will need to obtain written permission from each author or the executor of his/her estate. Writing to each of 619 authors will be an arduous labor-intensive task.

## Conclusion

The Library of Congress has assembled a unique multimedia and audiovisual resource in the Archive of Hispanic Literature on Tape. It is now committed to converting it to electronic format and making the product available as soon as possible to provide wider access to this diverse resource. Given the current budgetary constraints forecast for the Library and the federal government, the automation project of the Archive cannot be undertaken with appropriated funds. Instead, we are interested in discussing how retrospective conversion to an electronic format might be accomplished cooperatively. The Fundación MAPFRE América has already signaled its interest in collaborating with the Hispanic Division on a pilot project to digitize the archive. We hope to explore with the joint SALALM-LASA Scholarly Resources Task Force support of the project among librarians, scholars, and professional organizations. Once we have secured the necessary backing of the academic community we plan to seek additional financial assistance from foundations and philanthropic organizations interested in supporting this worthwhile project.

## NOTES

1. Francisco Aguilera, "Iberian and Latin American Poetry on Records," *Library of Congress Quarterly Journal* 14:2 (February 1957), 18.

2. Georgette M. Dorn, "Luso-Hispanic Recordings at the Library of Congress," *Latin American Research Review* 14:2 (1979), 178.

3. Francisco Aguilera, "Introduction," *The Archive of Hispanic Literature on Tape: A Descriptive Guide*, edited by Georgette M. Dorn (Washington, DC: Library of Congress, 1974), pp. v-vi.

4. Ibid.

5. Pedro Salinas, *El Contemplado* (Washington, DC: Library of Congress, 1950), HLP-1. Cassette copies of this and other recordings mentioned in this paper may be obtained for $9.50 each from the Library of Congress, Recorded Sound Section, Washington, DC 20540.

6. Conversation with Francisco Aguilera and Graciela Palau de Nemes of the University of Maryland, at the Library of Congress, February 28, 1968.

7. *Gabriela Mistral Reading Her Own Poetry* (Washington, DC: Library of Congress, 1971), HLP-2.

8. Dorn, "Luso-Hispanic Recordings at the Library of Congress," p. 175.

9. Aguilera, "Introduction," *The Archive*, pp. vi–ix.

10. In addition to the recordings by Salinas and Mistral, the Library of Congress issued the following LPs: *Readings by Julio Cortázar* (HLP-3) and *Two Colombian Poets: Eduardo Carranza and Germán Pardo García* (HLP-4). All four recordings are also available on cassette.

11. Dorn, "El Archivo de Literatura Hispánica de la Biblioteca del Congreso," pp. 52–53.

12. Georgette Dorn, "Expresiones de Literatura Chicana," *Ideas '92*. (University of Miami) 2:1 (1988), 98–101.

13. I am indebted to Sue Mundell, Assistant Editor of the *Handbook of Latin American Studies*, for guidance in formulating plans to automate and to convert electronically this rich multimedia resource, as well as for helpful comments on this paper. Ms. Mundell planned and carried out in 1994–1995, with generous funding from the Fundación MAPFRE América in Madrid and the Andrew W. Mellon Foundation, the retrospective conversion of the first 53 volumes of the *Handbook* and the production of the *Handbook*'s CD-ROM.

14. The Library's online catalog is available by telnetting to locis.loc.gov. One can search the 609 sound recordings cataloged to date by typing: find c "Archive of Hispanic Literature on Tape." For further documentation and search help, point your gopher to marvel.loc.gov, choose "Library of Congress Online Systems," then choose "Quick Search Guides to LOCIS."

# 14. The Latin Americanist Research Resources Pilot Project: A Distributed Model of Library Cooperation

Deborah Jakubs

The Latin Americanist Research Resources Pilot Project of the Association of Research Libraries (ARL) has faced and continues to face many challenges. It is, after all, a complex cooperative effort among 34 libraries of various sizes and collecting emphases, and its success depends on many factors. This paper reviews the very significant progress we have made toward increasing access to Latin American research materials. It is no wonder that the Latin American Project is the most advanced of the ARL pilots, given that many activities within SALALM are directed toward the same goals. We had a head start.

The meeting of ARL project bibliographers, added to the schedule on fairly short notice, was one event that indicated clearly the forward momentum within SALALM. Scheduled at a very inconvenient hour, during a pouring rain, the meeting was not expected to be well attended. It nevertheless attracted 35 librarians and bookdealers, who proceeded to discuss a wide variety of topics, including the results of the questionnaire recently sent to all project participants to survey each institution's experience with the project and the bibliographers' suggestions for scaling up.

The group's conclusions indicated unequivocally that they wish to move rapidly away from a pure pilot project. Specifically, the group decided to strengthen and diversify the table of contents database mounted on UT-LANIC and give it more of an identity (at present it contains some 300 tables of contents from Mexican and Argentine serials); to move into the area of monographs, perhaps by redirecting a fixed percentage of the acquisitions budget at each institution toward intensive collecting in a particular field or on a particular country; to utilize the World Wide Web to publicize the project and our distributed collection strengths; to cancel some of the widely held project serials; and to build on other initiatives that now exist, such as the regional consortia (Calafia, the California group; LANE, Latin America Northeast; and LASER, Latin America Southeast Region), the efforts of bookdealers who have been experimenting with serials databases (e.g., García Cambeiro and Editorial Inca), and HAPI (Hispanic American Periodicals Index). It became clear by the end of the meeting that we have at our disposal many building blocks for a distributed network of collections and services.

Although we do not yet know how the pieces will fit together, it is encouraging that there are so many efforts under way. Our colleagues, the bookdealers, have once again risen to the challenge of seeking new ways, utilizing technology, to assist libraries in gaining access to information and to a wide variety of publications. This is yet another step in a long collaboration among librarians, bookdealers, and publishers within SALALM. The prototype serials document-delivery operations represent only one way in which this is occurring; other services include providing MARC records to libraries for ease in ordering and cataloging, regular email communication, and new, flexible approaches to approval plans.

The regional consortia have become very effective in dealing with precisely the same questions of access, delivery, rationalization of resources, and collaboration that form the basis of the ARL project. For example, efforts within the consortia are directed at the persistent problem of access to newspapers from Latin America, and to sources for current news from the region. Other groups are sharing information on collection strengths, especially the availability of large microform sets, and designing special lending agreements. While it is true that basic, core collections must be available widely and on many campuses, individual bibliographers have also tended to concentrate their efforts on developing particular collection strengths, thus differentiating their institutions' collections from one another. The more we, our scholars, and our students know about each others' collections, the better we will be able to provide access to resources; and the regional consortia are making strides toward sharing that information, which is the basis on which a distributed collection, as envisioned by the Latin American Project, rests.

As we work with undergraduates and graduate students to gain access to resources that are not physically on our own campuses, we are helping to create within a new generation of scholars a consciousness of the importance and viability of a distributed system of Latin Americanist resources. This is not only one of the primary goals of the ARL project, but will be, in fact, the cornerstone of its success: the enthusiastic acceptance by faculty of the potential for much broader access to specialized research materials than is currently possible. Once they see that it can be done, and that it can work to their advantage, the model will be more appealing.

Hand-in-hand with increased access goes another goal, one that is of critical interest to university presidents and library directors: to demonstrate the economies of this approach, to create a cost-effective multiplayer system of access to diverse collections and electronic resources. We must be able to demonstrate that our project, especially once it has been expanded to include monographs, additional serial titles, and more digitized resources, will help contain the steeply rising costs of library acquisitions. This is not to say that it will allow us to cut budgets, but instead will make it possible to keep up with the cost increases while continuing to provide access to a wide array of resources.

We have learned many lessons from the ARL project. First, it is highly desirable to move away from a pilot phase and into the mainstream as quickly as feasible. In other words, a pilot serves only to test certain ideas; as Paul Conway commented in his paper on the Yale Open Book Project (Chapter 12), pilots serve their purpose and then disappear. In this case, the pilot is leading the way, indicating how we can provide information in new ways, but it will be best if the outcomes of the pilot are integrated into our daily operations and the work of our users in a seamless way; for example, it is not productive to look in yet another place for a subset of Argentine and Mexican journals. Our goal is to make it simple for users to have access to the journal articles and publications from nongovernmental organizations (NGO) they seek, without having to stop and think exactly where and how to get those particular materials.

We have learned that, for the most part, our internal library operations are not organized to facilitate the functioning of a distributed system. At their meeting, and in their questionnaire responses, many project bibliographers indicated that the internal bureaucracies within their libraries inhibit the effectiveness of a distributed system of access. For one thing, document delivery must improve significantly in both turnaround time and the capacity for users to generate requests directly if the distributed model is going to work. These and other aspects of library operations that underlie the project's success, and that of future distributed efforts, must receive attention from library administrators as well as from bibliographers and other concerned library staff.

We still face acquisitions problems. As we all know, Latin American journals are a dynamic body of materials. Some of the project journals have ceased publication, or have been published erratically, or are otherwise difficult to collect on a regular basis. The NGO publications have been especially slow in coming, but we will persist with this effort because of the importance of such resources to the work of many of our scholars and students. It may be advisable to adopt a different approach, perhaps to concentrate responsibility for NGOs in a smaller number of institutions, or to have all participating libraries report on the NGO publications that they are currently receiving, and commit to continue to receive them and catalog them expeditiously.

The distributed model represented by the ARL project has not yet been publicized as much as it deserves, partly because as a pilot it has taken many months to become functional. It is time for us to dedicate serious effort to publicizing the interdependence of our library collections, in anticipation of the major culture shift that will need to take place on our campuses as this model increasingly becomes the norm. Through the Task Force on Scholarly Resources of the Latin American Studies Association (LASA), some progress has been made in disseminating information to scholars about the project. A website can serve to expand this function, if it is carefully maintained and regularly updated.

Finally, the ongoing management of the project has been handled on different levels by various people, including a dedicated Project Coordinator. It will not be possible to maintain the labor intensity of this arrangement for the long run, and so we must consider other options. Can a system of distributed responsibilities for collections and access be successfully and efficiently managed by SALALM? Should it be delegated to a participating institution? Are there other models to examine?

What does the future hold for the Latin Americanist Research Resources Pilot Project? The Association of Research Libraries is giving increasing emphasis to global resources, as evidenced by its endorsement of a "tactical plan" that outlines steps toward a comprehensive program that moves beyond the pilot projects. This plan has been endorsed by the Association of American Universities (AAU) and has received continuing interest and support from the Mellon Foundation. The Center for Research Libraries (CRL) has also initiated a global resources project that complements the work of ARL, recommending as a first step a conference on foreign newspapers. The lessons of the Latin American pilot project will have a direct bearing on future developments in these global resources initiatives. All of these efforts, to be successful, must demonstrate the cost-effectiveness of a distributed model. It will also be critical for the participants to stand back from the intensity and complexity of the pilot phase and determine the best way to extend access to more and different research materials through the creative use of technology.

The Latin Americanist Research Resources Pilot Project has achieved a momentum that should soon bring it into the mainstream, building on the achievements of the regional library consortia and the many other encouraging efforts already under way within SALALM. There is no question that we will continue to face many challenges in meeting the goals of the project, but we have made a great deal of progress within our own libraries, with our regional partners, and in collaboration with our colleagues in SALALM and LASA.

# V. Media and Technical Services

# 15. Uso de OCLC-EPIC para identificar patrones de colección de material audiovisual sobre América Latina

Ketty Rodríguez

Debe ser de conocimiento común la crisis por la cual está pasando las colecciones en las bibliotecas académicas desde 1980. Esta crisis es producto de varios factores entre otros: (1) el aumento en la producción de publicaciones; (2) el aumento en precios de dichos publicaciones; (3) menos énfasis en colecciones especiales; y (4) la necesidad de permanecer tecnológicamente competitivo.

Aunque la crisis ha sido bien documentada en la literatura, su impacto no fue medido sistemáticamente hasta 1994 (Perrault 1994). Perrault estudió los patrones de adquisiciones para monografías de 72 bibliotecas académicas de ARL (Bibliotecas Académicas de Investigación) para los años 1985 y 1989. Encontró una reducción de 27.76% del total de monografías adquiridas cuando el año de 1985 fue comparado con el año 1989. El estudio identificó una disminución en el porcentaje de títulos únicos comparados con el total adquirido. Además encontró un aumento en el material básico (core material). La autora llega a la conclusión que hay menos diversidad y más homogeneidad en las colecciones de las bibliotecas académicas.

## Las colecciones sobre América Latina

Hay ciertos sectores dentro de la comunidad bibliotecaria donde el impacto de la crisis es mayor. Entre estos sectores se puede mencionar los estudios de área, colecciones especiales y las colecciones en idiomas extranjeros. Las colecciones de estudios de área que antes eran de moda en las bibliotecas ahora son consideradas como reliquias de una filosofía anticuada que enfatiza la propiedad de materiales en vez del acceso (Hazen 1993).

En algunas universidades estas colecciones (de área, especiales y de idiomas extranjeros) han sido integradas a la colección general para economizar en empleados. En el último caso (la de idiomas) vea Tabla 1. No solamente se ha reducido la adquisición de libros publicados en idiomas extranjeros pero se ha disminuido el control bibliográfico sobre aquellos adquiridos. Además, los récords preparados demuestran pobre calidad cuando se comparan con monografías domésticas (Leazer y Rohdy 1994).

Tabla 1. Adquisiciones para material no-seriado en ciencias sociales, de acuerdo al idioma, 1985–1989

| | 1985 | 1989 | Aumento o Disminución | % de Cambio |
|---|---|---|---|---|
| Total | 60,490 | 43,023 | -17,467 | -28.88 |
| Inglés | 31,151 | 26,929 | -4,222 | -13.55 |
| No-inglés | 29,339 | 16,094 | -13,245 | -45.14 |
| Francés | 3,351 | 2,006 | -1,345 | -40.14 |
| Alemán | 4,669 | 3,179 | -1,488 | -31.88 |
| Español | 5,034 | 2,941 | -2,093 | -41.58 |
| Ruso | 2,956 | 1,457 | -1,499 | -50.71 |
| Chino, Japonés y Coreano | 4,157 | 2,441 | -1,716 | -41.28 |

Fuente: Tomado y traducido de Perrault (1994: 87).

El énfasis en la colección de materiales sobre América Latina tiende a ser en disciplinas como historia, ciencias políticas, economía y literatura (Loring 1983; Perrault 1994). Se ha señalado que hay demasiado énfasis sobre monografías y no suficiente énfasis sobre material audiovisual (Hazen 1993). Quizás, en parte el problema es que la colección de material audiovisual impone una responsabilidad adicional en la biblioteca ya que requiere medios propios para almacenaje, preservación y uso de equipo.

El dilema encontrado por muchas bibliotecas es mejor ilustrado por este señalamiento hecho por un panel sobre prácticas en la distribución de recursos en la Universidad de Wyoming: "La biblioteca está consciente que el material audiovisual representa fuentes valiosas de información pero en este momento presenta tantos problemas que la situación exige precaución" (Shelton 1985: 28).

## Propósitos del estudio

Los materiales audiovisuales son muy efectivos como técnicas educativas. Considerando que el material audiovisual, particularmente los videos, se han convertido en un frecuente formato de publicación y debido a la proliferación, los costos tienden a ser competitivos, digamos, por ejemplo, con las monografías; es lógico suponer que a medida que pasa el tiempo el patrón en la adquisición de material audiovisual aumente de forma substancial.

El estudio tiene doble propósito: (1) intentar identificar patrones de colección para material audiovisual sobre América Latina en determinadas disciplinas, de acuerdo a la signatura topográfica de la Biblioteca del Congreso y de acuerdo a los encabezamientos de materia; y (2) evaluar la efectividad de búsqueda, usando el número de clasificación de la Biblioteca del Congreso, versus la búsqueda usando encabezamientos de materias.

## Metodología

Se utilizó la base de datos OCLC que cuenta con más de 4 millones de récords. Además, la gran mayoría de las colecciones sobre América Latina utilizan OCLC. Por lo tanto es lógico esperar una gran cantidad de récords sobre América Latina en esta base de datos. Debido a esta amplia cobertura de material sobre América Latina la base de datos OCLC resulta ideal para identificar patrones de colección.

Sin embargo, entre las desventajas de usar OCLC para el estudio la más importante es el costo de intentar realizar un estudio comprensivo. Por eso, este estudio está limitado a una muy pequeña muestra de números de clasificación de la Biblioteca del Congreso en ciertas disciplinas.

EPIC es un sistema de recuperación de información desarrollado por OCLC en 1992. Provee acceso a más de 50 bases de datos incluyendo la base de datos OCLC. Además, permite el uso de operadores boleanos y de operadores de proximidad. También es posible la búsqueda por campos específicos y por palabras o frases. EPIC es uno de los *interfaces* más poderosos y eficientes para accesar OCLC.

## Disciplinas seleccionadas

Este estudio se limita seleccionar una muestra de números de clasificación de *Latin America: A Conspectus Extracted from the Library of Congress Classification Scheme*, preparada por Laura Loring en 1983. Esta muestra se limita a ciertas secciones dentro de las disciplinas de historia, antropología, economía y literatura. Los criterios usados para seleccionar números de clasificación dentro de cada sección para cada una de estas disciplinas fueron los siguientes:

1. La posibilidad de que la materia se preste a ser presentada en forma audiovisual.
2. Selección de secciones de aquellas disciplinas que según la literatura tienden a recibir mayor cobertura en la literatura como, por ejemplo, historia.
3. Asumiendo que la región de América Latina en general y los países, como México y Argentina, reciben mayor cobertura estas secciones fueron incluidas.
4. Dentro de cada sección, he utilizado el criterio más amplio posible.

## Selección de números de clasificación

A continuación el desglose de números de clasificación de la Biblioteca del Congreso seleccionados para cada sección en cada disciplina.

Historia
América Precolombina. Los Indios
E 65 América Latina (general)
América Latina. América Española
F 1201 - 1392 México
F 1401 - 1419 América Latina (general)

Antropología; Etnología; Antropología social y cultural
GR Folklore por región o país
GR 114 América Latina (general)
GR 115 México

PN Drama; Representación dramática; Teatro
PN 2309 América Latina
PN 2310 México
PN 2450-2454 Argentina

## Selección de encabezamientos de materia

Los encabezamientos de materias fueron seleccionados de la siguiente manera: Una vez que se tenía el conjunto para cada disciplina usando los números de clasificación se desplegaban hasta un máximo de 5 récords para observar los encabezamientos de materia. De estos récords se seleccionó hasta un máximo de seis encabezamientos de materia. Luego aquellos seleccionados fueron buscados en la base de datos de OCLC, utilizando el campo de materia.

## Procedimiento

Esta muestra de números de clasificación de la Biblioteca del Congreso fue buscada en la base de datos en OCLC hasta mayo, 1996, usando el sistema de recuperación de información EPIC.

En EPIC los campos del número de clasificación de la Biblioteca del Congreso, identificados como (LC), y el campo de encabezamiento de materia identificado como (SU), son indizadas como palabras claves.

Una vez los números de clasificación fueron buscados en la base de datos de OCLC, el conjunto final de récords fue limitado a material audiovisual.

Es necesario señalar que el limitador usado en EPIC para restringir la búsqueda a material audiovisual es (med) para media. Esta categoría incluye lo siguiente: videos, películas y diapositivas.

## Análisis de data

La Tabla 2 presenta los resultados para diferentes búsquedas de números de clasificación para cada disciplina en la base de datos de OCLC. La Tabla 3 presenta los resultados obtenidos para las búsquedas de encabezamientos de materia para cada disciplina en la base de datos de OCLC.

Tabla 2. Búsqueda de números de clasificación por disciplina en OCLC

| Número de Clasificación | Disciplina o Sección América Precolombina | Total de Récords | Récords de Audiovisual | Porcentaje |
|---|---|---|---|---|
| E 65 | América Latina (general) | | | |
| | América Española | | | |
| F 1201-1392 | México | | | |
| 1401 - 1419 | América Latina (general) | 11,990 | 195 | 1.62 |
| GR | Antropología | | | |
| | Folklore (por región o país) | | | |
| GR 114 | América Latina (general) | | | |
| GR 115 | México (general) | 223 | 3 | 1.34 |
| HC | Historia económica y | | | |
| | Condiciones sociales | | | |
| HC 121-130 | América Latina | 2,636 | 12 | .45 |
| 131-140 | México | | | |
| PN | Drama; Representación | | | |
| | dramática; Teatro | | | |
| PN 2309 | América Latina | | | |
| 2310 | México | | | |
| 2450-2454 | Argentina | 440 | 1 | .22 |

Tabla 3. Búsqueda de encabezamientos de materia por disciplina en OCLC

| Disciplina o Sección | Encabezamiento de Materias | Total de Récords | Récords de Audiovisual | Porcentaje |
|---|---|---|---|---|
| E-F Historia | Indian Culture | | | |
| América Precolombina | | | | |
| Los Indios | Indians of México | 14, 996 | 664 | 4.42 |
| E 65 América | Antiquities | | | |
| Latina (general) | Teotihuacan | | | |
| América Latina | Latin America | | | |
| América Española | | | | |

| | | | | |
|---|---|---|---|---|
| F 1201-1392<br>México<br>1401-1419<br>América Latina (general) | | | | |
| GR<br>Antropología<br>Folklore (por<br>región y país)<br>GR 114<br>América Latina (general)<br>GR 115 México<br>(general) | Social Life and Customs<br><br>Folklore<br>Folk Festivals<br>Processions<br>Latin America<br>Mexico | 4,356 | 452 | 10.37 |
| HC Historia económica<br>y Condiciones sociales<br><br><br>HC 121-130<br>América Latina (general)<br>131-140<br>México | Economic Conditions<br>Social Conditions<br>Foreign Economic<br>Relations<br>Politics and<br>Government<br>History of 20th<br>Century Mexico | 9,877 | 158 | 1.59 |
| PN Drama<br>Representación dramática<br>Teatro<br>PN 2309<br>América Latina<br>2310 México<br>2450-2454<br>Argentina | Theater<br>Drama<br>Latin America<br><br>Drama<br>Mexico<br>Argentina<br>Latin America | 1,359 | 113 | 8.3 |

## Discusión

*Patrones en las colecciones de material audiovisual*

Se trató de identificar patrones de colección de material audiovisual según reflejados en la base de datos OCLC. Este análisis se llevó a cabo usando las Tabla 2 y 3. Para ello se tomó el número de clasificación y se limitó a los años 1980, 1985 y 1990 (vea Tabla 4). El mismo procedimiento fue aplicado a aquellos récords encontrados usando encabezamientos de materia (vea Tabla 5).

La Tabla 4 demuestra que el uso de números de clasificación para identificar material audiovisual no es efectivo. Quizás, parte del problema es que existen bibliotecas que no asignan números de clasificación al material audiovisual.

En términos generales los patrones de colección de material audiovisual reflejados en la base de datos OCLC para material sobre América Latina demuestran que este formato no ha crecido de la forma esperada. Sin embargo, con la excepción de la disciplina de antropología que demostró un decrecimiento en la colección de material audiovisual desde 1980 hasta 1990, fue posible identificar un patrón moderado de crecimiento para la disciplina de historia, mientras que en el resto de las disciplinas fue muy lento.

*Efectividad de los tipos de búsquedas*

Al evaluar la efectividad de los dos tipos de búsquedas, esto es por número de clasificación y por encabezamientos de materia, se tomó en cuenta cuatro criterios. Estos criterios incluyeron: tiempo tomado en realizar cada tipo de búsqueda, costo, el número de récords recuperados y precisión.

El uso de números de clasificación de la Biblioteca del Congreso como campo de búsqueda toma tres veces más tiempo que el uso de encabezamientos de materia en la base de datos de OCLC. Por lo tanto, como toma mucho más tiempo y como es mucho más tedioso, la búsqueda por número de clasificación tuvo un costo de $60.00 para cada disciplina mientras que el uso encabezamientos de materia resultó en un costo de $10.00 por cada disciplina.

Sin embargo el uso de números de clasificación permite una búsqueda más específica. Quizás ésta sea parte de la explicación del bajo número de récords recuperados para material audiovisual, según se demuestra en la Tabla 4.

Tabla 4. Patrón en la colección de material audiovisual por número de clasificación

| Disciplina | Número de Récords Audiovisual | 1980 | 1985 | 1990 |
|---|---|---|---|---|
| Historia de América Latina (general) | 195 | 6 | 3 | 9 |
| Antropología; Folklore | 3 | 0 | 0 | 0 |
| Historia económica y Condiciones sociales | 12 | 0 | 0 | 0 |
| Drama; Teatro Representación dramática | 1 | 0 | 0 | 0 |

Tabla 5. Patrón en la colección de material audiovisual por encabezamiento de materia

| Disciplina | Número de Récords Audiovisual | 1980 | 1985 | 1990 |
|---|---|---|---|---|
| Historia de América Latina (general) | 664 | 6 | 8 | 37 |
| Antropología; Folklore | 452 | 22 | 6 | 14 |
| Historia económica y Condiciones sociales | 158 | 3 | 4 | 8 |
| Drama; Teatro Representación dramática | 113 | 6 | 7 | 7 |

La Tabla 5 demuestra la efectividad de la búsqueda utilizando encabezamientos de materia para identificar material audiovisual. Se recomienda que para no perder especificidad se utilice el número de clasificación y luego se desplieguen varios récords y se utilicen los encabezamientos de materia utilizados en el récord con el debido cuidado. En este estudio se seleccionaron encabezamientos de materias generales, siempre intersectados con América Latina, o México o Argentina según fuera el caso.

De esta forma se aumenta el número de récords recuperados, aunque existe el riesgo de perder especificidad. Esta metodología resultó más efectiva para la recuperación de material audiovisual y permitió identificar patrones de colección ya que permitió la recuperación de mucho más material que la utilización del número de clasificación, según se demuestra en la Tabla 5.

## BIBLIOGRAFIA

Hazen, Dan C. 1993. "Latin American Studies, Information Resources and Library Collections: The Context of the Crisis." In Deborah L. Jakubs, ed., *Latin American Studies into the Twenty-First Century: New Forces, New Formats, New Challenges.* Papers of SALALM XXXVI, San Diego, California, June 1–6, 1991. Albuquerque, NM: SALALM. Pp. 267–271.

Leazer, Gregory H., and Margaret Rohdy. 1994. "The Bibliographic Control of Foreign Monographs: A Review and Baseline Study." *Library Resources and Technical Services* 39(1), 29–42.

Loring, Laura D. 1983. "Latin America: A Conspectus Extracted from the Library of Congress Classification Scheme." Master's thesis, University of California, Los Angeles.

Perrault, Anna H. 1994. "The Changing Print Source Base of Academic Libraries: A Comparison of Collection Patterns in Seventy-Two ARL Academic Libraries of Non-Serial Imprints for the Years of 1985 and 1989." Ph.D. dissertation, University of Florida.

Shelton, Diana. 1985. *Report of the Task Force on Allocation Practices.* Laramie: University of Wyoming [Ed259754] .

# 16. Latin American Websites for Catalogers and Technical Services Librarians

Barbara Stewart

Technical services librarians have always dreamed of the type of interconnectivity that the World Wide Web has brought us. What possibilities now loom before us—instant links to publishers; access to public catalogs, discussion lists, listservs, databases, replacing to a great degree previous telnet and ftp commands; the ability to perform quality authority control work in a manner never before possible; and, finally, the ability to improve subject and note access in our cataloging records.

This paper discusses Latin American websites for catalogers and other technical services librarians. Acquisitions librarians have always been aware of the difficulties of ordering and receiving Latin American and Hispanic peninsula materials. Many items have been available only by direct order, travel to the country itself, or long, protracted exchanges of snail-mail letters and invoices. Within the past five years, many Latin American publishers and vendors have acquired email addresses, and the race for vendors and publishers to establish websites has begun. Traditional vendor catalogs lend themselves extremely well to the web format; and with new security measures, web-based forms will soon become the preferred method for ordering library materials. The following section on Bookstores, Publishers, and Vendors lists many of our colleagues who are on the cutting edge of this new method for acquiring materials.

Latin American catalogers know the value of sharing documentation with colleagues, having participated for many years in collaborative projects. The web can help these same catalogers in many ways. Of primary importance is the assistance the web provides with authority control. Searching for biographical information about an author, or trying to locate a particular geographic location, has frequently required much time, effort, and legwork. The web adds a new dimension to searching for these topics. Catalogers can search for an email address of the author and direct questions to the author directly. If this is not possible, questions may be addressed to the home institution of the particular author. Appropriate discussion lists and listservs may be questioned about a particular topic. Finally, there are sites with extensive maps and town information. Name conflicts can sometimes be resolved by searching the library of the author's institution to discover early unpublished works or theses.

In addition to improved authority control, the web offers specific foreign language schedules, country codes and translation cutters, and Spanish- and Portuguese-related subject headings. Cataloging documentation is always helpful, and it exists at a variety of sites. Remember to cultivate cyber friendships—a colleague in another institution is a valuable resource in a search for information.

Foreign language sites are of great value to the technical services librarian. Dictionaries and grammar pages can be extremely helpful. How many of you have ever tried to catalog a book written in Euskara, the Basque language that is unrelated to any other language on earth? To help meet this challenge, one can now visit a Basque language site. The same can be said for a variety of Central and South American Indian languages that ARL (Association of Research Libraries) institutions love to collect. Sites dedicated to Náhuatl or Guaraní are very useful and frequently provide the opportunity to ask questions of the creator.

I would like to encourage technical services librarians to learn as much as they can about new technologies and to catalog Internet resources. Only by mastering, evaluating, and classifying the wide range of materials found on the World Wide Web will we be able to maintain our reputation as consummate classifiers and indexers of the world's knowledge. Protect yourself from outsourcing by becoming indispensable. Learn to create and manipulate digital documents and other computer applications. I wish us all the best of luck.

## Bookstores, Publishers, and Vendors

Alfaguara Global
**http://www.alfaguara.com**

Alianza Editorial
**http://www.anaya.es/Catalogo/CGA?act=D3400**

Almadraba Editorial
**http://www.edithermes.com/almad_cs.htm**

Asunto Impreso (Argentina). "Librería de la imagen."
**http://www.hq.satlink.com/asuntoi**

Azotea / Editorial Fotográfica (Argentina). See, in particular, the fotopoema of Quino's Mafalda.
**http://www.act.net.ar/azotea**

Base de Datos del ISBN; Formulario de Búsqueda. Keyword search of *Libros en Venta*, provided by the Ministerio de Cultura Programa PIC (Puntos de Información Cultural).
**http://www.mcu.es/pic/spain/ISBN.html**

Books in Print Search (Spanish and German)
**http://www.afb-adlers.com/docs/booksrch.htm**

Bosch, Casa Editorial
**http://www.boschce.es**

Casalini Libri
**http://www.casalini.com**

CELIAC (Centro Editorial en Literatura Indígena, Oaxaca, Mexico). Not-for-profit, indigenous-language publishing center in Oaxaca, Mexico.
**http://spgr.sppt.tulane.edu/TULing/IndigLang/CELIAC.html**

Centro de Servicios Bibliográficos, S.A. de C.V.
**http://www.amcham.com.mx/10-1-2.html**

CERLALC, Centro Regional para el Fomento del Libro en América Latina
**http://www.cerlalc.com**

ChilNET - Chile Business Directory - Actividad: Librerías. Includes addresses, faxes, email addresses, products, and services, the number of people employed by the company. The publisher's page is quite extensive. Most bookstores are located in Santiago, but other Chilean cities are also represented.
**http://www.chilnet.cl/rubros/LIBRER01.HTM**

CLACSO, Consejo Latinoamericano de Ciencias Sociales. Argentine "megasite."
**http://www.webcom.com/~clacso**

Club Internacional del Libro. Largest Spanish language mail order publisher.
**http://www.cilsp.com**

Cúspide Libros (Argentina). 15,000 technical and scientific books in 15 different catalogs.
**http://www.cuspide.com**

Ediciones Andrade (Mexico). Legal materials.
**http://www.jurisnet.com.mx/andrade.html**

Ediciones de la Rana Viajera (Uruguay). Electronic adventure books for children. La Casa Encantada is an interactive "choose your adventure" experience.
**http://www.chasque.apc.org/rfernand/ranaviaj**

Ediciones Destino (Spain). Spanish and Catalan titles; includes many excerpts.
**http://www.edestino.es**

Ediouro Livros (Brasil)
**http://www.ediouro-livros.com.br**

Editora FTD (Brasil)
**http://www.ftd.com.br**

Editora Manole (Brasil)
**http://www.cbl.com.br/manole**

Editora Objetiva (Brasil)
**http://www.objetiva.com**

Editoras Online (Brasil). Choose from Bertrand Brasil, Casa Jorge Editorial, Globo, Nova Fronteira, Salamandra, and many more.
**http://www.editoras.com/servico/editoras.htm**

Editorial Ariel
**http://www2.ariel.es/ariel**

Editorial Universitas
**http://www.artico.com/universitas**

Editoriales y Librerías (Biblioteca de la Universidad Complutense de Madrid)
**http://www.ucm.es/BUCM/0201ed.htm**

EDUNSA. Spanish language textbooks.
**http://www.globalcom.es/edunsa**

Espada~na Press. Emphasis on Mexican missions.
**http://www.west.net/~rperry**

Feria Internacional del Libro y la Lectura
**http://www.reuna.cl/filsa96/catalogo/c.html**

Grupo Anaya (Spain)
**http://www.anaya.es**

Grupo Editorial Sinos (Brasil)
**http://www.gruposinos.com.br**

Guía de Editores de España
**http://www.diret.com/editores/director.htm**

Howard Karno Books. New, rare, and out-of-print books about Latin America. Branches in California and Mexico. Many catalogs are available online. Each month a special item is featured. Order directly, bill credit card on file, or use a purchase order.
**http://www.cts.com/~karnobks**

Interbook : Librería Electrónica (Sevilla, Spain). Colorful, prize-winning page, offering prompt online service for books, CD-ROMs, multimedia, and video. Keyword searching available.
**http://www.disbumad.es/libreria/index.htm**

Latbook (Libros y Revistas Argentinas en Internet). Fernando García Cambeiro offers a database of more than 25,000 titles.
**http://www.latbook.com**

Latin American Bookstore (Ithaca, New York). Selling books in the humanities and social sciences since 1982. Excellent newsletter, *De Truchas y de Ranas*.
**http://www.latinamericanbooks.com**

León Sánchez Cuesta
**http://www.globalcom.es/saculib**

Librería de Porrua Hermanos y Cia. S.A. de C.V.
**http://porrua.com.mx**

Librería Linardi y Risso (Montevideo, Uruguay). Spanish and English language site from the most exquisite bookstore in South America, established in 1944, and based in the historic Casa del Vicario. Specializing in recent Uruguayan publications and Latin American rare and out-of-print materials. Blanket orders/ approval plans, and specially compiled subject bibliographies upon request.
**http://www.chasque.apc.org/lyrbooks**

Librerías de la Ciudad de Valencia (Spain). Keyword searchable.
**http://www.uv.es/~biblios/webuv/llif.html**

Librerías y Editorial El Ateneo. Colorful and Java-mad site.
**http://www.ateneo.com**

Libropolis. "La mayor librería en lengua española."
**http://www.libropolis.com**

Libros Argentinos en CD-ROM. English and Portuguese pages also available.
**http://www.librosarg.com**

Libros Latinos. "America's leading vendor of scholarly new and out-of-print publications from Latin America." Over 100 catalogs available.
**http://www.concentric.net/~libros**

LibroWeb. More than 1,000,000 titles.
**http://www.libroweb.com**

Los Andes Publishing (La Puente, California)
**http://www.losandes.com**

Luso-Brazilian Books. North American source for books from Brazil and Portugal.
**http://www.lusobraz.com**

MegaLibro. "Revista de la actualidad y las novedades editoriales de España."
**http://www.megalibro.com**

Mundi-Prensa. First publishing site on the web in Spain (1995).
**http://www.mundiprensa.es/mprensa/home.html**

Pan American Books (Washington, DC). A very prompt service at the lowest possible prices. Order by check, money order, or email.
**http://ourworld.compuserve.com/homepages/PanAmericanBooks**

Pehuen Portada (Chile). Homepage in Spanish, English, and German.
**http://www.cmet.net/pehuen**

Plaza & Janes Activa Multimedia (Spain)
**http://www.esegi.es/esegi/simo/texto/plazajan.html**

Portuguese Multilingual Books and Tapes
**http://www.esl.net/mbt/portuguese.html**

Puvill Libros. The first Spanish vendor to load its entire database into the OCLC Online Union Catalog.
**http://www.puvill.com**

SALALM Directory of Vendors
**http://latino.lib.cornell.edu/salalmlavendors.html#alphabeticalSBD**

Spanish BookDistributor (Miami, Florida). Well-constructed website.
**http://www.netpoint.net/sbd/sbd.html**

Universidad de Compostela, Servicio de Publicaciones, USC, Spain. Scientific publications exchange.
**http://www.usc.es/~spubl**

Vientos Tropicales / México Norte. Vientos Tropicales offers books from Belize, Costa Rica, Guatemala, Honduras, Nicaragua, El Salvador, and Panama. Mexico Norte covers new books from nineteen northern Mexican states. No catalog included, but an email address is listed.
**http://www.vientos.com**

## Library Acquisitions Department Websites

ANABISAI (Asociación Nacional de Directores de Bibliotecas, Redes y Servicios de Información del Sector Académico Universitario y de Investigación (Venezuela)
**http://www.cid.ve/congreso/anabisai.html**

Sector de Aquisições Bibliográficas (Universidade do Minho, Braga e Guimaraes, Portugal)
**http://www.sdum.uminho.pt/vgaquis-pt.htm**

Servicio de Adquisiciones, Biblioteca de la Escuela Universitaria de Estadística (Madrid, Spain)
**http://www.ucm.es/BUCM/est/0108.htm**

Servicios de la Hemeroteca Nacional Universitaria (Santafé de Bogotá, Colombia)
**http://www.icfes.gov.co/hemeroteca**

Sistema de Bibliotecas USACH (Universidad de Santiago de Chile)
**http://lauca.usach.cl/info/bibliotecas.html**

## Cataloging

### *Authority Control*

Authority Control (State University of New York at Buffalo). Best all-around authority site.
**http://wings.buffalo.edu/libraries/units/cts/ac**

Autores Latinoamericanos. Important site for checking Library of Congress classification numbers; created by Iván Calimano.
**http://www-lib.usc.edu/~calimano/bib_control/paises.html**

Concepto de Autoría Corporativa de Panizzi a Cutter. By Ofelia Solis Valdespino, CUIBUNAM.
**http://cuib.laborales.unam.mx/publicaciones/revista/r4a4rs.html**

GEONET Name Server. Excellent site for searching foreign geographic feature names; basis for the publications of the U.S. Board on Geographic Names (US BGN). Search with or without diacritics or special characters. Find out the difference between conventional, native, variant, and non-verified names.
**http://164.214.2.59/gns/html/index.html**

Non-Western Name Conventions
**gopher://liberty.uc.wlu.edu/00/library/human/eashum/nameconv**

Notable Citizens of Planet Earth Biographical Dictionary
**http://www.tiac.net/users/parallax**

***Cataloging Department Websites***

Cataloging Directorate (Library of Congress, Washington, DC). NACO, SACO, and much more.
**http://www.loc.gov/catdir/catdir.html**

Cataloguer's Toolbox (Memorial University of Newfoundland, Queen Elizabeth II Library, St. Johns, Newfoundland, Canada). Among the best cataloging department sites.
**http://www.mun.ca/library/cat**

Código de Catalogação Anglo-Americano
**http://www.silas.unsw.edu.au/students/RFATTAHI/rec92.htm**

Entrevista amb Alvar Garcia (Catalan)
**http://www.uv.es/biblios/mei3/AlvGarcia.html**

Princeton University Libraries Cataloging Division (Princeton, New Jersey). Many documents contained here may be applied to Latin American cataloging.
**http://infoshare1.princeton.edu/katmandu/cathome.html**

Procesos Técnicos (Biblioteca Nacional de la República Argentina)
**http://www.bibnal.edu.ar/procesos.html**

Sector de Catalogação (Universidade de Minho, Portugal)
**http://www.sdum.uminho.pt/vgcat-pt.htm**

Servicios Centrales (Biblioteca de la Universidad Complutense de Madrid)
**http://www.ucm.es/BUCM/centrales.html**

Situación Actual de la Biblioteca (Universidad de Buenos Aires)
**http://www.cpel.uba.ar/bib/situaci.htm**

TPOT (Technical Processing Online Tools) Cataloging (University of California, San Diego)
**http://tpot.ucsd.edu/Cataloging/catdept.html**

Universidad Politécnica de Puerto Rico. *El Politécnico* ed 7–17.
**http://www.pupr.edu/news/a3_ed7/biblio.htm**

***Cataloging Internet Resources***

Cataloging Internet Resources: A Manual and Practical Guide. Nancy B. Olson, editor.
**http://www.oclc.org/oclc/man/9256cat/toc.htm**

Intercat Catalog of Internet Resources. Searchable catalog of bibliographic records for Internet resources selected and cataloged by libraries around the world.
**http://www.oclc.org:6990**

### *General*

El Bibliotecario Electrónico, Servicio de Información, Colegio de Bibliotecarios de Chile, A.G.
**http://cdb.conicyt.cl:8010**

Conferencia Internacional sobre Principios de Catalogación: Sumario de Ponencias. Remarkable cataloging site, excerpted from the journal *Investigación Bibliotecológica* (Universidad Nacional Autónoma de México [UNAM], Centro Universitario de Investigaciones Bibliotecológicas). See "Relación entre los Principios de Catalogación y los Aplicables a Otras Formas de Trabajo Bibliográfico," by Andrew D. Osborn.
**http://cuib.laborales.unam.mx/publicaciones/revista/r1a3p1rs.htm**

SCATNews: Newsletter of the Standing Committee of the IFLA Section on Cataloging
**http://www.nlc-bnc.ca/ifla/VII/s13/scatn/news8.htm**

Spain OPACs. Approximately 50 links.
**http://www.rediris.es/recursos/mapas/OPAC/index.html**

Spanish Library of Congress Subject Headings
**http://www.ecnet.net/users/mfftc/wiu/guides/frglangs.htm**

Top 200 Technical Services Benefits of Library Home Page Development
**http://tpot.ucsd.edu/Cataloging/Misc/top200.html**

Universal Bibliographic Control and International MARC Core Programme (UBCIM)
**http://www.nlc-bnc.ca/ifla/VI/3/ubcim.htm**

## Language Sites

### *Dictionaries*

Diccionario Anaya de la Lengua. Approximately 30,000 definitions. All definitions are in Spanish.
**http://www.anaya.es/dict/Buscar?act=HAnaya.html**.

Guarani - Paraguayo = Guaraní-Ñanduti-Rogue. Access to the trilingual Guaraní-Español-Alemán Dictionary (over 1,400 entries).
**http://www.uni-mainz.de/~lustig/hisp/guarani.html**

Pedro's Dictionaries
**http://fonsg3.let.uva.nl/Pedros_dictionaries.html**

Spanish-to-English Dictionary
**http://grub01.physto.se:8080/cgi-bin/ssis/~calcato/espanol.html**

Web of Online Dictionaries
**http://www.bucknell.edu/~rbeard/diction.html**

***Language and Linguistics***

Buber's Basque Page. Introduction and description of Euskara, the Basque language. Includes an alphabet, a simple Basque dictionary, and links to many culturally related sites.
**http://weber.u.washington.edu/~buber/Basque**

Cataloging Foreign Language Materials: Resources for Catalogers. Ultimate site for foreign language cataloging; created by Cynthia Bertelsen. Links to Most Frequently Used Language and Country of Publication Codes and Translation Cutters. Princeton Vernacular Designators has sections for Catalan, Portuguese, Quechua, and Spanish. The CIA World Fact Book is useful for current country statistics. Includes useful maps, population estimates, official languages, states and departments, types of government, and political parties—all useful for cataloging census materials.
**http://www.vt.edu:10021/B/bertel/catalog.html**

Comp-jugador. Conjugates Spanish verbs in all tenses.
**http://csgwww.uwaterloo.ca/~dmg/lando/verbos/con-jugador.html**

Dartmouth College Language Resource Center (Hanover, New Hampshire)
**http://www.dartmouth.edu/~hr/lrc**

ECHO – EURODICAUTUM. Fill in query (in Spanish or Portuguese) and receive definitions from a database of official and technical terms.
**http://www.uni-frankfurt.de/~kurlanda/eurodicautom.html**

Foreign Language Resources on the Web
**http://www.itp.berkeley.edu/~thorne/HumanResources.html**

Galician Language Home Page (ILG, Instituto da Lingua Galega, Universidad de Santiago de Compostela, Spain)
**http://www.usc.es/~ilgas/welcome.html**

General Language Internet Resources from the University of Wyoming Libraries
**http://www.uwyo.edu/Lib/genlan.htm**

How Can I Learn Nahuatl? Just study this page!
**http://www1.iastate.edu/~rjsalvad/scmfaq/nahuatl.html**

Human Languages Page
**http://www.june29.com**
Tyler Jones has compiled this exceptional list of resources, a focal point for language-related information on the Net. For Spanish Lessons: **http://www.june29.com/Spanish**

IndigLang: Resources on Indigenous Languages of the Americas
**http://spgr.sppt.tulane.edu/TULing/IndigLang/IndigLang.html**

Lamson Library, Library of Congress Schedule for Foreign Languages (Plymouth State College, Plymouth, New Hampshire). Links to a multitude of foreign language sites, including the Diccionario de la Picardía Mexicana and Ejercicios de Gramática Española.
**http://oz.plymouth.edu/~library/lcforlang.html**

Language Reference Sources. Search by language or language family. Extensive list.
**http://www-sul.stanford.edu/depts/ssrg/linguist/langref.html**

Linguist List: Web-Accessible Linguistic Sources, Departments, and Information. Search archives of the *Linguist;* links to dictionaries, and much more.
**http://www.emich.edu/~linguist/datasources.html**

Maya Resources
**http://spgr.sppt.tulane.edu/TULing/IndigLang/maya.html**

MIT (Massachusetts Institute of Technology) Foreign Languages and Literatures
**http://web.mit.edu/fll/www**

Mundo Latino. Billed as the Spanish language Yahoo! See, in particular, the Guía Azul, an alphabetical listing of hispanohablantes en la red and the Escalera Temática of quality Latino websites. Links to the electronic version of Don Quixote de La Mancha (a beautiful facsimile reproduction of the first edition of the work).
**http://www.mundolatino.org**

Portuguese Language Page. Daily Extra of *O Jornal do Brasil*, the first Brazilian paper to jump on the Internet. Good for late-breaking news. Archives available from September 1, 1995. *Jornal Portugal* on the web is available as well (issues no. 1–3, 1995). A visit to the History of Portugal, Primary Documents, site might be worthwhile (links to a Spanish translation of the 1976 Constitution of the Republic of Portugal).
**http://humanities.uchicago.edu/romance/port**

Quechua Language Home Page. Barry Brian Werger's Quechua classes, lessons 1–3 available.
**http://www-robotics.usc.edu/~barry/quechua**

Universal Survey of Languages. Excellent, comprehensive site.
**http://www.teleport.com:80/~napoleon**

# 17. An Integrated System for Cataloging in the Field of Jurisprudence at the Ibero-American Institute

Markus Obert

The Ibero-American Institute is a lending library and research institute specializing in materials on Latin America, Spain, and Portugal. It supports research in all areas of Latin American, Spanish, and Portuguese studies, and promotes academic and cultural relations with the Iberian, Ibero-American, and Caribbean worlds. Located in Berlin, the Ibero-American Institute is the largest institution in Europe that collects Spanish, Portuguese, and Latin American library materials—published worldwide—on a multidisciplinary basis. Administratively, it is a tax-supported, not-for-profit corporation; access is free and open to the general public. The Institute is part of a federal foundation, the Prussian Cultural Heritage Foundation, which has responsibility for libraries, institutes, museums, and archives of the former state of Prussia dissolved in 1947.

The Institute's initial collection of of 120,000 volumes (1930) has grown steadily. The library now holds about 750,000 books and periodical volumes; 25,000 periodical titles, among these 4,500 current periodicals; a collection of maps totaling approximately 62,000 topographical and thematic maps and atlases; a photographic collection of 24,000 slides, photographs, and videos; a collection with 19,000 tapes, records, and compact discs; and a clippings file (dating back to 1930) containing more than 300,000 articles. Today the media collection includes prints, microforms, CD-ROMs, discs, and audio and videotape. The annual acquisitions budget exceeds $750,000, and the annual increase amounts to approximately 15,000 volumes; 1,200 slides, photographs, videos, and tapes; and 1,500 maps. Connected to the European interlibrary loan service, the Institute library receives more than 17,000 loan requests each year. A staff of 75 serves some 6,000 clients who borrow 120,000 books and periodicals annually.

## Development of Electronic Data Processing

The Institute's first step into the world of automated library systems dates to the end of the 1980s, when we determined that our traditional system of library service no longer met international standards. Even worse, like many other German libraries, we did not have a computer-based circulation or barcode system, nor software to manage the administrative functions of the library. In 1992 we faced the difficult task of choosing among nine different automated library systems, and decided in favor of Urica from McDonnel Information Systems (MDIS). At the time we were fully aware that turnkey systems—at least as far as the German market, with its very special requirements and standards, was concerned—did not exist. The complexity of developing the required computer programs, however, had been underestimated. Therefore the period from 1992 through 1994 was devoted to adapting to and debugging the new software. Nevertheless, since the beginning of 1995 we have been operating with part of the system in place. The Unix-based system is a local, integrated, online system. Recently, MDIS was bought out by Dynix Automated Library Systems, an Ameritech company, so that in two years we will move from Urica to the Horizon system. At present, we use a Hewlett-Packard mainframe computer. The server is connected via backbone to terminal servers and HUBs. Thirty terminals and 40 personal computers are in use.

As to the expediency of the programs, the library makes good use of the cataloging, retrieval, and circulation systems, as well as the provisional online public access catalog. Unfortunately, the acquisitions software can be used only to place orders with some of our booksellers. The serials software is not yet functioning.

*Cataloging*

At the end of 1994 we started cataloging and at present about 16,000 monographs, 5,000 essays, and 2,000 records have been cataloged; 270,000 volumes now have barcode labels. The cataloging of maps and photographs will begin at a later date. We estimate that 15,000 monographs, 5,000 articles, and 2,000 records are processed annually. In addition, more than half a million monographs are to be retroconverted. Because we need to locate our own sources of financial support for this phase, however, retrospective conversion will probably take at least 20 years. The approximately 400,000 essays will not be converted with Urica or Horizon, but may be scanned on another system.

*Retrieval and OPAC*

Since the Ibero-American Institute is not yet connected to the Internet, the advantages of the retrieval system can only be offered in the reading rooms. The OPAC provides access to materials cataloged or added to the collection since 1995. The terminals have search instruction screens. In Boolean combinations, users can search by author, title, keyword, subject heading, corporate author, and date of publication. Users no longer need to fill out call slips at the information desk. Hits can be requested by means of a special function key, so that the orders are sent directly to a printer in the stacks; open stacks are unusual in Germany.

*Circulation*

The circulation system runs without any problems.

*Serials*

The serials software will be put into practice with Horizon in 1998.

*Acquisitions*

To place orders with some of our booksellers, requests are entered in the computerized catalog. Order slips are printed and mailed to booksellers daily. Although online ordering by email is not possible, the OPAC does offer several improvements. For example, users are informed that a certain book is ordered, and the provisional catalog is updated when the book is received. As far as the further development of the integrated library system as a whole is concerned, the following goals have been established.

1996: Connection to the Internet, introduction of email; testing and debugging of Horizon software.

1998: Move from the current Urica system to Horizon; the OPAC available on the Internet.

1999: Production of CD-ROMs containing the bibliographic holdings of the Ibero-American Institute; quarterly or semiannual updates. Special bibliographies for music and law are in preparation.

## Documentation on Legal Information

The library houses a special collection of materials in jurisprudence of Latin America, Spain, and Portugal, the acquisition of which is financed in part by the German Research Society. Especially with respect to legal philosophy and constitutional and criminal law, there are noteworthy relationships between the German and the Hispanic legal systems. Because the seat of the German government, the state department, parliament, and most embassies will soon be relocated to Berlin, this collection will gain even more importance. Therefore, at present the library needs to be sure that its system is able to meet future demands. We have concentrated our efforts on improving bibliographic access to articles in periodicals and collective works in general, but especially in the field of law and jurisprudence.

And there is good reason to do so. Not only did the Institute have to suspend cataloging of articles in law more than five years ago, but we have also had to face the fact that the bibliographic situation in jurisprudence is unsatisfactory. In general, bibliographies and indexes make only sporadic reference to articles in law periodicals. The *Hispanic American Periodicals Index* and the *Handbook of Latin American Studies*, for instance, do not include legal journals. Bibliographies in monographs usually do not cite sources in law, or the selection criteria are unclear. Up-to-date special bibliographies and subject indexes do not exist.

Now, using the cataloging software, the Institute has not only resumed but also fundamentally improved the cataloging of articles. These improvements relate to the quality and speed of subject cataloging. (Cataloging means that we produce a catalog and index entry; we do not scan nor score the text nor do we produce abstracts). The old subject index, dating to 1958 and published in the bound Subject Catalog in 1977, has been completely revised. In the field of jurisprudence, in particular, we offer—and this is an essential point—a more accurate and comprehensive subject heading listing. In contrast to the old subject catalogs, codes, laws, court decisions, commentaries, and textbooks (even for special branches in the field of law) are now easy to find. In addition, we have been able to accelerate the pace of cataloging. The new system enables us to generate records for up to 3,000 articles per year, perhaps more, depending on the availability of descriptive cataloging staff. In comparison, prior to the installation of the new system, we produced only 500 catalog entries annually. We evaluate monographs and approximately 80 current periodicals. An average of 50 percent of the articles are documented. The library is mainly interested in Latin American, especially Central American and Caribbean, articles.

As far as the further development of the documentation on legal information is concerned, the following schedule has been established. In 1996 and 1997 the library has to do its utmost to bring the collection profile of law periodicals up to date, so that important periodicals are not missing, although we acknowledge that there might be gaps especially for Central America and the Caribbean countries. As soon as the Ibero-American Institute is connected to the Internet, the law documentation project will be available on the web, which will no doubt provoke a lively discussion of the purpose of this new bibliographic service. The international exchange of experience is essential to achieving the best possible results and avoiding duplication of effort. We also intend to list periodicals which at present are not included, and, because the subject headings are in German, English and Spanish indexes will be added. These indexes must be completed by the end of 1997, in time for incorporation into the OPAC in 1998.

# VI. Media and Education

# 18. Uso del Internet dentro de las bibliotecas latinoamericanas

Filiberto F. Martínez Arellano

El surgimiento y desarrollo de nuevas tecnologías para la transmisión e intercambio de información están motivando cambios en todas las actividades humanas. Sin duda alguna, el más representativo ejemplo de estas nuevas tecnologías es el Internet cuyo uso ha sido incorporado dentro de distintos ámbitos tales como el educativo, el gubernamental y el comercial. Las bibliotecas no han sido ajenas a la influencia de esta nueva tecnología y al igual que otras instituciones han incorporado dentro de sus actividades y servicios, en mayor o menor medida, esta nueva tecnología de la información.

Aunque los bibliotecarios hemos incorporando el uso del Internet dentro de muchas de nuestras actividades y servicios diarios, existe poca información acerca de la manera en la cual estamos haciendo uso de esta nueva tecnología dentro de nuestras instituciones.

Con la finalidad de coadyuvar a llenar ese vacío, se consideró conveniente el llevar a cabo una encuesta para obtener datos sobre el uso del Internet en las bibliotecas latinoamericanas. El presente documento incluye los resultados de dicha encuesta, la cual fue llevada a cabo por correo electrónico entre los integrantes de tres grupos de discusión BIBLIOMEX-L "Lista Mexicana de Bibliotecología", LADIG-L "Latin American Database Interest Group" y EDULAC "Educadores Latinoamericanos en Ciencias de la Información".

## Estudios sobre el uso del Internet en las bibliotecas

Dentro de la literatura abordando el tema del Internet y las bibliotecas podemos encontrar innumerables ejemplos de trabajos los cuales incluyen diversos aspectos relacionados con su aplicación en los distintos servicios que la biblioteca ofrece. Sin embargo, la gran mayoría de esos trabajos han sido enfocados hacia la descripción y promoción de servicios basados en esta nueva alternativa, o bien, a su importancia como punto central de la biblioteca virtual o biblioteca del futuro (Ladner y Tillman 1992). Muy pocos estudios han tenido como su punto central el estudio de la forma en que los bibliotecarios y las bibliotecas estamos haciendo uso del Internet.

Entre los pocos estudios que han tenido como su punto central el uso del Internet, los cuales nos ofrecen importantes datos al respecto, se encuentra una encuesta llevada a cabo por Ladner y Tillman (1992) en bibliotecas especializadas, otra encuesta efectuada por Basu (1995) entre bibliotecarios académicos y un estudio realizado por Bane y Milheim (1995) entre académicos.

Los resultados de estos estudios coinciden en que la comunicación por correo electrónico, la participación en listas de discusión y las búsquedas en bases de datos son las opciones más comúnmente utilizadas dentro del Internet. Asimismo, estos estudios indican que los usuarios del Internet tenían gran experiencia en el uso de computadoras y que el uso del Internet había sido menor. Sin embargo, la razón de esa diferencia estaba relacionada con el reciente surgimiento y desarrollo de esta nueva tecnología. Estos estudios también encontraron que el aprendizaje sobre el uso del Internet no había sido a través de un entrenamiento formal y sistemático, sino que el autoaprendizaje había sido la opción mayormente utilizada. Adicionalmente, en aquellos casos en que los encuestados habían recibido un entrenamiento formal, la duración de los cursos fue muy variada no existiendo un estándar.

En relación al uso del Internet dentro de las bibliotecas latinoamericanas, existen dos estudios que han abordado este asunto. Mattes llevó a cabo en 1995 una encuesta por correo electrónico sobre el impacto del Internet en las bibliotecas mexicanas. Desafortunadamente, muy pocas bibliotecas respondieron a esta encuesta por lo que no pudieron obtenerse datos específicos sobre la forma en la cual el Internet era utilizado dentro de estas bibliotecas (Mattes 1996). No obstante lo anterior, la respuesta de una de las bibliotecas respondiendo a esta encuesta nos da una idea de como esta nueva tecnología de la información es utilizada (Soto Fuentes 1995):

> En la Universidad de Monterrey implementamos un servicio de envío de la editorial de la Jornada a nuestros usuarios a través del correo electrónico...
>
> El correo electrónico nos fue (y es) de utilidad para contestar preguntas de referencia...
>
> En Integer...tenemos un servicio de entrega de fotocopia del TimesFax, un resumen de 8 páginas del *New York Times* (llega en un archivo que se lee en Acrobat Reader....
>
> También estamos utilizando Internet para verificar referencias antes de pedir materiales, entramos al servidor Z39.50 de la Biblioteca del Congreso.
>
> Para clasificar materiales también entramos a ese servidor y a RLIN, además de otras bibliotecas.
>
> Hemos contactado a diversos proveedores a través de Internet....
>
> Los colegas de Bibliomex también me ayudaron a definir algunas obras de consulta a adquirir por mi Centro de Información.
>
> Por Internet nos comunicamos (y hacemos pedidos obviamente) con nuestro proveedor...

Por otra parte, Urbizagastegui (1996) llevó a cabo un análisis de como seis listas de discusión en español sobre asuntos relacionados con la Bibliotecología y Ciencias de la Información estaban siendo utilizadas. Su análisis indicó que 40 por ciento de los mensajes incluidos utilizaban las listas como una fuente de referencia para obtener información.

Indudablemente, el uso del Internet ha modificado la forma en la cual se llevan a cabo las actividades dentro de nuestras bibliotecas y los siguientes ejemplos son evidencias de lo anteriormente mencionado:

> Al introducir Internet como herramienta de trabajo diario, los procedimientos de operación en el Departamento [Técnico] han cambiado, se aprovecha más el tiempo, el desempeño de las actividades es más fácil, se agiliza la comunicación interna y se adquiere más conocimiento sobre el uso de las nuevas tecnologías (Rodríguez García, bibliotecario mexicano, 1996).
>
> ...Te permite tener acceso a recomendaciones que dan colegas de materiales interesantes que se hayan publicado...
>
> ...Puedes pedir proformas y combinar con otra tecnología que es el fax obteniendo proformas para compras de material en poco tiempo...
>
> ...Puedes revisar OPACs y ver que han adquirido grandes Unidades de Información en una materia dada y del registro puedes tomar el nombre de una editorial...
>
> ...Te informan de direcciones de catálogos en línea a los cuales puedes tener acceso y revisar el tipo de tratamiento que se les da a los materiales...
>
> ...Para solicitar préstamo interbibliotecario...
>
> ...Para ganar tiempo y recursos en la comunicación... (Arguedas, bibliotecaria costarricense, 1996)

## Encuesta por correo electrónico

Como ha sido mencionado anteriormente, con la finalidad de obtener datos sobre el uso del Internet dentro de las bibliotecas latinoamericanas se llevó a cabo una encuesta entre los integrantes de tres grupos de discusión: BIBLIOMEX-L "Lista Mexicana de Bibliotecología", LADIG-L "Latin American Database Interest Group" y EDULAC "Educadores Latinoamericanos en Ciencias de la Información". Un cuestionario (ver Anexo) fue elaborado y distribuido por correo electrónico entre los integrantes de estos tres grupos de discusión. El cuestionario fue enviado durante los últimos días del mes de noviembre de 1995 y las respuestas se recibieron durante ese mes y el de diciembre.

Puesto que el principal objetivo de este estudio era conocer la forma en la cual los bibliotecarios y las bibliotecas estaban utilizando las nuevas tecnologías de información, el uso del correo electrónico se consideró la opción tecnológica más congruente para llevar a cabo este estudio. Por otra parte, el uso del correo electrónico para llevar a cabo encuestas tiene una serie de ventajas sobre el correo normal ya que constituye una opción más rápida y económica para el envío y obtención de información. No obstante esta serie de ventajas, también existen una serie de desventajas. Quizá la mayor desventaja es que el cuestionario no es anónimo y por lo tanto puede existir rechazo para su contestación ya que los respondientes pueden ser fácilmente identificados. A fin de vencer la reticencia para su contestación, el investigador deberá de asegurar a las personas e instituciones participantes el carácter confidencial de los datos.

En relación al número de respuestas recibidas, cabe hacer mención que 55 personas decidieron autoparticipar en la encuesta enviando su respuesta al cuestionario recibido por correo electrónico. Asimismo, cabe señalar que la encuesta despertó gran entusiasmo e interés entre los participantes. En algunos casos, el cuestionario fue distribuido por los mismos participantes a otros colegas los cuales no pertenecían a estas listas de discusión. Asimismo, en algunos casos, junto con las respuestas al cuestionario fueron recibidas peticiones para conocer los resultados de la encuesta.

El cuestionario fue diseñado para ser contestado de forma rápida y sencilla debiendo los participantes únicamente marcar las opciones correspondientes dentro de diez grandes rubros. La identificación de la ciudad y país de origen de los encuestados así como el tipo de institución fueron los primeros rubros incluidos dentro del cuestionario. A continuación se les solicitó que indicaran el tipo de actividades que llevaban a cabo dentro de sus instituciones.

La experiencia en el uso de computadora y el Internet así como el promedio semanal utilizando las diferentes opciones en el Internet fueron los siguientes aspectos dentro del cuestionario. Las opciones del Internet incluidas dentro de la encuesta fueron el uso de correo electrónico (email), grupos de discusión (listservs), servicio de noticias y artículos (Usenet), acceso remoto a otras computadoras (Telnet), transferencia de archivos (FTP, consulta de Archie, Verónica, catálogos de bibliotecas [OPACs]) y uso del World Wide Web a través de Mosaic o Netscape.

A los participantes también se les requirió que indicaran las actividades de la biblioteca dentro de las cuales estaban utilizando el Internet y la forma en la cual aprendieron a utilizar esta tecnología. Asimismo, también se les solicitó que indicaran el número de personal y si el usuario de la biblioteca tenía acceso directo al Internet.

## Resultados de la encuesta

La mayoría de las respuestas fue recibida de BIBLIOMEX-L "Lista Mexicana de Bibliotecología". Como puede observarse en la Figura 1, 60 por ciento de las 55 respuestas recibidas fueron de personas trabajando en instituciones mexicanas. No obstante lo anterior, también se recibieron las respuestas de colegas de otros países. El porcentaje y número de respuestas recibidas de los bibliotecarios de otros lugares fueron los siguientes: Perú 6 (11 por ciento), Costa Rica 5 (9 por ciento), Uruguay 4 (7 por ciento), Chile 2 (4 por ciento), Estados Unidos 4 (7 por ciento) y Alemania 1 (2 por ciento).

Los resultados incluidos en la Figura 2 indican que la mayoría de las personas respondiendo a esta encuesta laboraban en bibliotecas universitarias (54 por ciento). No obstante lo anterior, el número de encuestados laborando en bibliotecas especializadas y en centros de información fue también considerable (22 por ciento y 11 por ciento respectivamente). Por otra parte, únicamente una respuesta correspondiente a una institución gubernamental, otra de una escuela de bibliotecología, dos respuestas de centros de investigación y tres de otro tipo de instituciones fueron recibidas. Cabe hacer mención que ninguna respuesta de una biblioteca pública fue enviada. Estos resultados pueden ser explicados por el origen y desarrollo del Internet los cuales han sido prominentes dentro de las instituciones de educación superior. En relación al tamaño de las instituciones, este fue muy variable existiendo instituciones con un reducido número de personal, menos de diez, hasta aquellas con más de dos mil miembros.

La Figura 3 muestra los resultados correspondientes al tipo de actividades que los encuestados desarrollaban dentro de sus instituciones. Cabe hacer mención que los encuestados indicaron todas aquellas actividades que llevaban a cabo por lo cual existieron respuestas múltiples. Los resultados indican que la mayoría de los encuestados desarrollaban actividades de servicios al público (49 por ciento), seguidas por aquellas teniendo a su cargo actividades de carácter administrativo (36 por ciento) y de procesos técnicos (31 por ciento). Los porcentajes correspondientes a las actividades de investigación y docencia únicamente alcanzaron 22 y 20 por ciento respectivamente.

Los resultados correspondientes a las actividades y servicios de la biblioteca dentro de las cuales se estaban utilizando el Internet son presentados en la Figura 4. Como puede observarse, las actividades dentro de las cuales se estaba usando el Internet predominantemente fueron el acceso a fuentes de referencia electrónicas (72 por ciento), la obtención de artículos en revistas electrónicas (53 por ciento) y el acceso a bases de datos e índices comerciales (51 por ciento). No obstante lo anterior, las actividades correspondientes al área de selección y adquisición de los materiales bibliográficos así como las de procesos técnicos también alcanzaron proporciones considerables. Treinta y seis por ciento de los encuestados mencionaron utilizar el Internet para la selección de materiales y 29 por ciento para la adquisición de estos. Adicionalmente, 24 por ciento de los encuestados indicaron usar el Internet como un medio de acceso a los catálogos de otras instituciones para efectuar su catalogación y 14 por ciento como un medio de acceso a servicios de catalogación.

Por otro lado, la encuesta encontró que en 42 instituciones (76 por ciento) los usuarios tenían acceso directo al Internet (Figura 5). Estos resultados junto

Figura 1. Países incluidos en el estudio

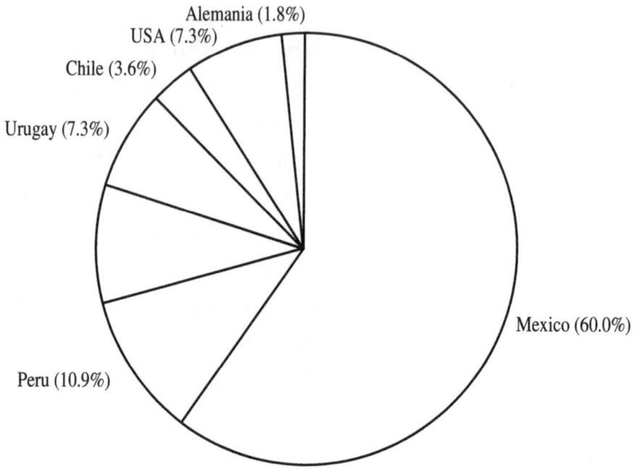


Figura 2. Tipo de institución

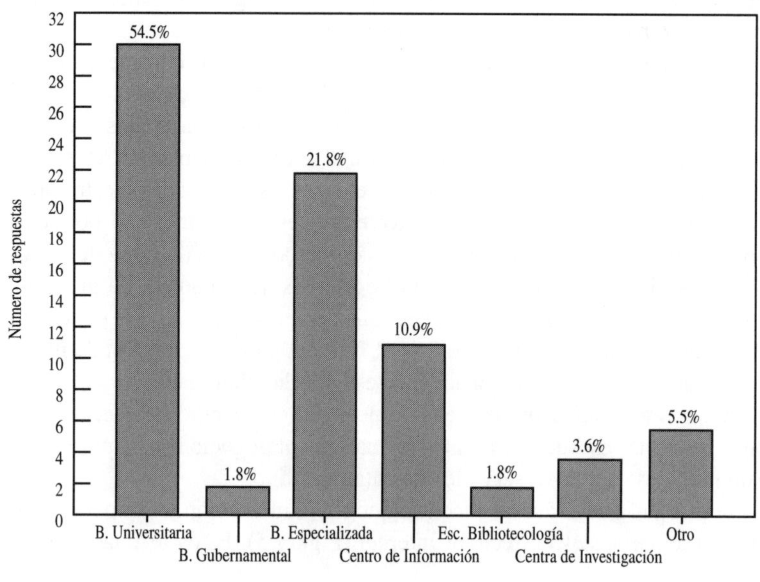

Figura 3. Tipo de actividad desarrollada

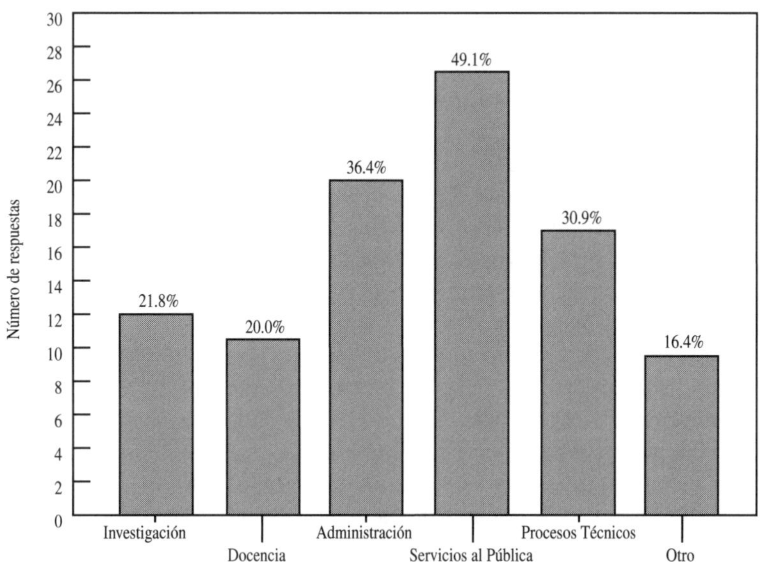

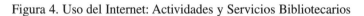

Figura 4. Uso del Internet: Actividades y Servicios Bibliotecarios

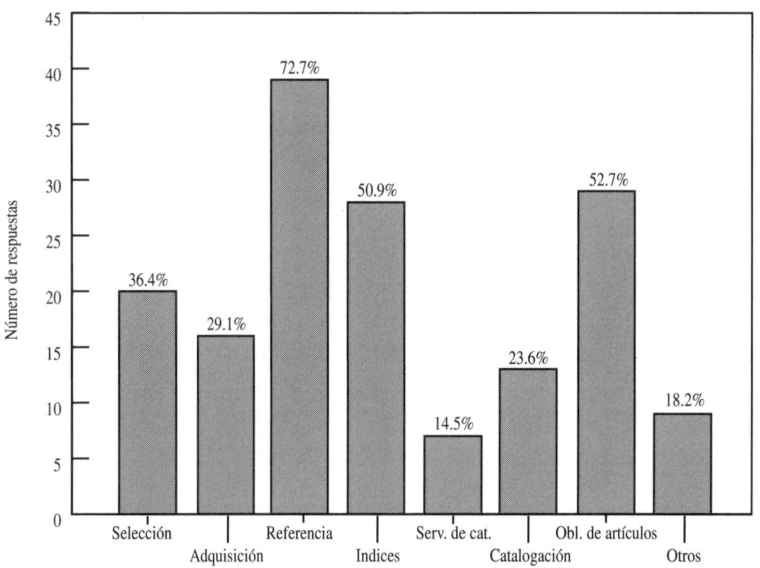

con los anteriormente mencionados son un indicador de que el área que mayormente está siendo modificada por el uso del Internet es la de servicios al público. No obstante lo anterior, aunque en menor medida, el Internet también está siendo utilizado dentro de las áreas de selección, adquisiciones y procesos técnicos.

Los resultados correspondientes a la utilización de las distintas opciones existentes en el Internet para obtener información son mostrados en la Figura 6. Estos resultados nos indican que la opción predominantemente utilizada fue el correo electrónico (92 por ciento). Otras opciones considerablemente utilizadas fueron: grupos de discusión (65 por ciento), acceso remoto a otras computadoras por Telnet (63 por ciento), acceso al web usando Netscape (58 por ciento) y consulta a catálogos de otras bibliotecas (53 por ciento). Por otra parte, tal y como se puede observar en la Figura 7, las opciones con mayor promedio de horas semanales de uso fueron el correo electrónico (7.3 horas por semana) y el acceso remoto a otras computadoras por Telnet (5.5 horas por semana).

En relación a la experiencia en el uso de computadoras, la encuesta encontró que los participantes tenían gran experiencia, pues como puede ser observado en la Figura 8, el 54 por ciento de los encuestados tenía una experiencia de 6 a 10 años en el uso de computadoras. Asimismo, el promedio general de años utilizando computadoras fue de 8.3 años. Por otra parte, aunque el número de años de experiencia en el uso del Internet fue menor, esta pudo considerarse representativa de acuerdo al surgimiento y desarrollo del Internet durante los dos últimos años. La Figura 9 indica que la mayoría de los participantes en la encuesta tenían una experiencia en el uso del Internet entre 1 y 2 años (32 y 23 por ciento respectivamente). Asimismo, el promedio general de años habiendo usado esta herramienta fue de 2.3 años. El menor número de años en el uso del Internet es consistente con el surgimiento y desarrollo de esta tecnología de la información durante los dos últimos años.

La Figura 10 incluye los resultados relacionados con la forma a través de la cual los encuestados habían aprendido a utilizar el Internet. La opción mencionada por la gran mayoría fue autoaprendizaje (80 por ciento). Otras opciones significativas fueron: información de manuales (44 por ciento) y por medio de un colega (33 por ciento). En relación al uso de cursos formales para el aprendizaje del Internet, los encuestados indicaron que estos fueron ofrecidos en su mayoría por la unidad de cómputo (29 por ciento). Otra significante opción de aprendizaje fue a través de información obtenida directamente de la red (27 por ciento). En relación a duración de los cursos formales, la Figura 11 nos muestra que la mayoría de estos tuvieron una duración de 1 a 5 horas.

## Análisis de los resultados

Los resultados de la encuesta anteriormente señalados son consistentes con los obtenidos en otros estudios como los llevados a cabo por Ladner y

Figura 5. Usuarios con acceso al Internet

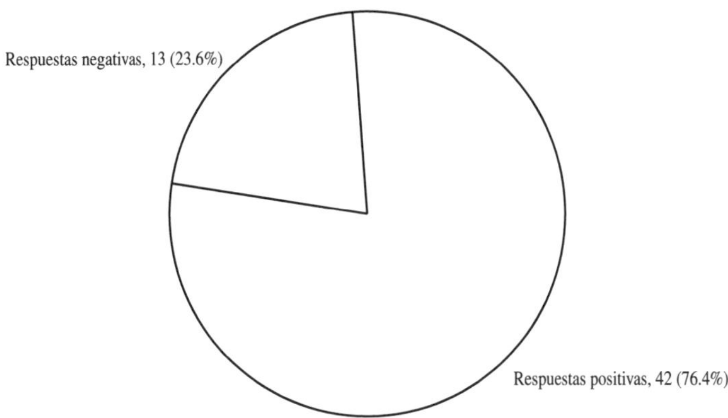


Figura 6. Opciones en el Internet: Frequencia semanal de uso

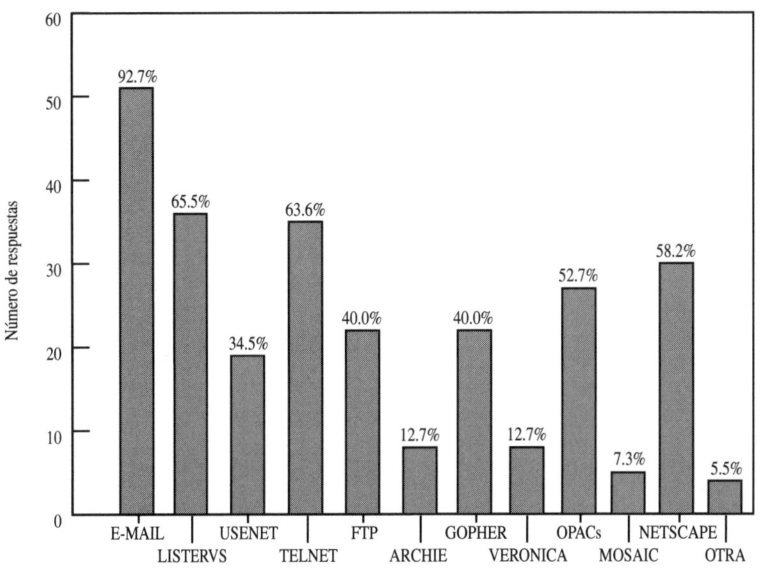

Figura 7. Opciones en el Internet: Promedia semanal de horas empleadas

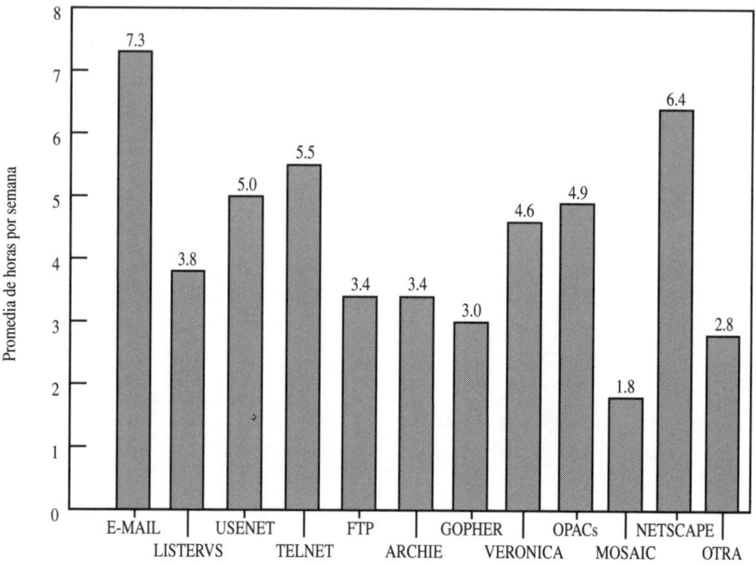


Figura 8. Experiencia usando computadora

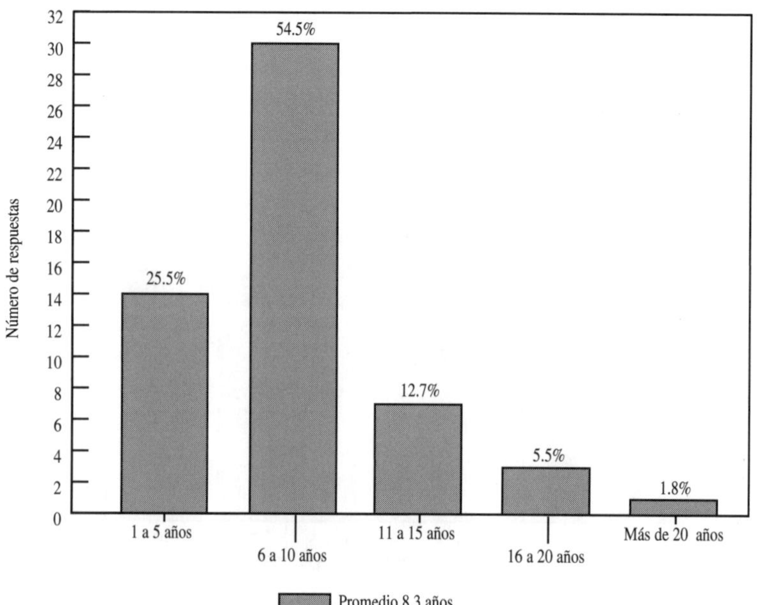

Figura 9. Experiencia usando el Internet

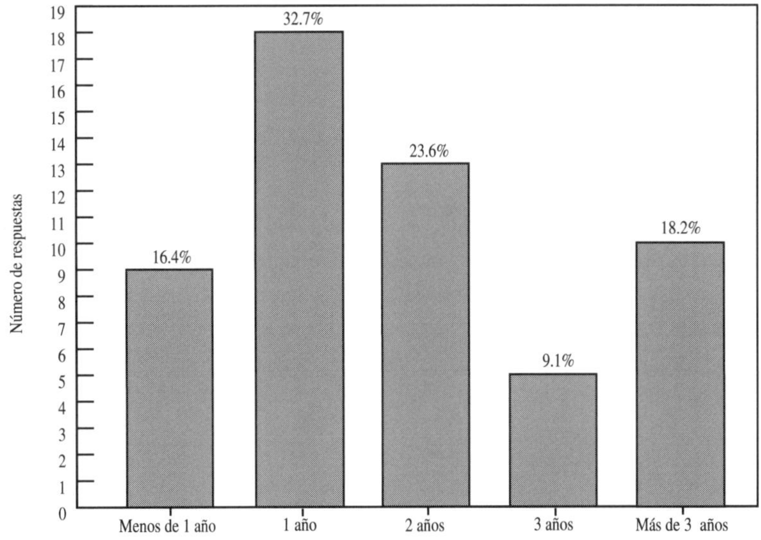

Número de respuestas

16.4% 32.7% 23.6% 9.1% 18.2%

Menos de 1 año | 1 año | 2 años | 3 años | Más de 3 años

Promedio 2.3 años

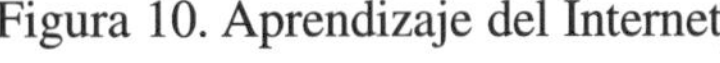

Figura 10. Aprendizaje del Internet

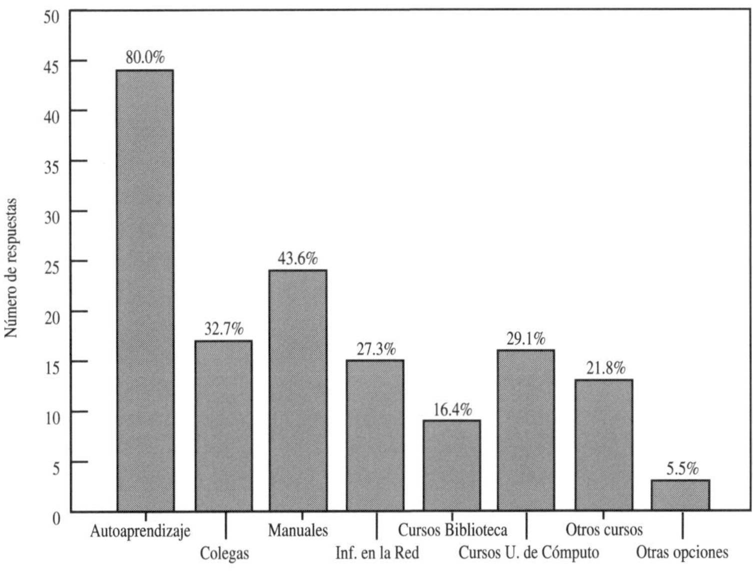

Figura 11. Duración de los cursos

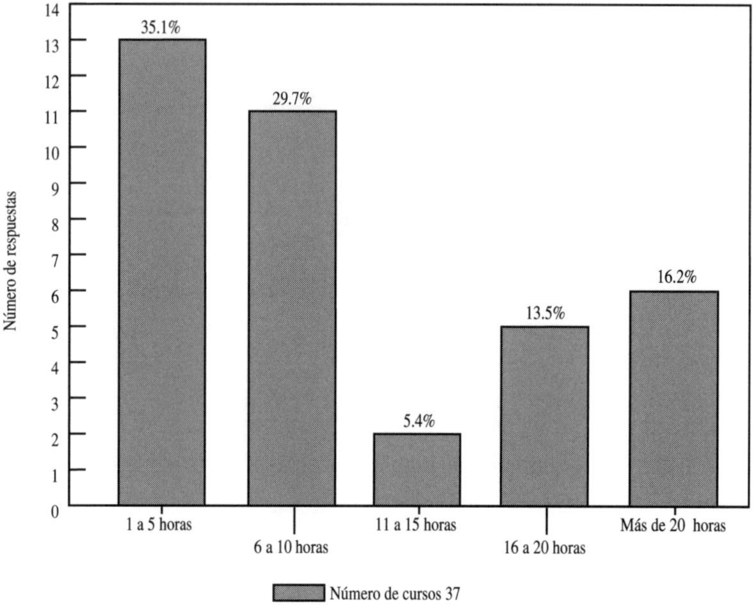


Tillman (1992), Basu (1995) y Bane y Milheim (1995). Asimismo, estos resultados son similares a los obtenidos por otras encuestas de carácter general sobre el uso del Internet.

En relación al país de origen de las personas que participaron en esta encuesta, cabe hacer mención que la mayoría de ellas laboraban en bibliotecas ubicadas en México. Lo anterior puede tener su explicación en el hecho de que una de las listas utilizadas para llevar a cabo el estudio agrupaba a bibliotecarios mexicanos. Sin embargo, la ausencia de varios países latinoamericanos fue notable. Resultados similares han sido encontrados por otras encuestas como la llevada a cabo por City Net (1995) la cual incluyó 8,935 usuarios del Internet. Esta encuesta encontró que el 59 por ciento de los usuarios encuestados fueron usuarios de Estados Unidos y solamente un 66 por ciento de México. Adicionalmente, ningún otro país de Latinoamérica a excepción de Brasil (0.44 por ciento) fue incluido dentro de los resultados de esta encuesta. Por otra parte, un estudio (Brown 1994) sobre el origen de los participantes internacionales en diez listas de discusión sobre asuntos bibliotecarios encontró muy pocos participantes de Latinoamérica: México 10 participantes, Brasil 13, Cuba 2 y

Venezuela 3. Indudablemente, los resultados de esta encuesta, al igual que los de otros estudios, reflejan el marcado desequilibrio que existe en el uso de los recursos de información disponibles.

Respecto al tipo de institución de las personas respondiendo a la encuesta, la mayoría de ellas prestaban sus servicios en bibliotecas universitarias, bibliotecas especializadas o centros de documentación. Por otro lado, las actividades que los encuestados desarrollaban dentro de sus instituciones fueron principalmente servicios al público. Evidentemente, la principal actividad dentro de las cuales se utiliza el Internet es servicios al público. Esto es similar a los resultados de encuestas a nivel mundial sobre los principales usos del Internet (Proyecto Hermes 1995) las cuales han encontrado que uno de los principales usos del Internet es el obtener materiales de referencia e información en línea. Los bibliotecarios también han usado el Internet para obtener respuesta de una manera rápida a preguntas de referencia (Lanier y Wilkins 1994).

Aunque el uso del Internet está siendo incorporado dentro de la mayoría de las actividades que tienen lugar dentro de las bibliotecas, su utilización dentro de las actividades de servicios al público es predominante. Lo anterior ha motivado comentarios respecto a que el uso del Internet dentro de las actividades de procesos técnicos ha permanecido inexplorado, existiendo posibilidades que no han sido utilizadas (McCombs 1994). Entre las actividades de procesos técnicos que pueden ser apoyadas por el Internet se han mencionado: completar información de materiales solicitados, acceso a catálogos y listas de editores, requisiciones y adquisición de materiales a través del Internet, envío de registros catalográficos de los materiales adquiridos previamente a su entrega y lógicamente el uso de otros catálogos para llevar a cabo la catalogación de los materiales (McCoy 1995).

Por otra parte, las personas que tenían a su cargo actividades de carácter administrativo tuvieron un considerable porcentaje dentro de los resultados de la encuesta. Estos resultados son similares a los arrojados por otras encuestas generales como la llevada a cabo por City Net (1995), la cual encontró que 39 por ciento de los usuarios del Internet ocupaban puestos de carácter administrativo. Contrariamente, aunque las personas reportando actividades de docencia e investigación alcanzaron niveles representativos, estas fueron minoría en comparación con aquellas que realizaban otro tipo de actividades. Lo anterior puede constituir una evidencia de que el uso del Internet dentro de nuestras instituciones permanece a niveles directivos y que su uso no ha sido generalización hacia el personal que lleva a cabo actividades de docencia o investigación.

Este problema es de carácter general y ha sido mencionado por Brown (1994) quien señala que solo 10 por ciento del personal académico de las universidades utilizan los recursos del Internet. En este sentido, el bibliotecario tiene un gran campo de acción para instruir al personal académico sobre la gran variedad de recursos de información existentes en el Internet. Sin embargo, primeramente es necesario una comprensión de las amplias posibilidades de estos recursos por el bibliotecario.

Al igual que los resultados encontrados en otros estudios (Bane y Milheim 1995), las herramientas del Internet primordialmente utilizadas fueron el uso del correo electrónico y las listas de discusión. Rowland (1994) señala que los bibliotecarios han sido asiduos usuarios del correo electrónico y los grupos de discusión para establecer comunicación con otros individuos y los resultados de esta encuesta apoyan este hecho. La utilización de estas opciones es importante elemento para que el bibliotecario interactúe con colegas dentro y fuera de la disciplina las cuales deben de ser aprovechadas para difundir el papel e importancia de sus actividades para apoyar las actividades académicas.

Los resultados de esta encuesta también nos indican que al igual que muchos de los usuarios del Internet, los bibliotecarios hemos aprendido a utilizar esta herramienta por medio del autoaprendizaje. El uso del Internet ha creado gran entusiasmo y un gran número de personas, incluyendo a los bibliotecarios, han aprendido a usarla por autoaprendizaje. Lo anterior es loable; sin embargo, esto conlleva una serie de riesgos. Uno de estos radica en que el aprendizaje del Internet sea únicamente enfocado hacia el nivel operativo, es decir, hacia el cómo hacer las cosas en lugar del porqué. Por lo tanto, uno de los aspectos claves dentro del aprendizaje de esta nueva herramienta no deberá ser únicamente el cómo, sino también el porqué y el para qué de su utilización dentro de las actividades bibliotecarias.

## Conclusiones y recomendaciones

Estos resultados nos ofrecen un panorama general de la forma en que los bibliotecarios y las bibliotecas estamos haciendo uso de las nuevas tecnologías de la información así como los efectos que estas tienen dentro de nuestras organizaciones y actividades. Por la naturaleza exploratoria de este estudio, sus resultados son de caracteres generales y muchos de ellos necesitan mayor investigación; sin embargo, estos nos permite establecer las siguientes conclusiones y recomendaciones.

Los bibliotecarios hemos incorporado el uso de la tecnología dentro de muchas de las actividades y servicios que llevamos a cabo en nuestras bibliotecas. No obstante lo anterior, los resultados de esta encuesta muestran una fuerte tendencia hacia su aplicación dentro del área de servicios. Si bien es cierto que la razón de ser de la biblioteca es el ofrecimiento de servicios, no debemos de olvidar que para proporcionarlos adecuadamente también son necesarias otro tipo de actividades dentro de las cuales es factible la utilización de esta herramienta. Tal es el caso de los procesos técnicos donde su aplicación al Internet no ha sido totalmente explorada.

Por otro lado, los resultados de esta encuesta no muestran grandes diferencias con las encuestadas llevadas a cabo entre los usuarios generales del Internet. Por ejemplo, los usuarios de todo tipo obtienen materiales de referencia e información en línea del Internet y los bibliotecarios también lo hacen. Los investigadores y profesores utilizan el Internet para comunicarse por correo electrónico, participar en listas de discusión, efectuar búsquedas en bases de datos usando Telnet y los bibliotecarios también llevan a cabo este tipo de actividades. Quizá por el carácter general de la encuesta, estos resultados no difieran substancialmente de los resultados obtenidos por encuestas de carácter general. Sin embargo, lo anterior es una evidencia de que los bibliotecarios tenemos que incorporar un valor añadido a nuestras actividades a fin de diferenciarlas de las que efectúan otro tipo de usuarios del Internet.

Al igual que muchos otros usuarios del Internet, los bibliotecarios hemos aprendido a utilizarla por autoaprendizaje. Nos ha faltado un aprendizaje formal y sistemático acerca del uso de esta herramienta el cual nos permita identificar su papel como un medio que facilita las actividades que llevamos a cabo. Por lo anterior, las escuelas de bibliotecología deberán de incluir el aprendizaje de esta nueva tecnología de la información dentro de sus programas de estudio, pues únicamente de esta forma el bibliotecario podrá utilizarla para adquirir, organizar y proporcionar a los usuarios los recursos de información que ellos necesitan.

## APENDICE

Cuestionario Enviado por Correo Electrónico

(1) CIUDAD Y PAÍS ______________________

(2) TIPO DE INSTITUCIÓN

| | |
|---|---|
| Biblioteca Pública | [ ] |
| Biblioteca Universitaria | [ ] |
| Biblioteca Gubernamental | [ ] |
| Biblioteca Especializada | [ ] |
| Centro de Documentación o Información | [ ] |
| Escuela de Bibliotecología | [ ] |
| Centro de Investigación | [ ] |
| Otro (Especifique) | [ ] |

______________________

(3) TIPO DE ACTIVIDAD QUE EFECTÚA USTED EN SU INSTITUCIÓN

| | |
|---|---|
| Investigación | [ ] |
| Docencia | [ ] |
| Administración | [ ] |
| Servicios al Público | [ ] |
| Procesos Técnicos | [ ] |
| Otra (Especifique) | [ ] |

______________________

(4) EXPERIENCIA EN EL USO DE COMPUTADORAS

Años [ ] Meses [ ]

(5) EXPERIENCIA EN EL USO DE INTERNET

Años [ ] Meses [ ]

(6) PROMEDIO SEMANAL DE HORAS USANDO

| | |
|---|---|
| Correo Electrónico (E-MAIL) | [ ] |
| Grupos de Discusión (LISTSERVS) | [ ] |
| Noticias y Artículos(USENET) | [ ] |
| Acceso Remoto (TELNET) | [ ] |
| Transferencia de Archivos (FTP) | [ ] |
| ARCHIE | [ ] |
| GOPHER | [ ] |

VERÓNICA [ ]
Catálogos de Bibliotecas (OPACs) [ ]
WWW Empleando MOSAIC [ ]
WWW Empleando NETSCAPE [ ]
Otra Opción (Especifique) [ ]

______________________

(7) INDIQUE SI ESTÁ UTILIZANDO INTERNET PARA

Selección de Materiales [ ]
Adquisición de Materiales [ ]
Acceso a Fuentes de Referencia Electrónicas [ ]
Acceso a Bases de Datos e Indices Comerciales [ ]
Acceso a Servicios de Catalogación [ ]
Acceso a Catálogos para la Catalogación de Sus Materiales [ ]
Obtención de Artículos de Revistas Electrónicas [ ]
Otra Opción (Especifique) [ ]

______________________

(8) COMO APRENDIÓ A UTILIZAR INTERNET

Autoaprendizaje [ ]
Por Medio de un Colega [ ]
Por Medio de Manuales o Información Escrita [ ]
Información en la Red [ ]
Curso Ofrecido por la Biblioteca [ ]
Especifique Número de Horas [ ]
Curso Ofrecido por la Unidad de Cómputo [ ]
Especifique Número de Horas [ ]
Otro Curso Formal [ ]
Especifique Número de Horas [ ]
Otra Opción (Especifique) [ ]

______________________

(9) NÚMERO DE PERSONAL EN SU INSTITUCIÓN [ ]

(10) EN EL CASO DE BIBLIOTECAS Y CENTROS DE DOCUMENTACIÓN EL USUARIO TIENE ACCESO DIRECTO A INTERNET

SÍ [ ] NO [ ]

(11) COMENTARIOS ADICIONALES

## BIBLIOGRAFIA

Arguedas, Leda. 1996. [ledaa@cariari.ucr.ac.cr]. *Correo electrónico*. En IWETEL [iwetel@saranet.es], abril 12.

Bane, Adele F., y William D. Milheim. 1995. "Internet Insights: How Academics Are Using the Internet". *Computers in Libraries* 15:2 (febrero), 32–36.

Basu, Geetali. 1995. "Using Internet for Reference: Myths and Realities". *Computers in Libraries* 15:2 (febrero), 38–40.

Brown, Jeanne M. 1994. "The Global Computer Network". *International Information and Library Review* 26 (1), 51–65.

City Net. 1995. *City Net Survey Demographics*. [http://www.city.net/cnx/survey_fall95.html].

Ladner, Shary J., y Hope N. Tillman. 1992. "How Special Librarians Really Use the Internet." *Canadian Library Journal* 49 (junio), 211–215.

Lanier, Don, y Walter Wilkins. 1994. "Ready Reference via the Internet." *RQ*, 33:3 (primavera ), 359–367.

Mattes, Daniel. 1995. [dmattes@ua9000.dcc.anahuac.mx]. *Impacto de Internet en las Bibliotecas*. En BIBLIOMEX-L [bibliomex-l@ccr.dsi.uanl.mx], agosto 29.

———. 1996. [dmattes@ua9000.dcc.anahuac.mx]. *Replay: Pregunta*. Mensaje enviado a Filiberto F. Martínez [vp24qanb@ubvms.cc.buffalo.edu], enero 9.

McCombs, Gillian M. 1994. "The Internet and the Technical Services: A Point Break Approach." *Library Resources and Technical Services* 38:2 (abril), 169–177.

McCoy, Patricia Sayre. 1995. "Technical Services and the Internet." *Wilson Library Bulletin* 67:7 (marzo), 37–40

Proyecto Hermes Project. 1995. *The Fourth WWW Consumer Survey*. [http://www-personal.umich.edu/~sgupta/hermes/survey4].

Rodríguez García, Ariel. 1996. [rgarcia@dewey.rhon.itam.mx]. *Respuesta*. Mensaje enviado a Filiberto F. Martínez [vp24qanb@ubvms.cc.buffalo.edu], enero 5.

Rowland, Lucy M. 1994. "Libraries and Librarians on the Internet." *Communication Education* 43:2 (abril), 143–150.

Soto Fuentes, Saúl.1995. [ssoto@mail.integer.mx]. *Reply: Impacto de Internet en las Bibliotecas*. En BIBLIOMEX-L [bibliomex-l@ccr.dsi.uanl.mx], agosto 29.

Urbizagastegui, Rubén. 1996. [ruben@pop.ucr.edu]. *[Uso de listas de discusión]*. En BIBLIOMEX-L [bibliomex-l@ccr.dsi.uanl.mx], febrero 7.

# 19. As tecnologias da comunicação e a educação escolar

Leila Maria Ferreira Salles
Débora Mazza

Este trabalho discute a contribuição das tecnologias da comunicação buscando as inovações que elas podem suscitar na educação escolar.

As tecnologias da comunicação já estão presentes em todos os ramos das atividades humanas. "Do mesmo modo como outrora, com a revolução industrial, as máquinas mecânicas libertaram o homem do esforço físico, hoje, as máquinas passam a fazer parte do trabalho intelectual de cálculo, armazenamento de dados, etc." (Ripper, Braga, Moraes 1993:410). A inserção das tecnologias da comunicação faz parte da realidade contemporânea e, como um dado de realidade, altera o processo de trabalho e as relações humanas.

Embora o custo destas tecnologias, na sociedade brasileira, ainda torne proibitivo a sua aquisição e utilização em escala nacional no sistema escolar público, acreditamos que os interesses econômicos envolvidos vêm reduzindo os custos e tornando inevitável a pressão para consumo em massa de computadores, multimídia, televisores e vídeo-cassetes nas escolas.

As discussões na área educacional apontam para caminhos e interpretações divergentes quanto a essa questão, ora afirmando que a escola deve incorporar os recursos existentes na sociedade para não se tornar obsoleta, sobrevalorizando as potencialidades da tecnologia; ora postulando que a escola é pobre, a merenda é péssima, o giz quebra, faltam carteiras, as bibliotecas são precárias e o salário recebido pelo professor é irrisório, negligenciando-se assim as contribuições que poderiam advir da utilização de inovações tecnológicas no ambiente escolar.

Deve-se ainda levar em consideração que a incorporação dos novos recursos tecnológicos pode desencadear um certo receio de que o professor possa vir a ser subsituído por eles, eliminando-se com isso o lado humano da educação, o que pode gerar preconceitos com relação à utilização dessas novas tecnologias no contexto educacional.

O uso de computadores no sistema educacional, por ser uma tecnologia típica deste fim de século e só recentemente estar sendo incorporada às escolas, pode ilustrar as discussões que fizemos anteriormente. Nas escolas o computador tem sido utilizado para ensinar sobre computação, através de aulas de informática onde é utilizado para que o aluno adquira conceitos computacionais, como noções de funcionamento do aparelho e de programação ou é utilizado para o ensino de conceitos das diferentes disciplinas. E é aqui, nesta última postura, que a literatura na área tem procurado discutir as diferenças e as implicações pedagógicas do uso de computadores na escola.

A esse respeito, Valente (1993) tem apontado que quando o computador assume o papel de máquina de ensinar a abordagem pedagógica é a instrução auxiliada por computador. A idéia básica é do computador ensinando um determinado assunto ao aluno. Segundo Valente (1993:3), o uso do computador para ensinar tem sido apenas uma "versão computadorizada dos atuais métodos de ensino", onde substitui-se o papel ou o livro pelo computador. Permanece-se no paradigma instrucionista apenas informatizando os métodos tradicionais de educação. Já o uso de computador como ferramenta do processo de ensino e aprendizagem propicia, segundo Valente (1993:5), "as condições para os estudiantes excitarem a capacidade de procurar e selecionar a informação, resolver problemas e aprender independentemente". Neste paradigma construcionista a respeito da utilização de computadores na sala de aula a ênfase está na aprendizagem e não no ensino, onde o aluno é o construtor de seu próprio conhecimento. Segundo Valente, neste paradigma, o seu uso na educação provocaria o questionamento dos métodos de ensino tradicionalmente empregados, visto que os alunos não mais memorizariam as informaões mas sim seriam ensinados a buscar e usar as informacões adequando-se a escola ao mundo de hoje onde a velocidade das mudanças é rápida. Nessa situação o uso do computador nas escolas implica que "o professor deve deixar de ser o repassador de conhecimentos—o computador pode fazer isto e o faz muito mas eficientenmente do que o professor—e passar a ser o criador de ambientes de aprendizagem e o facilitador do processo de desenvolvimento intelectual dos alunos" (Valente 1993:6).

Assim, a recente produção científica a respeito das aplicações das novas tecnologias à educação tem atentado para as diferentes formas de sua utilização e suas implicações no processo de ensino e aprendizagem.

A literatura a respeito do uso de multimeios na escola tem também centralizado a discussão para o fato que a escola é um dos locais de aplicação destes recursos. Os multimeios estão mais intimamente associados a educação informal e, como o vídeo e a televisão, estão voltados para o entretenimento e o lazer. Já a educação formal tem objetivos diferentes, isto é, o da socialização dos conhecimentos socialmente produzidos. No entanto, as tecnologias da comunicação podem ser utilizadas na escola como complemento do trabalho do professor.

Isto coloca a necessidade da escola pensar urgentemente a sua relação com os meios de comunicação, deixando de ignorá-los ou considerá-los inimigos. A escola também não pode pensar em imitá-los, porque "nos meios predomina a função lúdica, de entretenimento, não a organização da compreensão do mundo e das atitudes" (Moran 1990:21).

A partir dessas reflexões decidimos coletar depoimentos de alunos, professores e diretores buscando caracterizar como os recursos tecnológicos são percebidos no processo de ensino e aprendizagem. Atentamos não para a experiência de uso das tecnologias da comunicação no ambiente escolar, mas sim para as expectativas e propostas de sua utilização inscritas no imaginário de diretores, professores e alunos. Para tanto trabalhamos com cinco escolas públicas de 1° e 2° graus localizadoas no município de Rio Claro, Estado de São Paulo, Brasil.

## A percepção da comunidade escolar

Desenvolvemos a pesquisa coletando depoimentos de diretores, professores e alunos de cinco escolas com as quais vimos trabalhando através de contatos com a Delegacia de Ensino do Município, cursos ministrados aos profissionais das escolas, estágios supervisionados a alunos da Faculdade. Portanto, sentimo-nos participantes e conhecedores da dinâmica de trabalho cotidiano destas escolas. Considerando a nossa história com as instituições, coletamos depoimentos de cinco diretores, dois professores e quatro alunos de cada uma das escolas; inteirando um total de 35 sujeitos envolvidos na pesquisa, que responderam a um questionário semi-estruturado. Selecionamos os alunos nas séries finais do 1° e do 2° graus contando com uma maior maturidade na análise das questões e elaboração das respostas.

Atentamos para os depoimentos da população escolar objetivando entender o processo de incorporação das tecnologias da comunicação no contexto escolar.

*Os diretores*

Os depoimentos dos diretores revelam que as tecnologias da comunicação viriam de encontro aos recursos necessários para que a escola cumpra a sua função social, qual seja, a de desenvolver um trabalho educativo consistente, interessante e envolvente; que favoreça a aquisição de conhecimentos significativos, previamente selecionados, e trabalhados pelos professores objetivando o crescimento e estimulando a participação dos alunos.

Os diretores descrevem os recursos necessários para que as escolas públicas apresentem um bom desempenho. Eles comentam que a administração escolar demanda recursos financeiros, materiais, humanos e físicos. A demanda financeira refere-se a destinação de verbas de acordo com a realidade escolar e a autonomia administrativa para poder aplicá-las. Os recursos materiais dizem respeito a existência de livros de pesquisa, acervo de fitas educativas, transporte para realizar atividades extra-classe, fitas de slides relacionadas com os conteúdos curriculares, computadores, etc. Os recursos humanos demandam um quadro funcional completo para a realização dos diferentes trabalhos (limpeza, merenda, secretaria, inspeção de alunos, guarda, equipa técnica de apoio pedagógico-bibliotecário, psicólogo, coordenador, orientador e supervisor). Os recursos físicos apontam para a manutenção e preservação dos prédios bem como para projetos de construção adequados à realização de atividades diversificadas tais como: recreação, esporte, dramatização, sala de televisão e vídeo, oficina de computação, biblioteca, laboratórios.

Na fala dos diretores as tecnologias da comunicação ajudariam a aparelhar a estrutura escolar e favorecer o processo de ensino aprendizagem. Elas aparecem no bojo dos recursos necessários para qualificar o espaço escolar.

Eles dizem que para se desenvolver um trabalho escolar qualitativo é necessário um local limpo, arejado, iluminado, com cadeiras e carteiras adequadas a faixa etária dos alunos, com recursos audio-visuais selecionados, com condições para realizar atividades extra-classe, com materiais gráficos para confecção de jornais, revistas, materiais didáticos, etc. As tecnologias da comunicação se inserem no quadro de necessidades de aparelhamento das condições de trabalho na escola. Elas se apresentam como ferramentas modernizadoras e facilitadoras da prática institucional. As tecnologias são meios, instrumentos que auxiliam os sujeitos do processo educativo.

Os diretores fazem, também, uma leitura política da relação Educação-Sociedade e Tecnologia, dizendo ser necessário valorizar a carreira do magistério, remunerar dignamente os profissionais da educação, formar permanentemente os educadores, adequar a escola às necessidades sociais, engajar a população escolar num trabalho coletivo, definir metas e prioridades ao alcance de todos, construir uma política educacional acessível, exequível e enviar o kit das tecnologias de comunicação.

Para os diretores é inegável que as tecnologias da comunicação estimulam a participação dos alunos e ajudam a desenvolver suas capacidades mentais e intelectuais, mas isso precisa se dar num contexto de elaboração sistematizada dos conteúdos e metodologias de ensino, relação dialógica professor-aluno-conhecimento, participação da comunidade nas definições das diretrizes escolares, capacitação permanente dos profissionais da escola.

Fica claro nos depoimentos dos diretores que os meios de comunicação podem auxiliar no processo educativo que visa o desenvolvimento integral do aluno-cidadão e a construção de uma sociedade democrática, desde que eles sejam aplicados, adequando-se à especificidade da educação escolar.

*Os professores*

Para os professores as tecnologias da comunicação relacionam-se, fundamentalmente, com o trabalho de sala de aula. Para eles uma boa aula é aquela que cumpre com os objetivos previamente estabelecidos, desenvolve o conteúdo num processo dialógico contando com a participação dos alunos e, consequentemente, favorece a assimilação e produção dos conhecimentos. Neste horizonte as tecnologias da comunicação aparecem como um dos recursos utilizados para que se desenvolva uma boa aula.

Os depoimentos dos professores explicitam que para se desenvolver um trabalho educativo qualitativo é necessário classes com número reduzido de alunos (máximo de 30), salário que possibilite dedicação exclusiva do professor à escola, bibliotecas com material de pesquisa atualizado, condições de realização de atividades de campo, salas adequadas para televisão e vídeo, projeção de slides, computador, máquina xerox.

Muitos professores fizeram propostas qualificando a prática docente. Eles dizeram ser necessário um processo permanente de reciclagem dos professores, interação efetiva escola-comunidade onde a escola diga com clareza sua proposta de trabalho e a comunidade explicite seus costumes, valores e expectativas frente a instituição; fixação do currículo mínimo e revisão dos instrumentos de avaliação, aumento salarial tendo em vista a valorização da carreira docente, definição da função social e dos diversos papéis no interior da escola, adequação do "produto" ofrecido pela escola aos avanços tecnológicos deste fim de século.

Na fala dos professores aparece, também, a consciência de que só com o giz, a lousa e a oratória não se consegue mais estimular a participação do aluno e desenvolver as suas capacidades mentais e intelectuais. O esforço do professor para atrair o interesse do aluno tem como concorrente os "vídeos-games, as sextas-sexy, os cines-trash, as bandas e grupos de rock, os jogos de computador, a internet, etc.". Eles acreditam que as tecnologias da comunicação ajudam a modificar a aparência obsoleta da didática escolar mas elas precisam ser incorporadas e digeridas tendo como ponto de partida a realidade e as curiosidades dos alunos e o desenvolvimento do currículo mínimo das disciplinas, num processo de relação dialógica.

As tecnologias da comunicação, no entender dos professores, apresentamse como uma ferramenta que facilita a operacionalização do trabalho docente.

*Os alunos*

O significado atribuido pelos alunos às tecnologias da comunicação no contexto escolar está vinculado a percepção do que é uma boa aula.

As falas apontam para a importância de uma aula onde tanto a transmissão/assimilação do conteúdo da disciplina como o relacionamento prefessoraluno caracterizado pelo respeito, compromisso pelo ensino e afetivo é primordial. As tecnologias da comunicação adquirem, segundo os depoimentos dos alunos, o papel de complementar o trabalho do professor facilitando o processo de ensino a aprendizagem.

A importância atribuida ao professor como núcleo do processo educativo perpassou todas as respostas dos alunos, seja quando falam das dificuldades que encontram quando alguns "profesores não se expressam de forma que compreendem", sugerem que "deve ter aulas para os professores de como é ser um bom professor", seja quando apontam as atividades que gostariam que integrasse o cotidiano escolar ou as suas propostas para a melhoria do sistema escolar.

Especificamente no que se refere à qualidade do ensino enfocam o papel do professor esperando que ele os motive para o estudo, mudando a dinâmica da sala de aula ao permitir a sua participação, trabalhos em grupos, seminários, leitura, pesquisa, música, poesia, dramatizações e que procure a fixação do conteúdo com vários exercícios sobre a matéria, ou, ainda, promovendo atividades extra classe como palestras, visitas a museus e excursões. Questionam, às vezes, a metodologia utilizada na sala de aula propondo que o professor "use vários métodos para decidir com o qual o aluno aprende mais," transmita "uma visão mais crítica do conteúdo", aproxime o conteúdo da "sua realidade para que ele se identifique com o assunto", ensine "várias vezes até que aprenda", "dê o direito de perguntar o que não entende". Propõem que o professor utilize na sala de aula matérias de jornais que facilitem a discussão de assuntos atuais como AIDS, doenças, política e economia. E sugerem, extrapolando a sala de aula, algumas mudanças curriculares que gostariam que fossem implantadas nas escolas, como aumento da carga horária das disciplinas Educação Física e Educação Artística e maior tempo de aula. Mais uma vez, como se vêa retornam ao que parece-nos ser o aspecto central de todos os depoimentos: que o papel do professor na condução do processo educativo é indiscutível, inclusive, quando dizem que a melhoria da qualidade do ensino implica também na valorização financeira do seu trabalho.

Os alunos apontam, também, o que esperam do comportamento dos seus pares na sala de aula: "fazer silêncio", "não irritar os professores com palhaçadas", "prestar atenção nas explicações". Com isso indicam a percepção de uma disciplina para o bom desenvolvimento do trabalho escolar. Nesse sentido, os alunos questionam, ainda, aspectos do cotidiano escolar que podem dificultar o trabalho do professor e o seu aprendizado como o número de alunos na sala de aula, a falta de funcionários e limpeza da escola.

A fala dos alunos a respeito da melhoria do ensino aponta para a necessidade de incorporação das tecnologias da comunicação nas escolas, pois contribuiriam no processo de ensino e aprendizagem. Mas parece-nos que o uso destes meios na sala de aula tem o sentido de auxiliar o trabalho docente já que vários expressam que o único recurso que as escolas precisam são "bons professores que expliquem bem a matéria" ou "eu acho que tem que ter um bom professor e só isso" ou ainda "o que precisa é ter mais cuidado ao selecionar professores".

Porém iso não significa que não percebam a importância de outros recursos ou mesmo que não gostariam que seu uso fosse difundido. Na fala dos alunos os recursos que visualizam como necessários na sala de aula vão desde "ter um bom giz que não quebre" até ter bibliotecas e laboratórios e equipá-las com vídeos, televisão, projetores e computadores. A fala mais freqüente é por bibliotecas melhores, laboratórios equipados, livros didáticos e uso de TV e vídeo. Talvez a televisão e o vídeo apareçam mais freqüentemente pelo fato de serem um equipamento disponível na maioria das escolas e por serem um item de consumo de mais fácil acesso à maioria da população.

O vídeo foi muitas vezes valorizado pelos alunos no sentido de "aprender melhor a matéria", "acompanhar visualmente o que o professor explica" ou para tornar a aula "mais prazerosa, mais legal", ou seja como um recurso complementar ao trabalho docente. Já quando se referem ao uso de computadores na sala de aula justificam a sua necessidade para "ter contato com o mundo" ou "porque estamos nessa era," dando a esse desejo uma conotacão que decorre de modismo.

Parece que nas falas dos alunos convivem duas situações opostas, de um lado a falta de recursos básicos nas instituições escolares quando reivindicam melhores condições didácticas traduzidas em acesso a livros, mapas e xerox, ou se queixam das mesas de estudo que estão em péssimas condições, giz de má qualidade, ausência de cortinas nas salas de aula, bibliotecas precárias e laboratórios sem uso ou com equipamentos quebrados. Por outro lado, reivindicam o uso mais freqüente de recursos audiovisuais e escolas equipadas com computadores, com aulas de informática onde as novas tecnologias da comunicação se incorporem ao cotidiano escolar.

Enfim, o retrato traçado pelos alunos mostra o cotidiano escolar resumido basicamente ao professor, seus alunos e o quadro negro convivendo com as expectativas de que outras tecnologias se tornem parte integrante das escolas.

## Conclusão

Este estudo tinha como preocupação inicial a discussão a respeito da incorporação das tecnologias da comunicação nas escolas tendo como pressuposto uma realidade que afirma a importância da absorção desses recursos sem problematizá-los, minimizando a contribuição dos demais aspectos determinantes do sucesso ou fracasso educacional. Isto é, que a escola corre o risco de absorver os recursos tecnológicos como solucionadores dos problemas educacionais reduzindo o problema da educação escolar a uma discussão meramente tecnológica. No entanto, a análise dos depoimentos, ao enfocar as expectativas e propostas de utilização das tecnologias da comunicação no contexto escolar, revelou que estas parecem centralizar-se em torno das tecnologias da comunicação como meios, instrumentos, que auxiliam os sujeitos do processo educativo e não como soluções para os problemas educacionais.

Porém, a ênfase dada as tecnologias da comunicação na educação por cada um dos segmentos parece-nos ser diferente. Para os diretores elas se inscrevem no quadro de necessidades de aparelhamento da escola. Para os professores elas ajudam a modificar aparência obsoleta da didáctica escolar e precisam ser incorporadas como um meio que facilita a operacionalização do trabalho docente. Para elas, embora seja um dos meios que facilita o processo de ensino e aprendizagem, as tecnologias da comunicação asseguram o envolvimento, o interesse maior dos alunos com as aulas e modernizam a escola permitindo a concorrência com os demais meios de comunicação social. Para os alunos a incorporação das tecnologias da comunicação tem por objetivo complementar o trabalho docente contribuindo para otimizar o processo de ensino e aprendizagem estando diretamente associada a percepção de uma boa aula. Assim, para eles o aspecto mais importante é uma aula onde o relacionamento professor-aluno é bom e a transmissão e assimilação dos conteúdos é assegurada.

Nesta perspectiva os meios de comunicação além de não eliminarem o papel do professor, ajudam-no a desenvolver sua tarefa principal que é a de obter uma visão de conjunto, educar para uma visão mais crítica, motivar o aprendizado dos conteúdos curriculares.

A análise destes depoimentos ajuda-nos a repensar o problema da educação escolar no Brasil. A escola continua sendo acusada de maximizar os processos de exclusão social, intelectual, cultural e econômica. Diante deste veredito é muito confortável absorver os recursos tecnológicos como solucionadores mágicos dos problemas educacionais, ou seja conceber a tecnologia como algo independente das relações sociais, de poder e de classe.

A educação no Brasil enfrenta problemas que, indiscutivelmente, extrapolam o âmbito escolar, tendo em seu conjunto causas relacionadas com as condições de vida e trabalho da população, bem como a inserção dependente da economia brasileira nas relações internacionais. Por outro lado, a escola não é um elemento passivo neste processo. Partindo-se deste pressuposto, entendemos que se faz necessário buscar soluções para os problemas da educação: número de jovens em idade escolar fora da escola, repetência, evasão, formação inadequada de profissionais da educação, salários que não oferecem condições dígnas de sobrevivência, sucateamento da estrutura escolar, ausência de recursos físicos-humanos e financeiros, tradicionalismo didático-metodológico.

As tecnologias da comunicação apresentam-se como um dos recursos que podem ajudar a reverter a situação em que se encontra o ensino público brasileiro. Isto só será verdadeiro se estes instrumentais forem incorporados considerando os nossos referênciais educacionais, econômicos e culturais.

Se a importação das tecnologias da comunicação implicar em transposição de modelos enraizados em outras realidades, isto representará um enorme desperdício de recursos e poderá ocasionar danos educacionais sérios. Estamos nos referindo a tendência moderna de se trazer modelos não só fora do nosso contexto cultural, mas também de fácil transposição e massificação. Estes modelos baseados em instrução programada tendem a restringir qualquer iniciativa de professores e alunos enquanto sujeitos construtores do conhecimento e potencialmente conscientes e criativos. Isto representaria, a curto prazo, uma geração educada com escassos estímulos quanto ao desenvolvimento da inteligência, da consciência e da criatividade, podendo vir a dificultar o país na produção científico-tecnológico, considerando que dentro do atual modelo económico a escassez de cidadãos conscientes e criativos poderá reforçar ainda mais os laços de dependência.

Neste sentido que colocamos como foco central da discussão a questão das condições de trabalho existentes nas escolas públicas que pesquisamos e da incampação das tecnologias da comunicação enquanto ferramentas facilitadoras no encaminhamento das reais necessidades da população escolar.

A questão que se coloca, portanto, não é a de se condenar a entrada das tecnologias da comunicação na escola e nem a de se deslumbrar frente a utilização desses meios, mas de como estas tecnologias podem ser incorporadas de modo a favorecer o processo educativo e o repensar as condiões de trabalho na instituição.

No caso brasileiro, se consideramos que a escola fundamental é um dos poucos, senão o único, bem cultural de acesso universal, o uso das tecnologias da comunicação pode trazer dividendos políticos para minimizar os processos de exclusão social, cultural, intelectual, educacional e econômica, sobretudo.

## BIBLIOGRAFIA


Arroyo, Miguel. 1995. "Educação Escolar e Cultura Tecnológica". Em *Paixão de Aprender II*. Petrópolis, R.J.: Vozes. Pp. 26–37.

Frigotto, Gaudêncio. 1995. "Construção Social do Conhecimento e Cultura Tecnológica". Em *Paixão de Aprender II*. Petrópolis, R.J.: Vozes. Pp. 15–25.

Gomes, Pedro G. 1990. "Senso Crítico: Uma Preocupação Educacional". Em *Série IDEIAS*, no. 9. S.P.: FDE. Pp. 31–37.

Leite, Lígia Silva. 1994. "As Tecnologias da Educação e da Comunicação e o Cotidiano do Ensinar e do Aprender". Em *Revista da Associação Nacional de Educação* 13 (20), 51–57.

Moran, José M. 1990. "Educação, Comunicação e Meios de Comunicação" e "Os Meios de Comunicação na Escola". Em *Série IDEIAS,* no. 9. S.P.: FDE. Pp. 13–17.

Nascimbem, N. M. S. 1988. "Relato de uma Experiência do Uso do Computador no Curso de Magistério". Em *NIED MEMO,* Núcleo de Informática Aplicada à Educação, no. 20. S.P.: Gráfica da UNICAMP.

Ripper, Afira V., Álvaro J. P. Braga e Raquel A. Moraes. 1993. "O Projeto Eureka". Em *Computadores e Conhecimento.* Pp. 409–418.

Secretaría Municipal de Educação de São Paulo. 1992. *Projeto Gênese: A Informática Chega ao Aluno da Escola Pública Municipal.* Relatório Técnico. S.P.: Prefeitura do Município de São Paulo.

Silva, Tomaz T. S., e Antônio F. Moreira, org. 1995. *Territórios Contestados: O Currículo e os Novos Mapas Políticos e Culturais*. Petrópolis, R.J.: Vozes.

Valente, J. A., e A. B. Valente. 1988. *Logo: Conceitos, Aplicações e Projetos*. S.P.: Editora McGraw-Hill.

Valente, José Armando. 1991. *Libertando a Mente: Computadores na Educação Especial*. Campinas, S.P.: Gráfica da UNICAMP.

Valente, José Armando, org. 1993. *Computadores e Conhecimento. Repensando a Educação*. Campinas, S.P.: Gráfica da UNICAMP.

# VII. Media in Latin America and the Caribbean

# 20. El potencial del Internet como fuente de información en América Latina

Eduardo Villanueva Mansilla

Cualquier aproximación a la problemática de la difusión del conocimiento sobre América Latina creada en los últimos años nos lleva a una manifestación de problemas hace bastante tiempo presentados en la literatura, tanto al nivel general de la comunicación como al específico de la difusión de información académica. Nada nuevo diremos si mencionamos las limitaciones de la comunicación sur-sur, de la industria editorial y de la actividad académica en la región latinoamericana.

Vamos a desarrollar el siguiente trabajo en tres etapas: primero una introducción a la presencia del Internet en la región, para luego acercarnos a las razones porque las que intuimos el estado de la cuestión. Finalmente, trataremos de proponer modos de anticipar las posibilidades de encontrar información valiosa en servidores de países de la región latinoamericana.

Pero antes de cualquier discusión, una aclaración: como casi cualquier estudio sobre el Internet, éste no puede pretender exhaustividad ni ausencia de generalizaciones. Las afirmaciones que hacemos se basan en nuestra experiencia antes que en la revisión de una literatura aún no muy amplia, y por lo tanto pueden ser y sin duda serán discutidos.

## Una apreciación sobre la presencia del Internet en América Latina

Hacer una historia de las redes de comunicación e información en América Latina es una de las tareas pendientes para los académicos de la región. Ante la carencia de estudios integrados y totalizadores sobre este tema, un panorama grueso, basado en diversidad de fuentes, es lo que queda como opción.[1]

Inicialmente, todas las redes de la región fueron logradas a partir de fines de la década de los ochenta (ver Cuadro 1), con otras naciendo en los primeros años de la década de los noventa. Esfuerzos previos, como redes bajo BITNET en Chile, o la gran experiencia de Alternex, parte de la red de comunicaciones alternativas, fueron más bien aislados.

La expansión de redes en el molde Internet fue posible, en la mayoría de casos, por el interés de los Consejos de Ciencia y Tecnología de cada país, con

Cuadro 1. Conexiones latinoamericanas al Internet a través de la NSFNET

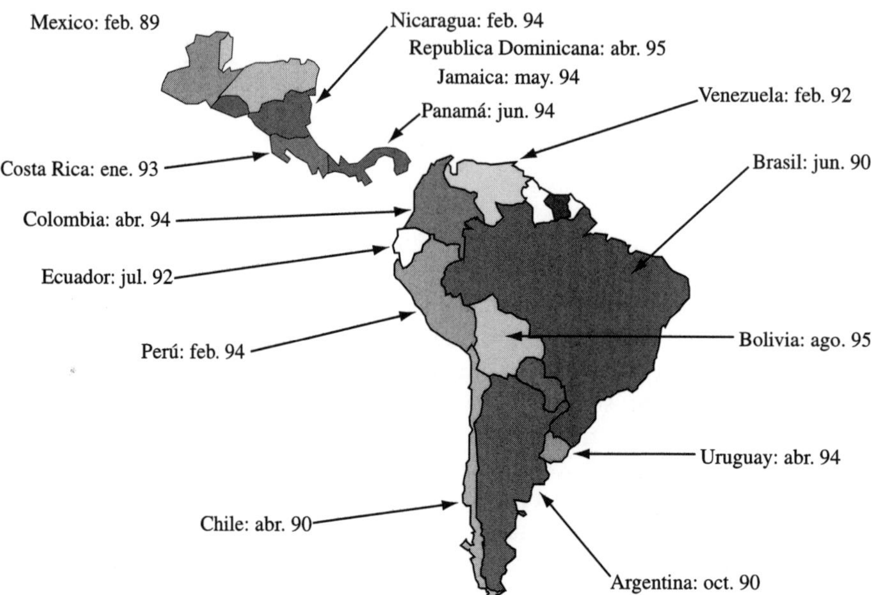


Fuente: ftp://nic.merit.edu/nsfnet/statistics/nets.by.country; 5 de enero de 1995.

excepciones como la peruana, donde el trabajo cooperativo fue la regla y la participación estatal ha sido ínfima por no decir inexistente; Bolivia, con un fuerte impulso de la cooperación técnica internacional; o Chile, con más presencia de algunas universidades privadas que del consejo nacional propiamente. En los últimos años, la presencia comercial ha crecido enormemente y en casi todos los países de la región en los que hay Internet, también existen proveedores comerciales de acceso (ver Cuadro 2 para el detalle de los niveles de conectividad en la región).

Siendo el Internet una red de comunicaciones, depende para su expansión de la calidad y difusión de las redes públicas de datos; en una región donde los servicios de telecomunicaciones han sido tradicionalmente de mala calidad, el efecto casi inmediato es la poca facilidad para su incorporación a la red.

La llegada del Internet por lo general ha significado una importante inversión para las instituciones académicas: el costo en equipos es importante, pero el costo del entrenamiento del recurso humano quizá sea el ingrediente más caro de la mezcla. Los centros de computación y escuelas de informática se han vistos recargados al tener que enfrentar una tecnología que por lo general estaba fuera de sus prioridades, marcadas no por los sistemas abiertos sino por las tendencias del mercado. El entrenamiento de personal de computación ha demandado un esfuerzo elevado, mientras que el entrenamiento de uso en Internet por lo general ha sido dejado como segunda o inexistente prioridad.

Esta situación se ve acompañada por una relativa ausencia de posibilidades de usar la red. Si bien el Internet había llegado a las universidades, se podría decir que sólo ha alcanzado el hall de visitantes antes que las oficinas y salas interiores: la mayoría de profesores tienen aun hoy que hacer esfuerzos importantes para poder usar la red sin incurrir en costos mayores, debido a la casi inexistencia de redes *internas*, un elemento tan importante como la conexión *externa* al Internet. El acceso facilitado por lo general se limitó al correo electrónico por un tiempo bastante significativo. El caso peruano puede servir como ejemplo para la situación latinoamericana, por lo que presentamos un resumen de la situación actual de la conectividad en el Perú (ver Cuadro 3).

La limitación al correo electrónico por cierto, no tiene nada de malo. Una buena conexión con el mundo exterior requiere de disponer de medios para reforzar la comunicación interpersonal antes que nada, pero la dificultad de acceder al Internet impide aprovechar, al menos como usuarios, los servicios "reales" de la Red.

Pero si comenzamos a buscar acceso a recursos informacionales, podemos ver que el acceso a los catálogos de las bibliotecas, uno de los recursos más importantes y básicos del Internet, es limitado. Por ejemplo, buscando a través del Gopher madre en Minnesota, son muy pocas las instituciones de la región que han puesto accesibles por Telnet sus catálogos, y también son muy pocas aquellas que, sea a través de un servidor para la W3 (World Wide Web), sea mediante circunloquios técnicos, hacen que sus catálogos estén sino disponibles al menos buscables a través de sus páginas W3 (ver el apéndice para una relación de puntos de acceso interesantes en América Latina).

Finalmente, los usuarios interesados en América Latina no tienen que prescindir del Internet, puesto que abunda información sobre la región en la Red. Entre las diversas fuentes tenemos los grandes catálogos de bibliotecas especializadas en el tema, las revistas electrónicas, los servicios de alerta bibliográfica de revistas electrónicas, las listas de discusión, tangencialmente los newsgroups de USENET, menos relevantes que lo anterior. Lo curioso es que toda esta riqueza se basa en iniciativas y energías desarrolladas en los Estados Unidos y otras zonas, no en los mismos países que nos interesan hoy.

Hasta aquí el repaso de la situación. Consideremos ahora algunos elementos más interpretativos de la situación de la conectividad latinoamericana.

Cuadro 2. Conectividad latinoamericana

25000
20000
15000
10000
5000
0

139 141 148 164 504 626 813 1165 1495 2262 5312 9027 13787 20113

Bolivia Ago-95
Republica Dominicana Abr-95
Nicaragua Feb-94
Panama Jun-94
Jamaica May-94
Ecuador Jul-92
Uruguay Abr-94
Perú Feb-94
Venezuela Feb-92
Costa Rica Ene-93
Colombia Abr-94
Argentina Oct-90
Chile Abr-90
Mexico Feb-89
Brasil Jun-90

Número de anfitriones a marzo de 1996

Fuente: ftp://nic.merit.edu/nsfnet/statistics/history.hosts; 14 de marzo de 1996.

Cuadro 3. Conectividad a la Red Científica Peruana:
Tipos de conexión

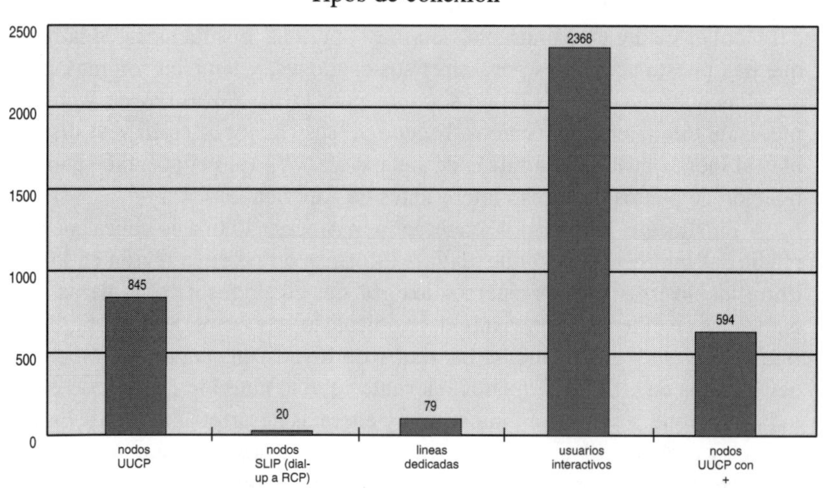


Fuente: Red Científica Peruana (RCP); 27 de mayo de 1996.

## Algunas intuiciones sobre las limitaciones del uso creativo del Internet en Latinoamérica

Una conclusión importante de cualquier revisión de los servidores Internet de la región latinoamericana, por rápida que sea, es que muchas instituciones han habilitado sus páginas W3 o sus Gophers casi porque *hay que* hacerlo, antes que porque haya claridad de *para qué* hacerlo. Abundantes páginas simplemente reemplazan al papel de los folletos institucionales, casi reproduciendo la diagramación de un documento impreso, y por cierto no añadiendo nada nuevo. Las ventajas de poner semejante información a disposición de los usuarios del Internet no son pocas: mayor actualidad de los datos (cuando se los actualiza adecuadamente), mayor flexibilidad para la ubicación de los mismos (cuando se organiza la página atendiendo al medio, no reproduciendo lo existente), facilidad y gratuidad de la información; mucho menor costo para añadir nueva información (el concepto de edición o tiraje carece de sentido en este contexto). Pero si bien este tipo de páginas justifica montar un servidor W3, no necesariamente lo explota a un mínimo de sus capacidades.

No buscamos descalificar la iniciativa: en realidad, el solo hecho de poner una página W3 sirve como primer paso para aumentar las maneras de contactar a las personas que trabajan o estudian en una universidad, lo que de por sí es bueno. También es cierto que el no estar en el Internet es equivalente a faltar a la fiesta, a no subirse al coche. La ausencia es mayor pecado que la poca o irrelevante presencia. Pero no es esto lo que hará interesante una página, al menos a la segunda visita.

El especialista latinoamericano interesado en saber que pasa en la región, académicamente hablando, tiene que buscar en sitios de países fuera de la región. Inclusive para encontrar noticias corrientes, es preferible recurrir a servidores genéricos, como el Latin American Newsletter, que a lo que ofrecen los cada vez más abundantes sitios de revistas y diarios de la región, puesto que usar éstos requiere un conocimiento muy directo de lo que sucede día a día en los países en donde se les edita, para poder ser de utilidad al extranjero o al observador casual.

En consecuencia, y a pesar de la carencia de estadísticas de movimiento de datos que sirvan para probar esta afirmación, es posible sostener desde una lectura cuidadosa de las diversas experiencias que conocemos, que el flujo es esencialmente de datos que llegan, antes que de datos que salen. Consideramos que es producto de dos grandes carencias: la falta de valor agregado en los servidores de la región, y la falta de comunicación entre los países de la región.

Sobre lo segundo, bástenos decir que es tema de otro tipo de reflexión. Sobre el primer punto, tendríamos que aceptar que la conectividad al Internet es sólo el primer paso, y que el poner información a disposición de la Red es un índice importante de desarrollo de la utilización del recurso Internet. Valor agregado no es tan sólo el montar un servidor WWW, es sobre todo poner información en él que haga del usarlo una actividad sino diferenciada al menos paralela a la consulta de fuentes en formato impreso.

Los servidores WWW no suelen presentar más información que la que normalmente se encontraría en documentos impresos de la institución (ver la lista de servidores de interés que se presenta como apéndice de este trabajo). No es esto malo, ni mucho menos, puesto que facilita el encontrar información que en otras circunstancias requeriría semanas de papeleo y cartas. Sin embargo, el componente más interesante de las páginas de las instituciones académicas de los Estados Unidos. no reside en la información sobre ellas mismas, sino en la información creada por y para la Red; en más de un caso es el resultado de la actividad de los usuarios del Internet, antes que de los encargados del mantenimiento del servidor.[2]

En base a lo presentado hasta aquí, podemos proponer las siguientes hipótesis para iniciar la búsqueda de una explicación al poco valor agregado disponible en los servidores Internet en América Latina:

1. falta de difusión del medio fuera de los grupos de especialistas involucrados en el montaje y mantenimiento de las redes
2. carencia de recursos para conectar plenamente todas las unidades de las distintas instituciones
3. escasez de compenetración entre los usuarios de las áreas más susceptibles de facilitar información de interés con la red.

Desarrollaremos los puntos, advirtiendo nuevamente que cualquier afirmación es más una hipótesis a investigar que una firme certeza respaldada por datos empíricos.

La creación de redes ha sido, en términos generales, tarea de unos pocos especialistas en los centros de computación y facultades de informática, antes que una actividad de compromiso masivo. La mayoría de las afirmaciones son generalizables a cualquier realidad. Un simple rastreo de servidores académicos en el Internet mostrará la clara prevalencia de las áreas de las ciencias exactas y naturales frente a las ciencias sociales y humanas, lo que es explicable porque la tecnología de información es usada siempre primero por aquellos que tienen la necesidad de manipular números antes que ideas. Como es lógico, en cualquier universidad equilibrada la meta final es poner tanta tecnología de información como sea necesaria en manos de aquellos que puedan necesitarla, pero muchas veces las prioridades establecidas por las limitaciones de presupuesto premian a aquellos que están más directamente en posición de hacer un uso "productivo" de computadoras.

En el área de conocimiento que nos interesa a los participantes de esta reunión, es fácil encontrar ejemplos de un desarrollo más pausado en la implementación de soluciones tecnológicas. Sin duda alguna, hay interesantísimas experiencias en la aplicación de tecnologías de información, pero lo general han sido posteriores a similares experiencias en las áreas de las "ciencias duras". Si podemos extraer una conclusión de todo esto, es que la iniciativa de utilización de tecnologías de información en las ciencias sociales y humanas ha sido por lo general el resultado de la facilidad de uso que la microcomputadora ha traído a nuestro ámbito, puesto que ha abaratado el acceso a recursos demasiado caros.

Los usuarios finales han estado relativamente fuera de la educación. Las universidades latinoamericanas producen grandes cantidades de publicaciones impresas en sus distintas áreas, las más de las veces con valiosa información producto de cuidadosas investigaciones, pero la difusión de estas publicaciones está en manos de la poca o ninguna capacidad de cada institución para distribuir y vender sus publicaciones. Y a pesar de eso, no han habido esfuerzos significativos para poner esas revistas en un servidor de listas, en un servidor de FTP o en una página de la W3, simplemente porque la brecha entre los creadores de información y los tecnólogos a cargo de semejantes servicios es por lo general difícil de ser cubierta. Los primeros pueden tener una intuición de para que es útil un servicio, pero no el conocimiento de cómo poner la información en servicio; los segundos pueden intuir que valiosa información está en las revistas, pero al no recibir iniciativas claras de los usuarios, carecen de motivación para acometer ellos mismos la tarea.

Debemos también considerar como un elemento en contra de la publicación electrónica, que el esfuerzo de montar una revista en un medio inestable y en crecimiento puede ser visto como un exceso de entusiasmo, cuando primero debería poder garantizarse la seriedad y prestigio de la revista impresa.

Si bien la gran mayoría de universidades líderes en la región están conectadas al Internet, por lo general la conectividad se limita a una amplia difusión del correo electrónico, y a la existencia de relativamente pocas opciones de uso de los servicios más potentes. Esto es lógico, puesto que el correo electrónico requiere una inversión baja en tecnología, mientras que el acceso a un servidor de FTP requiere acceso físico directo a la Red.

Este acceso está por lo general también disponible, pero salvo los muy entusiastas, el tiempo y la distancia que media entre una computadora con conexión al Internet y la oficina o salón de clase son factores decisivos para preferir cualquier otra tarea. Y si se dispone de la conexión, viene la segunda etapa: como y en que forma encontrar la información que se busca. Surfear en el Internet puede ser muy interesante, pero lograr respuestas a lo que se está buscando puede ser agotador. Un ejemplo casi cómico es la siguiente búsqueda sobre Perú en Infoseek, que como podemos ver da como resultado un par de páginas de profunda irrelevancia.

La ecuación Internet siempre incluye al correo electrónico, pero muchas veces se limita a éste. Conectar muchas computadoras a un servidor de correo electrónico es relativamente asequible, gracias a módems baratos y uso de centrales telefónicas compartidas; cuando se trata de ampliar los servicios no alcanza el teléfono, se necesita la red interna. Entonces se produce una curiosa paradoja: muchas instituciones ofrecen con mayor facilidad un servicio de conexión pseudo dedicada por línea telefónica (SLIP) al Internet, que la conectividad completa dentro del campus: profesores y alumnos pueden acceder a la Red desde sus casas, pero no en sus oficinas. Como se puede ver, esto requiere la computadora doméstica, y la disposición del profesor a gastar por su cuenta en el pago de las llamadas telefónicas.

Casi un corolario de lo anterior: el usuario final tiene todavía mucha distancia con Internet como para realmente aprovecharla. No estamos hablando de hacer páginas, sino simplemente usar la Red para encontrar algo más que simples datos interesantes. ¿Cuanto de relevante sobre, por ejemplo, noticias sobre el efecto Tequila o estudios comparados de patrones demográficos en América Latina, puede encontrarse en el Internet, rápida y fácilmente? Nos tomamos la libertad de presentar los resultados de un ejercicio hecho en un curso de bibliotecología de la Pontificia Universidad Católica del Perú, que sirven para explicar este punto.[3] (Ver Cuadro 4.)

Cuadro 4. Ejemplo básico de búsqueda de temas latinoamericanos en el Internet

Búsqueda por "Tequila Effect"

| Search Engine | Resultados totales | Resultados relevantes de los 10 primeros recuperados | Sitios latinoamericanos |
|---|---|---|---|
| Alta Vista | 10,000 | 8 | 0 |
| InfoSeek | 3 | 3 | 0 |
| Excite | 10 | 1 | 0 |
| Lycos | 79,790 | 1 | 0 |

Búsqueda por "Efecto Tequila"

| Search Engine | Resultados totales | Resultados relevantes de los 10 primeros recuperados | Sitios latinoamericanos |
|---|---|---|---|
| Alta Vista | 4,000 | 10 | 10 |
| InfoSeek | 0 | 0 | 0 |
| Excite | 10 | 0 | 1 |
| Lycos | 3,035 | 7 | 8 |
| Fantastico | 0 | 0 | 0 |

¿Qué nos queda claro de los resultados tan variados de las búsquedas? Que si un profesor o estudiante de economía quiere información sobre el tema en cuestión, sin una guía adecuada sobre que esperar de las fuentes disponibles y de las herramientas que debe usar para la búsqueda deseada, nada o muy poco sacará del Internet.

Se nos puede responder que el Internet es en realidad una fuente distinta de información, que debe usarse desde aproximaciones distintas a las que normalmente tendríamos cuando usamos revistas o libros; pero esto no sirve cuando un usuario frustrado encuentra que usar el Internet es "tiempo perdido".

El usuario final, que finalmente será el creador de cualquier valor agregado en un servidor Internet, tiene dificultades para familiarizarse con el medio desde el momento en que los resultados que busca son imprecisos o poco fiables. Un elemento que complica la situación es la inmensidad de la red, así como la cada vez mayor presencia de servicios comerciales, que pueden ofrecer información que tangencialmente es relevante para el tema que se busca, o que pueden estar haciendo conocer datos o servicios que guardan relación ligera o casi mínima con el tema, pero que igual aparecen como hit a la hora de hacer una búsqueda. Añadamos a esto la falta de tiempo y tranquilidad para usar el Internet (producto de las razones que mencionamos anteriormente), y tenemos que no es mucho el tiempo disponible para obtener resultados relevantes, lo que conspira contra la necesaria dedicación a la revisión detenida de páginas y la constante precisión de términos, imprescindibles para poder encontrar información relevante.

Otro elemento, que ya insinuamos antes: el medio no es todavía visto con el mismo respeto con que se ve el medio impreso. Desde minucias (¿cómo se hace una cita de una revista electrónica? y ¿cómo se cita una discusión en una lista de correo?) hasta la imagen de aventura y entusiasmo, por lo general ajenas a la "seriedad" académica, los usuarios tienden a considerar al Internet y en general a cualquier formato electrónico como un medio para conseguir información, pero poco adecuado para publicar información. Sumémosle a la combinación el medio al robo intelectual y al plagio, puesto que es tan fácil copiar de un texto electrónico, y encontramos los orígenes de una actitud aún desconfiada hacia la publicación electrónica.

Si el uso del Internet es bajo y poco sofisticado, es poco probable que hayan muchos ánimos a la hora de pensar en ser proveedores además de usuarios de la Red. No hay demasiada iniciativa cuando se carecen tanto de las costumbres como de las habilidades que el uso del Internet requiere, y la falta de familiaridad crea un círculo vicioso difícil de romper.

No tenemos intención de negar viabilidad a la expansión de la oferta de información sobre la región en el Internet. Sólo hemos querido ser realistas sobre las posibilidades, que como puede verse son bajas.

## Elementos de intensificación de valor agregado en los sitios del Internet en América Latina

Ciertamente, existen ya experiencias de publicaciones electrónicas en el Internet, como también existen algunas iniciativas interesantes con páginas W3 que, prefiriendo el contenido al continente, facilitan datos e información valiosa para los usuarios del ciberespacio.

Hemos logrado identificar varias revistas electrónicas, de alcance e intención algo limitadas aún. También hemos podido encontrar servidores que muestran de manera original lo que en principio no es más que información para el medio impreso.

Podemos proponer a partir de nuestra experiencia, algunos elementos de juicios para suponer que en un determinado país de América Latina se encontrará o no servidores con valor agregado.

1. Llegada temprana del Internet al país: permite mayor madurez en el montaje de servidores, así como mayor familiaridad en el uso de las herramientas.
2. Existencia de alguna red académica, manejada por los propios académicos o por un organismo coordinador o director de la actividad académica: sin desmerecer las alternativas cooperativas o los proveedores comerciales, la presencia o no de una red académica indica que las instituciones participan con personal calificado que necesariamente lleva su experiencia de regreso a la institución. Una red multipropósito (como lo es la Red Científica Peruana) tiene que atacar varios frentes al mismo tiempo y por lo tanto cuenta con menos recursos para difundir sin costo lo avanzado entre sus socios. Y una red comercial cobrará por entrenar o montar servicios, lo que está fuera de la cuestión para iniciativas que no producen réditos.
3. Servidores a disposición de alumnos: una de las claves del Internet es la participación de los estudiantes universitarios, los que pueden ofrecer una enorme dosis de creatividad y sobre todo gran cantidad de tiempo para la creación de servicios con valor agregado.
4. Un Consejo de Ciencia y Tecnología con una fuerte y clara presencia en las actividades culturales y científicas del país: el liderazgo de semejantes instituciones facilita no sólo la difusión de experiencias sino también el financiamiento de iniciativas (qué mejor ejemplo que la NSF).
5. Instituciones académicas con gran desarrollo en el área de la informática: mayor desarrollo significará mayores posibilidades de encontrar personas en condiciones de aportar por poco o ningún costo, y el acceso a la Red estará hasta cierto punto garantizado.
6. Incorporación de servicios electrónicos básicos (biblioteca automatizada, por ejemplo): es poco probable que una universidad financie o promueva iniciativas como las que pensamos si cuestiones básicas como el catálogo de la biblioteca no están ni a disposición de los usuarios internos.

Si una universidad reúne todos estos elementos, lo más probable es que puedan encontrar en sus páginas o servidores información relevante preparada para el medio. No estaríamos hablando de una simple página con fotos y datos administrativos de una institución, sino más bien publicación de información para uso en la Red, y con la intención de dirigirse a especialistas o interesados en temas que se tratan dentro de la universidad, no en la mera universidad.

No hemos encontrado aún muchos ejemplos de esto en América Latina; intuimos que es posible que aumenten poco a poco. Aquí es donde el rol del bibliotecario entra en juego. No sólo en su tradicional rol de organizador del conocimiento, sino sobre todo como difusor y capacitador .

La organización del conocimiento disponible a través del Internet es uno de los grandes desafíos que enfrentan los bibliotecarios: ¿cómo lograr que la creación de páginas web sea una actividad pensada no para la diversión sino para la recuperación de información?, ¿cómo trasladar las premisas de la organización para la recuperación a la hora misma de la creación o edición del documento? Pero estas tareas implican un ambiente donde efectivamente se crea información, no donde sólo se usa la información creada por otros.

Ubicar páginas, servidores o listas en el Internet, de utilidad para los usuarios propios, servirá para que estos poco a poco se incorporen activamente al ciberespacio. Así como escribir requiere una gran práctica de lectura, hacer páginas web exige familiaridad con el medio y sobre todo, confianza en la capacidad de dominarlo. Antes de eso, el usuario tiene que lograr moverse libremente en él, y sobre todo, encontrarle utilidad.

La tarea de darle valor de uso al Internet es principalmente labor de los bibliotecarios, los llamados a encontrar información dispersa, caótica y sobre todo poco estructurada y ponerla al alcance de aquellos que pueden aprovecharla. Mientras que el bibliotecario participe pasivamente en el Internet, como de alguna manera ha sucedido en buena parte de América Latina, la interacción del usuario final con la Red será pasiva.

Generar metadatos sobre el Internet, difundir su utilidad y las maneras prácticas de conducirse en él, son tareas propias de los bibliotecarios pero que están pendientes en la actividad latinoamericana. Los esfuerzos específicos son parciales, pero indican que la comprensión de este fenómeno comienza a ganar el espacio necesario. Confiemos en que pronto podamos ver una nueva actitud del usuario latinoamericano respecto al Internet, y que sea, al menos en parte, resultado del interés de los bibliotecarios en facilitar el acceso, el uso y el aprovechamiento de la red.

## APENDICE

### Puntos de Acceso Interesantes en América Latina

Esta no es una lista exhaustiva de todos los lugares interesantes en Sudamérica, pero sí trata de presentar una variedad de sitios que sirven como puntos de partida para la exploración. Los sitios han sido comprobados hacia mediados de mayo.

**Argentina**

El ministerio de Economía y Bienestar Social: http://www.mecon.ar/. Dentro de él, hay mucha información de otros organismos públicos, como por ejemplo el Instituto Nacional de Estadísticas.

La Universidad de Buenos Aires: http://www.uba.ar

La Universidad de La Plata: http://www.unlp.edu.ar/

La Red de Interconexión Universitaria: http://www.riu.ar

Startel, proveedor de acceso a Internet: http://www.startel.com.ar

**Bolivia**

Una de las últimas naciones sudamericanas en entrar a Internet.

Universidad Andina Simón Bolívar, nodo regional de Chuquisaca: http://www.uasb.nch.edu.bo

BOLNET, el proveedor de acceso: http://www.bolnet.bo

**Brasil**

La Rede Nacional de Pesquisa, o Red nacional de investigación: http://www.rnp.br

El Indice de Paginas WWW en la Universidade de Campinas: http://dcc.unicamp.br/~camcima/

Pontificia Universidad Católica de Rio de Janeiro: http://www.puc-rio.br

Universidad de São Paulo: http://www.usp.br

Jornal do Brasil Online: http://www.ibase.br/~jb/

Agencia Estado, base del Jornal do Estado do São Paulo: http://www.embratel.Net.br/~agestado/index.html

La biblioteca de la Universidad de São Paulo: telnet://bee08.cce.usp.br

**Chile**

Punto de entrada a Chile, con mapa sensitivo: http://sunsite.dcc.uchile.cl/chile/chile.html. También sirve como punto de entrada a la Universidad de Chile.

El Consejo de Ciencia y Tecnología: http://www.conicyt.cl/

La Pontificia Universidad Católica de Chile: http://www.puc.cl/

La Red Universitaria Nacional de Chile: http://www.reuna.cl/

La biblioteca de la Universidad de Concepción: telnet://cisne.bib.udec.cl

La biblioteca de la Universidad de Santiago de Chile: telnet://azapa.usach.cl

**Colombia**

La Universidad del Valle, en Cali, ofrece una página de entrada a Colombia: http://www.univalle.edu.co/Colombia.html

La Universidad de los Andes, en Bogotá: http://www.uniandes.edu.co

La Pontificia Universidad Javeriana, también en Bogotá: http://javercol.javeriana.edu.co/default.html.

**Costa Rica**

Universidad de Costa Rica: http://cariari.ucr.ac.cr/

Gobierno de Costa Rica: http://www.casapres.go.cr/

Instituto Tecnológico de Costa Rica: http://www.cic.itcr.ac.cr/cic.html

Diario La Nación: http://www.nacion.co.cr

CRNet, Red Nacional de Costa Rica: http://www.cr

TICONET Information services: http://www.ticonet.co.cr/

**Ecuador**

La Universidad de San Francisco: http://mail.usfq.edu.ec/root.htm

EcuaNet, Corporación Ecuatoriana de Información: http://www.ecNet.ec/

Diario Hoy: http://www.ecNet.ec/hoy/hoy.htm

Pontificia Universidad Católica del Ecuador: http://puce.edu.ec

**México**

La UNAM; Universidad Nacional Autónoma de México: http://serpiente.dgsca.unam.mx/

El ITAM, Instituto Tecnológico Autónomo de México: http://www.itam.mx

La Universidad de Colima, primera institución de la región en habilitar una biblioteca electrónica, si bien ésta no es todavía accesible por Internet: http://www.ucol.mx

El Colegio de México: http://www.colmex.mx

Biblioteca de la Universidad de Guadalajara: telnet udgserv.cencar.udg.mx

Biblioteca de la Universidad de las Américas, Puebla: telnet bibes.pue.udlap.mx.

Biblioteca de la Universidad de Monterrey: telnet umhp01.mty.udem.mx

Biblioteca del Instituto Superior Tecnológico de Monterrey: telnet mtecv2.mty.itesm.mx

**Perú**

La Red Científica Peruana: http://www.rcp.net.pe. Dentro de las páginas de la RCP hay acceso a múltiples páginas institucionales y algunas de medios, como la Revista Caretas (http://www.rcp.net.pe:80/CARETAS/) y el diario La República (http://www.rcp.net.pe/7)

La Pontificia Universidad Católica del Perú: http://www.pucp.edu.pe

La Universidad de Lima: http://www.ulima.edu.pe

**Uruguay**

El servidor Uruguay: http://bilbo.edu.uy/uruguay.html.
Universidad de la República: http://fisica.edu.uy/www-uru.html
Diario "El Observador", en versión electrónica: http://www.zfm.com/observador

**Venezuela**

Servidor oficial, en el MIT: http://venezuela.mit.edu/
REACCIUN, una red académica: http://www.conicit.ve/
Instituto Venezolano de Investigaciones Científicas: http://www.ivic.ve
Universidad Simón Bolívar: http://www.usb.ve
Universidad de los Andes: http://www.ing.ula.ve
Universidad Central de Venezuela: http://www.sagi.ucv.edu.ve
Biblioteca Nacional de Venezuela: telnet biblio.iabn.ve
Biblioteca del Consejo Nacional de Investigaciones Científicas y Tecnológicas: telnet dino.conicit.ve

**También**

Hay presencia del Internet en Panamá, Jamaica, Honduras, Nicaragua y varias islas nación del Caribe. Cuba tiene servidores fuera de su país, para eludir los problemas del bloqueo.

Paraguay no tiene aún conexión a Internet. Vale la pena mirar este servidor genérico: Enlaces con Universidades Iberoamericanas: http://www.docuweb.ca/~pardos/univer.html

## NOTAS

Nota del autor: Quisiera agradecer a Patricia Naka, Martín Tanaka y Carlos Acuña por las oportunas observaciones a este texto o las ideas que se presentan, y a Rosario Peirano tanto por la crítica como por la muy concienzuda revisión.

1. Véase la bibliografía, en la que hemos presentado todos los trabajos sobre el uso del Internet en América Latina que hemos podido revisar.

2. Entre los puntos que creo importante destacar es la presencia escasa de servidores de bibliotecas latinoamericanos en la Red, pero hay que aclarar que la razón de esto no depende tanto de la voluntad de las instituciones cuanto de las posibilidades técnicas y económicas de montar semejantes servidores. Otro elemento sobre el valor agregado: la ausencia de USENET en América Latina. No es el resultado de otra cosa sino de la carencia de recursos para administrar el tráfico que la participación en semejantes servicios implica.

3. El ejercicio consistió en interrogar, el mismo día y a la misma hora, a cuatro servicios de búsqueda en Internet (las llamadas "search engines"). Incluimos servicios orientados a búsquedas sencillas y sin mayor estructura, por oposición a servicios como Yahoo!, porque los servicios de búsqueda por palabra se parecen más a la forma como los usuarios finales hacen sus pedidos. Para el pedido de "Efecto Tequila" añadimos a Fantástico, un servicio supuestamente orientado a la comunidad hispano hablante del Internet, que fue el peor de todos. Alta Vista fue el más exitoso, como también lo ha sido en experiencias tales como la reportada por Tomaiuolo (ver bibliografía).

## BIBLIOGRAFIA

Cabezas, Alberto. "Internet: potencial de servicios en América Latina". *IFLA Journal* 21:1 (1995), 11–18.

Finlay, Karen y Thomas Finlay. "The Relative Roles of Knowledge and Innovativeness in Determining Librarians' Attitudes toward and Use of the Internet: A Structural Equation Modeling Approach". *Library Quarterly* 66:1 (1996), 59–83.

GVU's Third WWW Users Survey. http: //www. cc.gatech. edu/gvu/user_surveys/survey-04-1995/

Herrero Solana, Víctor Federico. "Revistas y boletines electrónicos: su localización en la red y su utilización en la biblioteca". *Investigación Bibliotecológica* 8:17 (julio 1994), 33–37.

The Internet Index. http://www.openmarket.com/intindex/

Jacobson, Thomas. "The Electronic Publishing Revolution Is Not 'Global' ", *JASIS* 45:10 (diciembre 1994), 745–752.

Pimienta, Daniel. "La comunicación mediante computador: una esperanza para el sector académico y de investigación del Tercer Mundo". *Ciencia de la Información* 24:3 (septiembre 1993), 163–168.

Rada, Juan F. "The Information Gap between North and South". *IFLA Journal* 20:1 (1994), 13–15.

Rodríguez, Ketty. "Barriers to Information Technology in Latin America and the Caribbean: Some Options". *The Electronic Library* 12:1 (1994), 29–35.

Su-Lien Sun y George Barnett. "The International Telephone Network and Democratization". *JASIS* 45:6 (julio 1994).

Summerhill, Craig. "Connectivity and Navigation: An Overview of the Global Internetworked Information Infrastructure." *IFLA Journal* 20:2 (1994), 147–157.

Tercer Foro de Redes Académicas de América Latina y el Caribe. Informe Final, Declaración de Caracas. Caracas, Venezuela, 18 al 22 de octubre de 1993. http://www.rcp.net.pe/VFORO/caracas.html

Tomaiuolo, Nicholas. Quantitative Analysis of Five WWW "Search Engines". http://neal.ctstateu.edu:2001/htdocs/websearch.html

Torres Vargas, Georgina Araceli. "La biblioteca virtual: algunas reflexiones en torno a su contexto conceptual". *Ciencia de la Información* 25:2 (junio 1994).

Villanueva Mansilla, Eduardo. *Internet: breve guía de navegación en el ciberespacio.* Lima: PUCP, 1996.

_________. "Internet in Latin America: The Benefits of the Personal Touch." *Information World Review* 107 (octubre 1995), 18–19.

# 21. La divulgación del conocimiento en las universidades públicas mexicanas: la distribución de sus publicaciones

Jesús Lau
Jesús Cortés

Las universidades mexicanas y el resto de instituciones de educación superior, como sus similares de otras latitudes, tienen en su misión tres funciones básicas: la enseñanza, la investigación y la extensión. Esta última, que tiene el objetivo de mantener una comunicación estrecha con la sociedad, ha sido tradicionalmente la más desarticulada y la que ha recibido menor atención. Sin embargo, es de esperarse que en los próximos años será objeto de especiales apoyos por parte del gobierno federal, ya que la difusión de cultura y extensión de los servicios se han incorporado dentro de las once Tareas de Atención Prioritarias susceptibles de ser apoyadas a través de los Fondos para la Modernización de la Educación Superior (FOMES) (México 1996).

Dentro de una amplia gama de actividades que se incluyen en la función de extensión, está la divulgación del conocimiento generado en aulas, laboratorios o centros de investigación. Esta labor de divulgación se realiza en México principalmente a través de la producción editorial, actividad que se abordará en este trabajo. La perspectiva no es de especialistas en temas educativos, sino de bibliotecarios que analizan la problemática de las editoriales universitarias y su efecto en las bibliotecas.

Los datos que aquí se presentan están tomados de la consulta de algunos materiales documentales, páginas electrónicas y de dos encuestas aplicadas a un número reducido de editores y bibliotecarios universitarios.

## El sistema de educación superior

Las instituciones de educación superior, es decir organizaciones que ofrecen formación a alumnos después de haber cursado la primaria, la secundaria y la preparatoria, están agrupadas en cinco subsistemas: universitario, tecnológico, universitario tecnológico, escuelas normales y mixto. El total de instituciones asciende a 794, de las cuales el 79 por ciento son financiadas con fondos gubernamentales (véase Tabla 1).

Tabla 1. Sistema de educación superior

| Sistema | Número de instituciones |
|---|---|
| Universidades[a] | 88 |
| Tecnológicos[b] | 112 |
| Universidades tecnológicas | 8 |
| Normales[c] | 326 |
| Instituciones mixtas[d] | 260 |
| Total | 794 |

a. 68 por ciento de los estudiantes.
b. Dependientes de la Secretaría de Educación Pública.
c. 66 por ciento de carácter público.
d. 260 escuelas pequeñas.

Fuente: México, Secretaría de Educación Pública, *Programa sectorial de educación, 1995–2000* (México: La Secretaría, 1996). Consultada en http://www.udg.mx:81/SEP/pse.html

Las características de las casas de estudio difieren mucho. La mayor parte de la población estudiantil es atendida por las llamadas propiamente universidades, las cuales atienden casi el 70 por ciento de la matrícula. Dentro de éstas, las que tienen mayor tamaño son las denominadas universidades públicas, que son las más antiguas en el país. El resto de las instituciones, que son numerosas, atienden pocos estudiantes. En este documento las instituciones que se analizan son las 39 universidades públicas, las cuales realizan la mayor parte de la producción editorial académica en México, quizá hasta en un 90 por ciento. El resto de las casas de estudio casi no publican libros o revistas, su producción individual en títulos no llega a los dos dígitos.

La Asociación de Editoriales de Instituciones de Educación Superior, A.C. (ASEDIES) agrupa a 45 socios, entre los cuales predominan las universidades públicas. Las causas de que la mayoría de las instituciones no publiquen material se debe, entre otros factores, a su poca o nula actividad de investigación. En la mayoría, las funciones académicas giran únicamente en torno a la docencia. Inclusive las grandes universidades y tecnológicos privados de reconocido prestigio carecen de actividad de investigación y de producción editorial.

## La generación de conocimiento

El escenario general de la producción del conocimiento en México puede resultar muy diferente al que se presenta en otros países, por lo tanto se describirán algunos aspectos sobresalientes en los que son más notables sus peculiaridades. Los datos aquí presentados podrían haber sufrido algunas modificaciones en virtud de la reciente crisis económica, sin embargo, la estructura fundamental del sistema de investigación en México sigue básicamente igual.

La mayor parte de la investigación científica en México es coordinada por el Consejo Nacional de Ciencia y Tecnología (CONACYT) y realizada principalmente por universidades y organismos gubernamentales. En las universidades privadas esta actividad, como se señaló, es casi imperceptible y, a diferencia de lo que sucede en Estados Unidos, en México las empresas privadas tampoco participan activamente en la investigación, aportando sólo el 21 por ciento de los recursos gastados en este rubro (CONACYT 1995).

Otro aspecto que conviene resaltar es el del personal que realiza las tareas de investigación. En México no existe una cultura sólida para la investigación, ni tampoco para escribir. Hasta ahora, pocos profesores universitarios consideran que dentro de sus actividades normales deba incluirse el investigar o, cuando menos, divulgar el resultado de sus experiencias y reflexiones a través de documentos escritos. La investigación es entonces una tarea básicamente de investigadores de tiempo completo, aunque esta situación está cambiando, gracias a una serie de estímulos concedidos por el gobierno federal, quien creó desde hace 12 años el Sistema Nacional de Investigadores (SNI), que otorga reconocimientos y subvención económica a aproximadamente 5,900 personas.

Existe una aguda centralización de las actividades de investigación; solamente la Universidad Nacional Autónoma de México (UNAM) concentra al 33 por ciento de los investigadores inscritos en el SNI. Por otra parte, las tres más grandes instituciones de educación superior del país, localizadas en el Distrito Federal, recibieron en 1994 el 43 por ciento de todos los recursos asignados para investigación en el sistema educativo mexicano. Las estadísticas del SNI muestran también, por otra parte, que las universidades públicas tienen el 65 por ciento de los investigadores, mientras que las universidades privadas sólo agrupan a un 2.5 por ciento. El porcentaje restante de investigadores se concentra principalmente en organismos federales (CONACYT 1995). (Véase Tabla 2.)

Tabla 2. Generación del conocimiento

| Tabla 2. Generación del conocimiento |
|---|
| La investigación es coordinada por CONACYT |
| Se realiza principalmente por universidades públicas y agencias del gobierno |
| La participación de empresas privadas es reducida |
| La centralización es un problema |
| La educación superior carece de una cultura de investigación |
| El SNI cuenta con 5,900 investigadores |

Fuente: CONACYT (Consejo Nacional de Ciencia y Tecnología), *1994 Indicators of Scientific and Technological Activities* (México: El Consejo, 1995).

Es entendible que la producción editorial está determinada, entre otros factores, por la actividad de investigación en las universidades y que, por lo tanto, la mayor parte de los títulos editados se concentran en las universidades que son líderes en investigación, mismas que en el caso de México están ubicadas en la zona metropolitana de la capital de la República.

## Infraestructura para la divulgación

Al hablar del problema de la divulgación del conocimiento en México, se debe hablar necesariamente de una falta de hábitos de lectura en el ciudadano común. El número de bibliotecas públicas que existían en el momento en que se extendió el uso de la TV era mínimo y, por lo tanto, la población no se había acostumbrado ni había aprendido a disfrutar de la lectura, cuando su atención fue absorbida por las imágenes sugestivas de los monitores. No obstante, es justo señalar que sí existe un fuerte mercado para revistas ilustradas, especialmente las románticas y de tipo sensacionalista (Lau 1993).

En México solamente una de cada 100 personas que saben leer acostumbra comprar libros con regularidad, existiendo una librería por cada 7 mil habitantes (Tabla 3). El 60 por ciento de estas librerías están en la Cd. de México. Por otro lado, más del 50 por ciento de la producción editorial total corresponde a los libros de texto gratuitos distribuidos por la Secretaría de Educación Pública (Rangel 1996).

Tabla 3. Infraestructura editorial

| |
|---|
| 88 % población mayor de 15 años es alfabeta |
| 1 de cada 100 personas compra libros con regularidad |
| 1 librería por cada 7,000 habitantes |
| 60% de las librerías están en la Cd. de México |
| 50% de los libros publicados son textos gratuitos de la SEP |
| Se redujo el número de editoriales (550 en 1995) |
| Se disminuyó la publicación de novedades editoriales (4,500 en 1995) |

Fuente: J. C. Rangel, "En 95, al libro, como en feria: ecos de la FIL'95 de Guadalajara". *Avión de papel: órgano de difusión de la Asociación de Editoriales de Instituciones de Educación Superior, A. C.*, Vol. 1, No. 2, febrero–abril de 1996, p. 9.

En los últimos años (Rangel 1996), se ha presentado una reducción drástica en la infraestructura y en la producción editorial: en 1980 había 1,315 editoriales, para 1990 se habían reducido a 880 y hacia 1995 solamente quedaban 550. Según las cifras de Rangel, en 1993, se editaron 6,045 novedades editoriales y en 1995 la cifra disminuyó a 4,500. El costo del papel registró un aumento del 120 por ciento tan sólo en 1995 y se sabe que para las grandes empresas papeleras resulta más atractivo el mercado de los pañales, servilletas y papel sanitario que el de la industria editorial, pues la edición de libros participa únicamente con el 1.5 por ciento del mercado total del papel.

La producción editorial de las universidades está consecuentemente determinada por la demanda de un mercado pequeño de lectores ya mencionados. En lo que respecta a la producción académica, la participación en la producción global del país puede considerarse importante: en 1987 las instituciones de educación superior publicaban una de cada cinco novedades editadas. Por otro lado, la producción de la UNAM es digna de destacarse, ya que por si sola participaba con el 5 por ciento de los volúmenes publicados en el país (Figueroa y Torres 1992).

## Publicaciones periódicas mexicanas

Con respecto a la publicación de revistas, en 1993 había en México 2,326 títulos vigentes que contaban con registro del International Serial Data System (ISDS), correspondiendo aproximadamente un 50 por ciento a las dedicadas a temas de ciencias sociales y humanidades (CONACYT 1995). Las revistas mexicanas enfrentan hasta cierto grado la problemática que la producción de libros, como son la calidad de contenido y la continuidad de su publicación.

En el año de referencia, el CONACYT promovió la realización de un proyecto para determinar cuántas de revistas reunían las características suficientes para ser incluidas en un Indice de Revistas Científicas Mexicanas de Excelencia. El resultado fue que únicamente 68 títulos cumplieron con una serie de indicadores propuestos, los cuales en este caso se referían básicamente a aspectos de tipo académico.

De las 68 revistas mencionadas (Apéndice 3), 40 de ellas, un 59 por ciento, cubren principalmente temas de ciencias sociales y humanidades. Por otra parte, regresando al tema de la centralización, solamente tres instituciones ubicadas en el Distrito Federal—la UNAM, la Universidad Autónoma Metropolitana y El Colegio de México—publicaban 32 de estos títulos, equivalentes a un 47 por ciento del total (Bonilla 1996).

## Labor editorial universitaria

Como se hizo mención, la labor editorial en las instituciones de educación superior de México está influida por una serie de mecanismos y acciones que las instituciones tradicionalmente han identificado como convenientes para cumplir con la función de extensión ("Programa Nacional", 1995). La Tabla 4 enlista estas actividades, con lo que es posible formarse una idea acerca de lo difícil que resulta prestar atención al rubro editorial, entre las múltiples tareas que cubre extensión, aunado a los pocos recursos asignados.

En un análisis efectuado en 1991 por la Comisión Nacional de Evaluación de la Educación Superior (CONAEVA), se identificaron los principales problemas que impedían el adecuado desarrollo de las actividades de extensión (véase Tabla 4), encontrando que una gran parte del personal adscrito a estas áreas no había recibido instrucción formal para realizar su trabajo ("Programa Nacional", 1995), de ahí que regularmente los administradores le concedan más atención y les resulte más fácil realizar actividades de promoción orientadas a deportes y recreación, que promover la labor editorial.

Al igual de lo que sucede en otras áreas administrativas, los departamentos editoriales tienen una alta movilidad de personal. Esto último está determinado, en gran medida, por la falta de continuidad en los programas universitarios, debido al cambio de autoridades rectorales cada cuatro o seis años. Según un cuestionario hecho por los autores (Apéndice 1), que se discute más adelante, de ocho editores encuestados, todos excepto uno tienen un promedio de doce años en el puesto.

Otro aspecto digno de mencionarse es que la Secretaría de Educación Pública, pese a que las instituciones de educación superior públicas prácticamente sobreviven gracias al presupuesto asignado por ésta, no puede imponerles procedimientos para realizar sus actividades, ya que las universidades disfrutan de autonomía. Lo que sí puede y hace la Secretaría es condicionar el apoyo proporcionado a proyectos especiales, otorgando recursos adicionales únicamente a las instituciones que presentan proyectos viables y bien fundamentados.

Tabla 4. Programas más comunes de extensión

| |
|---|
| Difusión artística |
| Divulgación científica y tecnológica |
| Educación continua |
| Vinculación con los sectores productivo y social |
| TV y radiodifusoras |
| Producción editorial |
| Servicio social |
| Deportes |
| Patrimonio cultural |

Fuente: México, Secretaría de Educación Pública, *Programa sectorial de educación, 1995–2000* (México: La Secretaría, 1996). Consultada en http:/www.udg.mx:81/SEP/pse.html

Las universidades tienen que buscar la posibilidad de compaginar una misión de divulgación con la de obtener ingresos que permitan al menos recuperar sus costos. La producción editorial es con frecuencia muy dispersa en cuanto a la variedad de temas abordados, pero al mismo tiempo estos temas llegan a ser exageradamente técnicos, reduciendo con esto la posibilidad de que puedan ser adquiridos. En los departamentos editoriales es común que se carezca de políticas claras para hacer una selección adecuada de los materiales a editar, así como de personal con la suficiente capacidad para dar estilo y formato atractivos a un escrito. Por deficiencias en la planeación o por problemas del personal encargado, no se realiza una adecuada promoción de los materiales, generando almacenes sobresaturados de ejemplares y recursos potenciales desaprovechados (Figueroa y Torres1992).

Para nadie es un secreto que las editoriales universitarias mexicanas responden muchas veces a gustos o intereses particulares de la administración vigente. Por adorno personal o compromisos contraídos, se autoriza la edición de documentos que difícilmente encontrarán un lector interesado en adquirirlo.

Recientemente se ha añadido el problema de algunas universidades que tratan de aparentar una abundante labor de investigación, mediante la aprobación de escritos que no reúnen la calidad necesaria. A esto se suma que los profesores e investigadores universitarios han empezado a recibir estímulos económicos por la publicación de artículos y libros, con lo que se propicia una mayor presión para imprimir títulos sin mercado. En ambos casos, se observa que se concede una alta importancia a la publicación de materiales, pero no se vigila qué tanto estos materiales son distribuidos y consultados. En México se carece de instrumentos que auxilien la evaluación del impacto de los trabajos publicados a través de citas hechas por otros autores, tales como el Social Science Citation Index, que a pesar de sus limitantes, permite realizar evaluaciones.

## Opciones de editores y bibliotecarios

Para confirmar la problemática hasta ahora discutida acerca de las editoriales académicas, se hizo un sondeo entre algunos editores y bibliotecarios. La población estudiada no representa el amplio universo de actores en los campos bibliotecario y editorial, sin embargo da una idea de su sentir.

La encuesta enviada a editores se circunscribió a los miembros más activos de ASEDIES, excluyéndose a la UNAM por su gran tamaño atípico. Las respuestas recibidas fueron de ocho casos, los que reportaron producir entre 10 y 20 títulos por año, excepto en dos de los casos que tuvieron una producción de aproximadamente 70 títulos anuales, sumando una producción total de 220 títulos. En cuanto a revistas, la producción la esperada por los encuestadores, ya que reportaron 29 títulos en las ocho universidades, lo cual implica que publican menos de 4 títulos por institución. Se les preguntó en que áreas del conocimiento publicaban más libros, predominando ciencias sociales con 54 por ciento seguido por un 28 por ciento, en humanidades y artes. Tecnología y ciencias puras se mantuvieron a la zaga de la producción editorial, representando

15 por ciento. El porcentaje restante de 7 por ciento fue declarado como producción de temática indefinida (otros).

Casi todos los casos reportaron tener librerías propias y participar en ferias de libros, y solamente la mitad reportó tener representantes libreros en la Ciudad de México, así como contar con catálogos impresos actualizados. Esta última respuesta mostró que la mitad de los casos no contó con este instrumento práctico de mercadotecnia. Finalmente, tres casos más reportaron promover material a través del Internet y solamente uno de ellos paga inserciones en medios de difusión. Los directores editoriales tienen relativamente poco en sus puestos, es decir un promedio de tres años, deduciéndose que posiblemente sus nombramientos estén sujetos a los cambios rectorales de las casas de estudio.

Otro cuestionario fue enviado a la lista de discusión *Bibliomex* por medio del Internet, contestando 17 bibliotecarios de instituciones de educación superior, para indagar las dificultades que tienen para adquirir material editorial universitario. La mayoría, es decir 15, señaló que tiene mayor dificultad para comprar este material que el representado por editoriales comerciales. Asimismo, el 88 por ciento afirmó que les resulta más fácil comprar el material publicado en el extranjero, que el de las editoriales universitarias mexicanas.

Los bibliotecarios señalaron también que la información requerida para adquirir las obras la proporcionan generalmente los mismos usuarios y 7 de los informantes, el 41 por ciento, los obtienen directamente de los catálogos editoriales. Esto significa que posiblemente la producción editorial universitaria no se adquiere tan frecuentemente como el material comercial, pues la mitad de los casos no consultan los catálogos para comprar obras, ya que el usuario es quien debe identificar y describir los datos del título que sugiere.

Los mecanismos de distribución utilizados para adquirir el material fueron principalmente a través de compra directa a las editoriales académicas, reportando 13 casos esta respuesta, lo que hace un 77 por ciento; 7 de ellos respondieron pedirlo a un distribuidor general y otro contestó comprarlos en ferias y exposiciones de libros. En otras palabras, la mayoría de los bibliotecarios encuestados no utilizan los servicios de un proveedor. Esto se puede tomar como un indicador de que éstos posiblemente no trabajan dicho material.

La pregunta final de este cuestionario fue enfocada a pedir una comparación sobre cual era el problema principal de la producción editorial universitaria, cuestionándose qué problema era mayor, si la calidad del contenido o los mecanismos de distribución, señalando el 82 por ciento de los bibliotecarios que el problema de distribución era más serio que la calidad del contenido y solamente tres difirieron en la anterior respuesta. Estos resultados corroboran lo que es una creencia generalizada en México, razón por la cual la ASEDIES busca que los editores cuenten con los conocimientos esenciales de comercialización ("Talón de Aquiles", 1995–1996).

Los bibliotecarios de universidades públicas han colaborado poco para reducir los enormes problemas de las editoriales. Existen algunos aspectos en los que podría haber una mayor participación, misma que brindaría amplios beneficios. Por ejemplo, la compilación de fuentes de acceso a la producción editorial y la catalogación en la fuente de las obras. En México son realmente raros los libros que aparecen con dicho proceso. La asignación de los números ISBN es con frecuencia anárquica por la falta de conocimiento de la importancia de este número, algo que los bibliotecarios deberían demandar (Figueroa y Torres 1992).

## Adquisición de obras universitarias

Si bien conseguir materiales editados en universidades mexicanas es difícil en el mismo territorio, esto debe ser más complicado para bibliotecas extranjeras. No existen proveedores/libreros de publicaciones universitarias, como tampoco existen catálogos que listen la producción nacional y se carecen de mecanismos para promoción y venta de los materiales.

Para vencer estos problemas se pueden realizar acciones como solicitar catálogos a las universidades públicas y ordenar los materiales a través de proveedores, quienes pueden recibir comisiones mayores que los que obtienen de editoriales comerciales. Otro mecanismo para conocer la producción de universidades es consultar sus páginas electrónicas en Internet, que empiezan a proliferar, y solicitar información a ASEDIES quien puede proporcionar datos de sus afiliados (véase Tabla 5). Adjunto a este documento (Apéndice 2) se presenta un directorio de las principales universidades públicas, así como un listado de las revistas que se consideran las mejores en el plano nacional (Apéndice 3) (Bonilla 1996). Ambas herramientas pueden ser usadas para contactar los editores citados, como para seleccionar títulos de publicaciones periódicas.

Los compradores extranjeros de publicaciones universitarias deben estar conscientes que los editores carecen de buenos o suficientes medios de comunicación, tales como teléfono, fax o correo electrónico. Igualmente, es raro que puedan recibir pagos a través de tarjetas de crédito.

Tabla 5. Limitaciones editoriales de universidades

| |
|---|
| Carencia de un catálogo único de producción nacional |
| Mecanismos de pago lentos |
| Poca promoción |
| Carencia de personal especializado |
| Potencial del Internet inexplorado |
| Mercado de reducido para temas cubiertos |
| Poca infraestructura de comunicaciones en editoriales |
| Tiempos de respuesta lentos |
| Conclusiones |

La producción editorial universitaria se concentra en un grupo reducido de instituciones, las cuales en su mayoría son de carácter público, es decir financiadas con fondos gubernamentales.

La adquisición y conocimiento de novedades bibliográficas generadas por las universidades no es fácil para clientes del extranjero, como tampoco para nacionales, por la carencia de repertorios que concentren la producción nacional. En la mayoría de los casos, deben hacerse contactos con cada universidad para saber lo que editan y comprar sus obras. Estos factores limitan seriamente la distribución de las publicaciones universitarias en el extranjero, limitando también, por lo tanto, la diseminación del conocimiento generado por los investigadores nacionales y de aquellos que escriben en las casas de estudio mexicanas.

La producción académica de libros y revistas es importante tomando en cuenta el total de títulos publicados a nivel nacional. Es muy posible que la producción universitaria equivalga al 20 por ciento de la producción nacional de libros y revistas, producción que está enfocada principalmente a las ciencias sociales y a las humanidades.

Los bibliotecarios académicos consideran que existen dificultades para adquirir libros editados por las casas de estudio, incluso superiores que las que implica comprar material extranjero similar. Consideran ellos también que la escasa venta de obras universitarias se debe más bien a un problema de distribución, que la mala calidad del contenido.

El acceso a las redes de cómputo mundiales, como el Internet, está facilitando la promoción de las novedades bibliográficas, ya que algunas universidades han creado páginas electrónicas, donde incluyen información sobre los títulos publicados. Es de esperarse que en un plazo corto aprovechen las ventajas del Internet para organizar y dar a conocer la producción nacional en solo repertorio electrónico, del cual se pueden derivar otros impresos o digitalizados. Si los cambios mencionados se realizan, la comunidad mundial conocerá las aportaciones de las universidades públicas mexicanas, facilitando la adquisición de sus novedades bibliográficas.

Las universidades mexicanas tienen que reconocer que su función no sólo consiste en editar publicaciones, sino en divulgar el conocimiento, tanto para apoyar internamente sus funciones de docencia e investigación, como para compartirlo con la sociedad.

## APENDICE 1

Universidad Autónoma de Ciudad Juárez,
Dirección de Recursos Informativos
(Mayo 1996)

Cuestionario sobre Producción y Distribución
de Publicaciones Universitarias

Le rogamos contestar las preguntas siguientes, sus respuestas servirán para una ponencia sobre editoriales universitarias mexicanas que se presentará en la Cd. de Nueva York. Contestar el cuestionario no le llevará más de cinco minutos. Le suplicamos que si no tiene a la mano los datos exactos, proporcione una cifra aproximada.

1. ¿Cuántos títulos editados por su universidad tienen en venta?
   Libros __________
   Revistas ________

2. ¿Cuál es su producción anual en títulos de libros?

3. ¿En qué áreas publica más su universidad?
   ______% Ciencias sociales ______% Ciencias puras
   ______% Tecnología ______% Humanidades y artes
   ______% Historia ______% Otros

4. Señale con una cruz los medios de distribución que utiliza. Puede marcar varios.
   ( ) Librería(s) propia(s)
   ( ) Representantes en la ciudad de México
   ( ) Asisto a ferias de libros. ¿Cuántas por año?_____
   ( ) Cuento con catálogo impreso actualizado
   ( ) Promuevo a través de Internet
   ( ) Pago inserciones en medios de difusión

5. ¿Cuánto tiempo tiene en el puesto el Director Editorial?
   ______ Años
   ______ No se cuenta con Depto. editorial

¡Gracias por su colaboración! Indique si desea recibir copia de la ponencia.

Sí ___ No ____

Favor de enviar vía fax a Dr. Jesús Lau, Director de Recursos Informativos, UACJ.

Fax No. (16) 11 31 68, Tel. (16) 11 31 67, Email: jlau@uacj.mx

Universidad Autónoma de Ciudad Juárez
Dirección de Recursos Informativos
(Mayo 1996)

Cuestionario sobre Publicaciones Universitarias Mexicanas

A continuación se presenta un cuestionario de sólo 6 preguntas. Las respuestas serán muy útiles para una ponencia que se está preparando acerca de la producción y distribución editorial de las universidades mexicanas.

Les pedimos dirigir sus respuestas a cualquiera de nuestras direcciones personales de email o vía fax. Posteriormente divulgaremos a través de este mismo FORO una síntesis de los resultados.

1. Adquirir libros producidos por editoriales universitarias mexicanas le cuesta

( ) Menor dificultad que los libros de editoriales comerciales
( ) La misma dificultad
( ) Mayor dificultad

2. ¿Piensa Ud. que en promedio le resulta más fácil adquirir libros o revistas de universidades extranjeras que los producidos por universidades mexicanas?

( ) Sí ( ) No

3. Regularmente ¿Cómo integra la información necesaria para solicitar materiales de editoriales universitarias? Señale la más importante.

( ) Los datos los proporcionan los usuarios que solicitan el documento
( ) Los obtengo en los catálogos editoriales de las universidades
( ) No requiero reunir los datos, pues adquiero los materiales en ferias o exposiciones
( ) La obtengo de otras fuentes (Especificar)

________________________________________

4. Excluyendo los libros de la UNAM, ¿Qué mecanismos utiliza para conseguir libros producidos por editoriales universitarias? Señale sólo el más importante para Ud.

( ) Los solicito a un distribuidor general
( ) Me comunico al departamento editorial de la universidad respectiva
( ) Adquiero los libros en ferias y exposiciones
( ) Otro (Especificar)

________________________________________

5. ¿Considera Ud. que el principal problema de las universidades mexicanas con respecto a su producción editorial radica en que

( ) Es necesario mejorar la calidad de su contenido
( ) Es necesario mejorar los mecanismos de distribución

6. ¿Tiene algún comentario que quiera agregar con respecto a este tema?

________________________________________
________________________________________
________________________________________

# APENDICE 2

## Directorio de Universidades Públicas
## Compilado por Jesús Lau y Jesús Cortés
## (Mayo 1996)

**Universidad Autónoma de Aguascalientes**
Av. Universidad No. 2100
20100 Aguascalientes, Ags.
Tels. (49) 12 33 45, 14 31 07, 12 34 04, 14 60 70
Fax (49) 14 32 22 y 14 55 91

**Universidad Tecnológica de Aguascalientes**
Carretera a la Cantera Km. 5
Apartado Postal 637
20000 Aguascalientes, Ags.
Tels. (49) 18 46 86, 18 46 87, 18 73 77, 18 70 78,
Fax (49) 18 58 09

**Universidad Autónoma de Baja California**
Av. A. Obregón y J. Carrillo s/n
21100 Mexicali, B.C.
Tels. (65) 54 24 92, 53 46 42, 52 48 25, 52 95 40,
53 46 52, 54 20 27, 54 22 00
Fax (65) 53 44 61, 52 23 79

**Universidad Autónoma de Baja California Sur** *
Lázaro Reynosa Ramírez
Siderurgia2785, Álamo Jud **
Carretera al Sur Km. 5.5
Apartado Postal 19B
23080 La Paz, B.C.S.
Tels. (112) 1 18 70, 1 11 40, 1 05 69, 1 07 55, 1 15 50
Fax (112) 1 07 77

**Universidad Autónoma de Campeche**
Av. Agustín Melgar s/n
Apartado Postal 204
24030 Campeche, Camp.
Tels. (981) 6 52 43, 6 22 02, 6 26 18, 6 22 44
Fax (981) 6 52 43

**Universidad Autónoma del Carmen**
Av. Concordia y Av. 56 s/n
24180 Ciudad del Carmen, Campeche
Tels. (938) 2 58 62, 2 11 33, 2 58 06, 2 08 67, 2 58 40
Fax (938) 2 58 62

* Miembro ASEDIES
** Dirección revisada

**Universidad Autónoma de Coahuila**
Blvd. V. Carranza y Lic. Salvador González Lobo
25280 Saltillo, Coah.
Tels. (84) 14 87 83, 15 73 92, 15 81 55
Fax. (84) 14 81 55

**Universidad Autónoma Agraria Antonio Narro**
Domicilio conocido
Buenavista
25315 Saltillo, Coah.
Tels. (84) 17 31 84, 17 36 64, 17 30 22
Fax (84) 17 30 22

**Universidad de Colima**
Av. Universidad No. 333
28000 Colima, Colima
Tel. (331) 2 54 36
Fax (331) 4 41 77

**Universidad Autónoma de Chiapas**
Fernando Lara Piña
Jefe del Departamento Editorial
Blvd. Dr. B. Domínguez Km. 1081
Col. Universitaria
Apartado Postal 1051 y 1053
29050 Tuxtla Gutiérrez, Chis.
Tels. (961) 5 08 27, 5 10 21
Fax (961) 5 06 64

**Universidad de Ciencias y Artes del Estado de Chiapas** *
Andrés Fábregas Puig
Av. Sur Poniente 1460
Tuxtla Gutiérrez, Chis.
Tels. (961) 3 71 74, 1 38 73

**Universidad Autónoma de Chihuahua**
Escorza y V. Carranza
31000 Chihuahua, Chih.
Tels. (14) 15 79 44, 16 28 17, 15 27 22, 15 24 27
Fax (14) 14 93 85

**Universidad Autónoma de Ciudad Juárez ***
Jesús Lau Noriega
Av. López Mateos No. 20
Circuito PRONAF
32310 Cd. Juárez, Chih.
Tel. (16) 11 31 67
Fax (16) 11 31 68

**Universidad Nacional Autónoma de México**
Torre de Rectoría 6o. piso
Ciudad Universitaria
04510 México, D.F.
Tels. (5) 6 16 19 36, 6 22 12 80 al 85, 6 22 12 87
Fax (5) 5 50 87 72

**Universidad Autónoma Metropolitana**
Blvd. M. Avila Camacho No. 90 5o. piso
Col. El Parque
53390 Naucalpan, Edo. de México
Tels. (5) 5 76 39 75, 5 76 46 33, 5 76 38 86,
5 76 79 00
Fax (5) 5 76 68 88

**Universidad Autónoma Metropolitana - Atz.**
Valentín Almaraz M.
Jefe de la Sección Editorial
Av. San Pablo 180
Col. Reynosa, Tamps.
Del. Azcapotzalco
México, D.F
Tel. (5) 7 24 44 23
Fax (5) 7 24 44 22

**Colegio de México ***
Sergio López Avalos
Camino al Ajusco 20
México, D.F
Tel. 6 45 59 55 ext. 3139
Fax 6 45 04 64

**Universidad Pedagógica Nacional ***
Juan Carlos Rangel
Coordinador
Carretera al Ajusco No. 24
Col. Héroes de Padierna
Delegación Tlalpan
14200 México, D.F.
Tel. (5) 6 45 49 65
Fax (5) 6 45 09 65

* Miembro ASEDIES
** Dirección revisada

**Instituto Politécnico Nacional ***
Ingnacio Flores Calvillo
Director de Publicaciones
Tresguerras No. 27 **
Centro Histórico
06040 México, D.F
Tel. 7 29 63 00 ext. 46326
Fax 7 09 48 07

**Universidad del Valle de México ***
José Antonio Otón Mato
Tehuantepec 250
Col. Roma Sur
México, D.F.
Tel. 2 64 79 33
Fax 5 74 04 22

**Universidad Juárez del Estado de Durango**
Constitución No. 404 sur
34000 Durango, Dgo.
Tels. (181) 2 01 44, 2 02 44, 6 30 32, 2 56 05,
6 30 32
Fax (181) 2 95 13

**Universidad de Guanajuato ***
Jesús Rosales
Alonso 12 **
Centro
36000 Guanajuato, Gto.
Tel. (473) 2 57 02

**Universidad Autónoma de Guerrero**
Edif. Nuevo de Rectoría
39 070 Chilpancingo, Gro.
Tels. (747) 2 59 24, 2 25 36
Fax (747) 2 29 10

**Universidad Autónoma de Hidalgo**
Abasolo No. 600
42000 Pachuca, Hgo.
Tels. (771) 5 31 33, 5 10 67, 5 10 76, 5 10 68
Fax (771) 5 53 40

**Universidad Tecnológica de Tula-Tepeji**
Carretera a Tula-Tepeji Km. 8
Ejido del Carmen
Col. 61 Tula de Allende
42800 Tula, Hidalgo
Tels. (773) 2 19 71, 2 12 14
Fax (773) 6 07 88

**Universidad de Guadalajara ***
Jesús Anaya Rosique
Calderón de la Barca 280 **
44260 Guadalajara, Jal.
Tels. (3)6 15 87 42, 6 15 75 99 y 6 15 76 66

**Universidad Autónoma del Estado de México**
Instituto Literario No. 100 Ote.
50000 Toluca, Edo. de México
Tels. (72) 13 47 32, 15 95 89, 14 40 80, 14 48 04, 14 44 48, 14 49 80
Fax (72) 14 55 56

**Universidad Autónoma de Chapingo**
Américo Flores
Km. 38.5 Carr. México-Texcoco-Chapingo
56230
Tel. (595) 4 98 88

**Universidad Tecnológica de Nezahualcóyotl**
Calle Benito Juárez s/n
Col. Benito Juárez
57000 Nezahualcóyotl, Edo. de México
Tel. 7 30 30 37
Fax 7 30 19 24

**Colegio de Michoacan ***
Valentín Juárez
Martínez de Navarrete No. 505
Fraccionamiento Las Fuentes
59690 Zamora, Mich.

**Universidad Michoacana de San Nicolás de Hidalgo**
Ciudad Universitaria
Edif. TR. Planta Alta
58030 Morelia, Mich.
Tels. (43) 16 70 20, 16 88 34
Fax (43) 16 88 35

**Universidad Autónoma del Estado de Morelos**
Av. Universidad No. 1001
Col. Chamilpa
62210 Cuernavaca, Mor.
Tels. (73) 13 65 97, 11 22 88
Fax (73) 13 34 95

* Miembro ASEDIES
** Dirección revisada

**Universidad Autónoma de Nayarit**
Ciudad de la Cultura Amado Nervo
Nervo Torre de Rectoría 3er. piso
63190 Tepic, Nayarit
Tels. (321) 3 31 72, 3 31 76, 3 31 78, 79 y 80, 3 38 39, 3 38 47
Fax (321) 3 66 05

**Universidad Autónoma de Nuevo León**
Ciudad Universitaria
Torre de Rectoría 8o. piso
Nicolás de los Garza
64000 Monterrey, N. L.
Tels. (83) 52 31 18, 52 55 81, 76 41 40
Fax (83) 76 77 57

**Universidad Autónoma Benito Juárez de Oaxaca**
Ciudad Universitaria
Ex-Hda. de 5 señores
68120 Oaxaca, Oax.
Tels. (951) 1 05 66, 6 38 65
Fax (951) 6 53 44

**Universidad Tecnológica de la Mixteca**
Carretera a Acatlima Km. 2.5
69000 Huajuapan de León, Oax.
Tel. (953) 2 10 50, 2 02 14

**Benemérita Universidad Autónoma de Puebla ***
Luis Enrique Sánchez Fernández
Director General de Fomento Editorial
Av. Maximino Avila Camacho 406 **
72000 Puebla, Pue.
Tel. (22) 42 79 33

**Universidad Autónoma de Querétaro ***
Jorge Lara Ovando
Centro Universitario
Cerro de las Campanas
Apartado Postal 184
76010 Querétaro, Qro.
Tel. (42) 13 42 42 ext. 142
Fax (42) 16 35 37

**Universidad de Quintana Roo**
Blvd. Bahía s/n Esq. Ignación Comonfort
Apartado Postal 10
77010 Chetumal, Quintana Roo
Tels. (983) 2 92 65, 2 83 88, 2 96 34
Fax (983) 2 96 56

**Universidad Autónoma de San Luis Potosí**
Alvaro Obregón No. 64
78000 San Luis Potosí, S.L.P.
Tels. (48) 12 02 82, 12 34 61, 12 33 00, 12 36 39
Fax (48) 18 19 21, 14 03 72

**Universidad Autónoma de Sinaloa ***
Roberto Moreno
Burócratas 274 -3 **
Col. Burócratas
80000 Culiacán, Sin.
Tel. (67) 15 59 92

**Universidad de Occidente**
Benito Juárez No. 435 Pte.
Col. Centro
81200 Los Mochis, Sin.
Tels. (67) 5 10 61, 2 66 17
Fax (67) 5 39 00, 16 17 08, 16 17 06

**Universidad Autónoma de Sonora ***
Jesús Armando Zamora A.
Director de Publicaciones
Rosales y Transversal
Apartado Postal 106
83000 Hermosillo, Son.
Tel. (62) 13 35 87
Fax (62) 13 35 87

**Instituto Tecnológico de Sonora**
5 de Febrero No. 818 Sur
85000 Cd. Obregón, Son.
Tels. (641) 7 07 83, 7 04 91, 7 08 51, 7 04 31, 7 03 71, 7 01 91, 7 01 21, 7 01 35
Fax (641) 7 02 44, 7 07 31

**Universidad Juárez Autónoma de Tabasco**
Av. Universidad s/n
Ciudad Universitaria
86040 Villahermosa, Tabasco
Tels. (93) 12 29 93, 12 72 11, 12 72 08 al 11
Fax (93) 12 16 37

**Universidad Autónoma de Tamaulipas ***
Jorge Aurelio Luiz García
Dirección de Fomento Editorial
Matamoros No. 8
Col. Centro
87000 Cd. Victoria, Tamps.
Tels. (131) 2 91 17, 2 85 11, 2 70 00
Fax (131) 2 00 70

**Universidad Autónoma de Tlaxcala ***
Paula Catalina
Av. Universidad No.1
90070 Tlaxcala, Tlax.
Tel. (246) 2 14 22

**Universidad Veracruzana ***
José Luis Rivas
Circuito Gonzalo Aguirre Beltrán s/n **
Zona Universitaria
91090 Xalapa, Ver.
Tel. (281)18 59 80

**Universidad Autónoma de Yucatán**
Calle 60x57 No. 491-A
Col. Centro
97000 Mérida, Yuc.
Tels. (99) 24 81 10, 24 92 82, 24 80 00, 24 86 63, 24 88 85
Fax (99) 28 25 57

**Universidad Autónoma de Zacatecas**
Jardín Juárez No. 147
Col. Centro
98000 Zacatecas, Zac.
Tels. (492) 2 91 09, 2 64 55, 2 29 24
Fax (492) 4 21 92

## Otras Instituciones

**Instituto Nacional de Antropología e Historia ***
Adriana Konzevik
Dir. de Publicaciones
Alvaro Obregón 151-3 **
Col. Roma
06700 México, D.F
Tel. (5) 2 07 45 73
Fax (5) 2 07 46 33

**Asociación Nacional de Universidades e Instituciones de Educación Superior ***
Carlo Rosas Rodríguez
Tenayuca 200
Col. Sta. Cruz Atayac
Delegación Benito Juárez
03310 México, D.F.
Tels. 6 04 38 00, 6 04 07 34
Fax 6 04 42 63

* Miembro ASEDIES
** Dirección revisada

# APENDICE 3

## Indice de Revistas Científicas Mexicanas de Excelencia

| Título | Patrocinador | Ant. | Period. |
|---|---|---|---|
| **Ciencias Exactas** | | | |
| 1. Bol. de la Soc. Mat. Mex. | Sociedad Mat. Mexicana | 39 | Semestral |
| 2. Rev. Mex. Astron. y Astrof. | UNAM. Inst. de Astron. | 21 | Semestral |
| 3. Mathesis | UNAM. Fac. de Ciencias | 13 | Trimestral |
| 4. Revista Mex. de Física | Sociedad Mex. de Física | 45 | Bimestral |
| **Ciencias Aplicadas** | | | |
| 5. Agrociencia | Inst. de Inv. y S. Agr. Chapingo | 29 | Trimestral |
| 6. Ciencia Forestal | SARH-INIFAP | 20 | Semestral |
| 7. Instrumentación y Desarrollo | Soc. Mex. Instrumentación | 5 | Anual |
| 8. Micología Neotropical Aplicada | Colegio de Postgraduados | 6 | Semestral |
| 9. Terra | Soc. Mex. Ciencia del Suelo | 12 | Semestral |
| **Ciencias Humanas** | | | |
| 10. QUIPU, Rev. Lat. Hist. C. y T. | Inst. Iberoam. de Est. de C. y T. | 1 | Semestral |
| 11. Anuario Hist. de Derecho Mexicano | UNAM. Inst. de Inv. Jurídicas | 6 | Anual |
| 12. Bol. Mexicano de Derecho Comparado | UNAM. Inst. de Inv. Jurídicas | 47 | Trimestral |
| 13. Crítica Jurídica | UNAM. Inst. de Inv. Jurídicas | 3 | Anual |
| 14. Anales Inst. de Inv. Estéticas | UNAM. Inst. de Inv. Estéticas | 58 | Anual |
| 15. Cuadernos de Arq. Mesoamericana | UNAM. Fac. de Arquitectura | 11 | Semestral |
| 16. Estudios de Cultura Náhuatl | UNAM. Inst. de Inv. Históricas | 25 | Anual |
| 17. Historia Mexicana | El Colegio de México | 40 | Trimestral |

| Título | Patrocinador | Ant. | Period. |
|---|---|---|---|
| 18. Nueva Revista de Filología Hisp. | El Colegio de Mexico | 48 | Semestral |
| 19. Alteridades | UNAM. Iztapalapa | 6 | Semestral |
| 20. Crítica | UNAM. Inst. de Inv. Filosóficas | 29 | Cuatrimestral |
| 21. Dianoia | UNAM. Inst. de Inv. Filosóficas | 20 | Anual |
| 22. Estudios Cult. Contemporánea | Universidad de Colima | 12 | Cuatrimestral |
| 23. Estudios de Hist. Novohispana | UNAM. Inst. de Inv. Históricas | 29 | Cuatrimestral |
| 24. Estudios Jaliscienses | El Colegio de Jalisco | 5 | Trimestral |
| 25. Geografía y Desarrollo | Col. Mexicano de Geogr. Postgrad. | 8 | Anual |
| 26. Revista Int. de Filosofía Pol. | UAM-Iztapalapa | 2 | Semestral |
| 27. Rev. Latinoam. de Est. Educativos | Centro de Estudios Educativos | 24 | Trimestral |
| 28. Literatura Mexicana | UNAM. Inst. Inv. Fil., Est. y Lit. | 5 | Semestral |
| 29. Revista Mexicana de Psicología | Sociedad Mexicana de Psicología | 12 | Semestral |
| 30. Nueva Antropología | Nueva Antropología | 20 | Semestral |
| **Ciencias Naturales** | | | |
| 31. Anales Inst. Biología "Botánica" | UNAM. Inst. de Biología | 65 | Anual |
| 32. Anales Inst. Biología "Zoología" | UNAM. Inst. de Biología | 65 | Anual |
| 33. Acta Botánica Mexicana | Instituto de Ecología | 7 | Trimestral |
| 34. Acta Zoológica Mexicana | Instituto de Ecología | 11 | Trimestral |
| 35. Boletín Soc. Botánica Mexicana | Sociedad Botánica de México | 51 | Semestral |
| 36. Fitotecnia Mexicana | Soc. Mexicana de Fitogenética | 7 | Semestral |
| 37. Folia Entomológica Mexicana | Soc. Mexicana Entomológica | 34 | Semestral |
| 38. Revista Hidrobiológica | UAM-Iztapalapa | 4 | Semestral |
| 39. Revista Latinoam. de Microbiología | Asoc. Latinoam. de Microbiología | 37 | Trimestral |
| 40. Revista Mex. de Fitopatología | Soc. Mexicana de Fitopatología | 15 | Semestral |
| 41. Revista Mex. de Micología | Soc. Mexicana de Micología | 10 | Anual |
| 42. Archives of Medical Research | IMSS | 25 | Trimestral |
| 43. Rev. de Salud Pública de México | Inst. Nal. de Salud Pública | 37 | Trimestral |
| 44. Investigación Clínica | Inst. Nal. de Nutrición S. Z. | 47 | Semestral |

| Título | Patrocinador | Ant. | Period. |
|---|---|---|---|
| **Ciencias Sociales** | | | |
| 45. Economía Mex. | CIDE | 17 | Semestral |
| 46. Estudios de Asia y Africa | El Colegio de México | 29 | Cuatrimestral |
| 47. Foro Internacional | El Colegio de México | 35 | Trimestral |
| 48. Gestión y Política Pública | CIDE | 3 | Semestral |
| 49. Argumentos | UAM-Xochimilco | 8 | Semestral |
| 50. Comunicación y Sociedad | Universidad de Guadalajara | 9 | Cuatrimestral |
| 51. Cuadernos del Sur | Cuadernos del Sur Oaxaca | 3 | Cuatrimestral |
| 52. El Trimestre Económico | Fondo de Cultura Económica | 61 | Trimestral |
| 53. Eslabones | Soc. Nal. de Estudios Regionales | 4 | Semestral |
| 54. Estudios Demográficos y Urbanos | El Colegio de México | 28 | Cuatrimestral |
| 55. Estudios Económicos | El Colegio de México | 9 | Trimestral |
| 56. Estudios Sociológicos | El Colegio de México | 12 | Cuatrimestral |
| 57. Frontera Norte | El Colegio de la Frontera Norte | 6 | Trimestral |
| 58. Iztapalapa | UAM-Iztapalapa | 16 | Semestral |
| 59. Rev. Mex. de Cs. Políticas y Soc. | UNAM. Fac. de Cs. Políticas y Soc. | 40 | Trimestral |
| 60. Revista Mexicana de Sociología | UNAM. Inst. de Inv. Sociales | 56 | Trimestral |
| 61. Política y Gobierno | CIDE | 1 | Semestral |
| 62. Relaciones Internacionales | UNAM. Fac. de Cs. Políticas y Soc. | 22 | Trimestral |
| 63. Revista Sociológica | UAM-Azcapotzalco | 65 | Cuatrimestral |
| **Ciencias de la Tierra** | | | |
| 64. Atmósfera | UNAM. Centro de Ciencias Atmos. | 7 | Trimestral |
| 65. Ciencias Marinas | Univ. Aut. de Baja California | 21 | Semestral |
| 66. Geofísica Internacional | UNAM. Inst. de Geofísica | 30 | Trimestral |
| 67. Revista Int. de Contaminación | UNAM. Centro de Ciencias Atmosf. | 10 | Semestral |
| 68. Revista Mex. de Cs. Geológicas | UNAM. Instituto de Geología | 18 | Semestral |

Fuente: Marcial Bonilla, “Indice de revistas mexicanas de excelencia”, *Academia* (marzo-abril 1996), pp. 12-19.

## REFERENCIAS

Bonilla, Marcial. 1996. "Indice de revistas científicas mexicanas de excelencia". *Academia* (marzo-abril ), 12-19.

CONACYT (Consejo Nacional de Ciencia y Tecnología). 1995. México. *1994 Indicators of Scientific and Technological Activities*. México: El Consejo.

Figueroa A. H., y G. A. Torres. 1992. "Alternativas de trabajo bibliotecario para la difusión del libro universitario". En *Memoria XXIII Jornadas Mexicanas de Biblioteconomía*, 17 al 19 de septiembre de 1992. Mérida, Yucatán: AMBAC; Universidad Autónoma de Yucatán. Pp. 199-214.

Lau, J. 1993. "Research in the Outskirts of Science: The Case of Mexico". *International Journal of Information and Library Research* 5(1), 39-46.

México. Secretaría de Educación Pública. 1995. *Guía de proyectos FOMES 1995*. México: La Secretaría.

______. 1996. *Programa sectorial de educación, 1995–2000*. México: La Secretaría. Consultada en http:/www.udg.mx:81/SEP/pse.html

"Programa Nacional de Extensión de la Cultura y los Servicios". 1995. *Revista de la Educación Superior*, no. 95 (julio–septiembre), 98–165.

Rangel, J. C. 1996. "En 95, al libro, como en feria: ecos de la FIL'95 de Guadalajara". *Avión de papel: órgano de difusión de la Asociación de Editoriales de Instituciones de Educación Superior, A. C.* Vol. 1, No. 2 (febrero–abril), 9.

"Talón de Aquiles". 1995–1996. *Avión de papel: órgano de difusión de la Asociación de Editoriales de Instituciones de Educación Superior, A. C.* Vol. 1, No. 1 (noviembre 1995–enero 1996).

# 22. Estrategias y políticas de información y tecnología: el futuro deseable

Saadia Sánchez Vegas

> ...En suma, lo que mal se conoce, mal se puede comprender, controlar, desviar o transformar, y cuando se desconoce, o se conoce mal el carácter mismo del proceso se está mucho más a la merced del azar o de la necesidad histórica que se imponen a las voluntades individuales o sociales, tanto más desprevenidas o ingenuas cuanto más ignorantes de las razones del acontecer, y tanto más expuestas a ser instrumento del azar que de la propia necesidad histórica que se quiere superar.
>
> Graciela Soriano de García Pelayo (1996: 138)

En la presente ponencia se pretende abordar el problema de la información e incorporación tecnológica en América Latina y de las políticas nacionales y regionales de información y tecnología de manera exploratoria, apuntado a la reflexión. Hemos estructurado la ponencia en tres partes. En una primera parte, enunciamos ciertas premisas como marco de referencia teórico-social. En una segunda parte, nos abocamos a una reflexión crítica sobre la presencia de América Latina en Internet; para terminar en una tercera parte, con un enunciado esquemático de orden metodológico y teórico de lo que consideramos son aspectos medulares de posibles políticas de información y tecnología, desde una perspectiva que aspira trascender lo nacional y llevarnos a una reflexión sobre lo regional en términos de un futuro deseable.

Más que desarrollar exhaustivamente las premisas que aquí se enuncian, se trata de traer a discusión (o mejor aún a debate) un tema complejo: la pertinencia de políticas de información y tecnología en América Latina, a partir del cual se han gestado numerosas discusiones, sobre el que se han volcado no pocos esfuerzos teóricos e incluso prácticos, y se ha escrito abundantemente desde organismos internacionales como Unesco, a instancias oficiales y académicas desde la perspectiva de cada país, tema que ha cobrado y perdido vigencia histórica en distintas coyunturas, pero cuyos avances e impacto en materia de diseño, instrumentación y logro de objetivos y metas de desarrollo distan de ser realmente satisfactorios.

Nuestra perspectiva política y teórica es latinoamericanista, y pretendemos recobrar la vigencia histórica de las políticas nacionales de información y tecnología, situándola en el contexto de un nuevo paradigma tecnosocioeconómico en franco proceso de consolidación a nivel mundial.

El nuevo paradigma tecnosocioeconómico viene determinado por el desarrollo de las denominadas nuevas tecnologías de información. Dicho en otros términos, este paradigma está definido por el auge e incorporación social de una onda de innovaciones tecnológicas vinculadas al advenimiento de la computación y su convergencia con las telecomunicaciones y medios audiovisuales, aplicables a distintos campos de la actividad individual y social.

Como ideal complementaria, debemos indicar que en lo relativo al contexto mundial nos situamos en la denominada era de la globalización, cuyo eje central lo constituyen las tecnologías de información, telecomunicaciones y comunicación electrónica, y que la concebimos como definitoria de la etapa actual de acumulación de capital, y cuya expresión concreta es la internacionalización financiera.

Asimismo, asistimos a un reacomodo de la correlación de fuerzas internacionales y dominio de la economía mundial caracterizado por una multipolaridad del poder económico compartido por los Estados Unidos, Japón y el Mercado Común Europeo. En este contexto y ante esta realidad, los países latinoamericanos, con mayor o menor éxito, hacen múltiples esfuerzos por diseñar políticas económicas (y deseablemente sociales) dirigidas a corregir sus desequilibrios macroeconómicos y macrosociales, con miras a insertarse de manera más favorable, e idealmente competitiva, en la economía mundial.

Aunado a estas políticas económicas nacionales, se han gestado esfuerzos en pro de políticas de integración latinoamericana bajo esquemas de cooperación subregionales y de acuerdos bilaterales, fundamentados en realidades económicas y comerciales afines y estructuradas (Ferrero Costa 1994). En términos de la deseable integración regional o de integración única bajo un proyecto común para América Latina, la perspectiva es menos optimista, dadas, según Ferrero Costa, las diferencias existentes entre los países de la región, de orden geográfico, demográfico y niveles de desarrollo. Esto último entra en dramática contradicción con el hecho mismo de que ante la multipolaridad del poder económico arriba mencionada, es precisamente la integración de una economía regional lo que le daría a América Latina como región la posibilidad de integrarse de manera realmente competitiva a la economía mundial.

No se trata de emitir un juicio valorativo en torno a estos procesos sino de asumirlo en su dimensión objetiva, esto es contrario a la retórica—por lo demás ideológica—de la globalización como promisoria de un mundo igualitario y equitativo, equidad ésta que viene dada por un supuesto "acceso universal", esto es, de "todos", sin barreras espaciales ni temporales, ni distinciones histórico-culturales, a la información y conocimiento, mediante el uso masivo de las tecnologías que hacen posible su organización y distribución.

Así, partimos de la premisa de que la incorporación tecnológica per se y las bondades intrínsecas a esa tecnología no se traducen mecánicamente en beneficios en una sociedad. Las tecnologías (como tampoco la es la información) no son neutrales, sino que las mismas son productos sociales e históricos que se corresponden con las especifidades contextuales, esto es, económico-sociales, políticas y culturales de aquellas sociedades dentro de las cuales se han generado y desarrollado. La tecnología es un fenómeno social activo y dialéctico que afecta, impacta y moldea el contexto social donde se inserta, y al mismo tiempo es afectada y moldeada por este mismo contexto.

Sin embargo, podemos afirmar que la transferencia de tecnologías—y también la transferencia de productos informacionales—en América Latina, con mayor o menor proporción, se ha dado y aún se da, soslayando lo anteriormente dicho.

En general, la transferencia e incorporación tecnológica ha operado como una variable exógena, bajo una política de compra y adquisición proveniente de los países de economías avanzadas sin haber con ello generado, lo que Ignacio Avalos (1991:34) refiere como el "dominio tecnológico". Es decir, no ha habido una aprehensión del hecho tecnológico ni una incorporación realmente ventajosa a los procesos productivos que se han pretendido transformar. Nos permitimos extrapolar una expresión de Graciela García Pelayo, para apuntar que la tecnología se ha incorporado en las realidades latinoamericanas con un carácter teleológico, cuyo "fin es ponerse a nivel de" los países altamente industrializados. De esta manera, se ha incorporado como factor exógeno a su tiempo y espacio, y como parte de un proceso transculturador.

La transferencia de tecnología, y corremos el grave riesgo de que lo mismo nos esté ocurriendo con la transferencia de información, ha operado dentro de lo que la autora arriba citada categoriza conceptualmente como un proceso *discrónico*, esto es, "como consecuencia de un desarrollo mecánico, inorgánico, incoherente, desestructurado expuesto a las influencias exteriores de sociedades más avanzadas y a las imprevisibles contradicciones internas" (Soriano de García Pelayo 1996:136) .

En razón de lo anteriormente dicho, se requiere imprescindiblemente de una voluntad política que le corresponde al estado asumir como parte sustancial de sus políticas económicas y sociales, bajo la forma de una coherentemente diseñada política nacional de información y tecnología, que se articule orgánicamente a las metas y objetivos de desarrollo de la nación. Esto último debe comprenderse en su cabal significado: No se trata de incorporar más tecnología ni más información. El problema no es la abundancia, sino la *relevancia* para satisfacer las demandas y requerimientos de información de los distintos sujetos sociales y de la sociedad en su conjunto.

Por otra parte, y sobre esto debemos alertar, lo democratizable no puede limitarse al ámbito del estado. Lo que sí creemos es que los roles del estado en los distintos países deberán estar ligados a la competitividad, al desarrollo, a la equidad, a la consolidación de la sociedad civil, esto es, a la participación ciudadana, a la descentralización y transferencia de competencias a la gestión local, en definitiva, al fortalecimiento de la relación del individuo con lo público. La democratización, como bien indica Sangmeister, "no es una mera cuestión de instituciones, sino también de realización efectiva de los derechos sociales del ciudadano" (1994:188).

Lo democrático, y sobre esto insistimos, no puede quedarse entonces en el ámbito de la institucionalidad estatal, sino que esencialmente pasa por una acción colectiva, por un esfuerzo sinérgico y sistémico, que se construye con la voluntad política de los distintos actores sociales, y que debe surgir de los individuos mismos, de su devenir cotidiano.

En este contexto, situamos nuestra convicción de que las redes de comunicación electrónica, siendo Internet la de mayor predominio, tienen por su misma organización descentralizada, el potencial de permitir un acceso democratizador a la información para los países que conforman este gran conglomerado heterogéneo que es la región latinoamericana. Pero ese potencial no viene dado por la existencia misma de la tecnología, ni siquiera de la información, sino que debe diseñarse, instrumentarse y desarrollarse, es decir volcarse en esfuerzos coherentes y coordinados y concretarse en estrategias, políticas, programas y planes específicos de información e incorporación tecnológica en concordancia con las políticas económicas y sociales de una nación dada.

Nos corresponde, a todos como sujetos sociales que somos, al estado y otros sectores sociales, definir y debatir, sobre cuál información es relevante, sobre su operatividad y viabilidad, sobre el cómo adecuar de manera significativa y ventajosa la transferencia de tecnología y de información a nuestras necesidades de educación, investigación, progreso y participación ciudadana.

De vital importancia y, más aún, imperativo, es el generar y crear fuentes de referencia y de conocimiento confiables y con alto control de calidad relativas a aquellas áreas críticas e imprescindibles para el apoyo a la toma de decisiones de los distintos actores sociales, y en función de los objetivos micro y macrosociales que se pretendan alcanzar. Estos aspectos son medulares en el diseño de políticas nacionales, subregionales y regionales de información. Se trata, pues, en última instancia, de generar e incentivar un uso creativo de la información y la tecnología para así garantizar un valedero retorno social para las naciones latinoamericanas.

Aunque hemos reiteradamente insistido en que es responsabilidad de los estados y de los distintos programas de integración subregional el propiciar políticas nacionales, subregionales y regionales de información y tecnología, somos nosotros los profesionales, las organizaciones no gubernamentales (ONGs), las comunidades universitarias y académicas, los que ocupamos cargos con poder de decisión en las distintas instancias gubernamentales, los agentes últimos del cambio. Es a nosotros como agentes sociales a quienes nos corresponde responsablemente actuar sobre las distintas instancias decisorias, y hacer de las redes telemáticas, redes "humanas" de comunicación que nos permitan incidir de manera organizada sobre los objetivos y acuerdos nacionales, e incluso subregionales y regionales.

A la luz de lo expuesto, consideramos que se hace imperioso aunar voluntades políticas y esfuerzos por "construir nuestra propia imagen" (Barbero 1995:90), por saber de nosotros mismos, por contar nuestra heterogeneidad, y también por comunicarnos en nuestra propia lengua. Articulemos el esfuerzo, con la tecnología que tenemos en nuestras manos, en función de la equidad social, y condición esencial para ello, es la democratización del acceso a la información y a las tecnologías que hacen posible su distribución, "la desconcentración del uso" y la perspectiva del "alcance global" (Barbero 1995:64), la ampliación de la participación ciudadana, y consubstancializado con todo esto, el estímulo al pluralismo ideológico y conceptual.

## América Latina y su presencia en Internet de cara al sur

En un contundente artículo, Carlos Leañez Aristimuño, de la Unión Latina, señale que el español es la segunda lengua de difusión intercontinental: 320 millones de personas que ocupan el 10 por ciento de las tierras del planeta y representan el 6 por ciento de la población mundial son hispanófonos. Es la primera lengua extranjera en los Estados Unidos: en tanto que más del 10 por ciento de sus habitantes hablan español y un creciente número de anglófonos lo aprende, además, es una de las cinco lenguas habladas por más del 10 por ciento de los habitantes de la Unión Europea, y es por supuesto, la lengua principal desde México hasta la Tierra del Fuego. También, prosigue Leañez Aristimuño, es portadora de una de las literaturas más extraordinarias de estos tiempos (Leañez Aristimuño 1996:5).

En franco contraste, sólo el 1 por ciento de la documentación científica es en español. Cabría preguntarse, de los vastísimos recursos existentes en el Internet, qué porcentaje se encuentra en español? ¿Cuántos y qué calidad de esos recursos se corresponden a y con América Latina?

Sin tener datos empíricos exhaustivos sobre esto, basta con una sesión de "navegación" en el Internet, para descubrir sin asombro, que tal y como lo expresa el autor citado, "el español no nos da acceso al mundo contemporáneo" (Leañez Aristimuño 1996:5). La realidad es que el inglés predomina, sin competidor cercano, en la literatura publicada por medios impresos y en el Internet, relativa a áreas del conocimiento que nos son fundamentales para el desarrollo y competitividad tales como bio-medicina, informática, tecnología, gerencia, finanzas, comercio y educación, por mencionar algunas.

En materia de recursos informacionales de y sobre América Latina en el Internet—y aunque existen importantísimos esfuerzos a los cuales me referiré seguidamente—podemos afirmar que en comparación con los recursos que provienen del mundo desarrollado, la desproporción resulta preocupante. En el Internet solo el 0.6 por ciento corresponde a América Latina y el Caribe (Edaz-Albertini 1996). Desde el punto de vista informacional somos "pensados" desde otras latitudes. Carecemos de un espacio discursivo propio: somos un constructo que proviene del norte, que no nos cuenta y que poco nos tome en cuenta. La realidad que confrontamos está signada por una unidimensionalidad norte-sur que debe ser modificada, si en verdad se pretende alcanzar una mayor competitividad internacional y una integración activa—no marginal ni periférica—al devenir histórico mundial.

Sin embargo, tenemos razones para sentirnos optimistas. Hoy por hoy, se están realizando esfuerzos significativos en materia de desarrollo de redes de servicios y comunicación en el Internet desde América Latina, y desde una perspectiva latinoamericanista. Para el último semestre de 1995 la tasa de crecimiento de América Latina en el Internet alcanzó el 62 por ciento comparado con el 42 por ciento de crecimiento para el resto del mundo (Edaz-Albertini 1996). También muestra clara de esta presencia es el recientemente celebrado "V Foro de Redes de América Latina y el Caribe" (Perú, 13–20 de abril de 1996 y el VI Foro, Chile, septiembre 1996) el cual reunió, desde una perspectiva pluralista y auténticamente participativa, a especialistas de distintas disciplinas, verdaderos agentes de cambio y actores comprometidos en estos importantes desarrollos.

Los esfuerzos a los que hacemos mención son provenientes de los sectores universitarios/académicos, de ONGs y de organismos internacionales, como la OEA, LASPAU, la Organización Panamericana de la Salud, por mencionar solo algunos. Mención especial merece el esfuerzo que en la actualidad realiza la Association for Progressive Communications (APC) que conecta en cinco continentes, con particular énfasis en América Latina, 20 redes de ONGs en pro de la paz, la justicia social y económica, la resolución de conflictos, y la defensa del ambiente.

Cabe mencionar que también se han diseñado interesantes programas de interconexión nacional y presencia en el Internet con intervención y subvención directa de los estados. Tal es el caso de Cuba que, pese a sus imponderables dificultades, ha logrado un importante y sistemático desarrollo de su red de información biomédica.

En el caso de Venezuela, se ha diseñado un proyecto de interconexión oficial denominado PLATINO (Plataforma de Información Oficial) que además de aspirar a la interconexión de todas las instancias estatales, de la zona capital, conjuntamente con la plataforma de interconexión universitaria (REACCIUN), aspira a proveer acceso al Internet a escala nacional.

En lo relativo a redes universitarias y académicas, en Venezuela existen dos proyectos, ambos operativos, de interconexión y de enlace al Internet, uno de estos, ya mencionado, es la Red Académica de Centros de Investigación y Universidades Nacionales (REACCIUN) antes SAYCIT instrumentado tempranamente en los años ochenta, concebido como una asociación civil del estado sin fines de lucro y tutelado por el Consejo Nacional de Ciencia y Tecnología (CONICIT), y otro denominado Red Universitaria Nacional (RUN) de más reciente conformación y operatividad.

Los tres proyectos, sustentados en parte por la red de telecomunicaciones que provee la Compañía Nacional de Teléfonos de Venezuela, están teoréticamente concebidos de manera complementaria y suplementaria. Sin embargo, su instrumentación se ha caracterizado por cierta incoherencia de carácter técnico y financiero. Pero estas razones no son las más significativas. Podemos afirmar que la ausencia de una política estructurada de información y de incorporación tecnológica, esto es, de objetivos claros y definidos de desarrollo de una infraestructura nacional de información y tecnología por parte del estado, limita la congruencia y beneficios potenciales de estos proyectos. Pese a ello, y afortunadamente, existe un verdadero esfuerzo y voluntad política provenientes de sectores comprometidos de las universidades nacionales, del CONICIT, IVIC, del sector petrolero con su Red de Información Petrolero y Petroquímica, y la Biblioteca Nacional de Venezuela por consolidar una infraestructura telepática y de servicios de información de alcance nacional y en función de un aprovechamiento integral de los recursos existentes en el Internet.

Por otra parte, en varios países latinoamericanos se han conformado redes universitarias y no gubernamentales de gran alcance y con una realmente significativa presencia en el Internet. Tal es el caso del Perú. Chile, Brasil, Argentina y México dan cuenta de muy significativos desarrollos en materia de redes y de presencia activa en el Internet. Asimismo, esfuerzos sistemáticos de interconexión y de participación en el Internet se están realizando en Ecuador y Bolivia, y con distintos niveles de operatividad, en varios de los países de Centroamérica y del Caribe. Para un análisis e inventario exhaustivo del desarrollo de redes latinoamericanas de interconexión y enlace al Internet, referiremos a los lectores a las ponencias y resoluciones del "V Foro de Redes de América Latina y el Caribe".

## Elementos teoréticos y metodológicos para una política de información y tecnología

Conceptualmente una política es un conjunto de principios, declaraciones, lineamientos, decisiones, instrumentos y mecanismos que persiguen el desarrollo de un sector, en el mediano y largo plazo, dentro del marco de objetivos globales de desarrollo socioeconómico y cultural.

El diseño de una política, específicamente de información y tecnología, pasa por una condición esencial, cual es, la delimitación del alcance que la misma tendrá. Metodológicamente requiere ser diseñada en fases de trabajo que implican un esfuerzo articulado, por una parte, de detección de prioridades de atención, y de determinación de áreas problemáticas o nudos críticos, y por otra parte de determinación de soluciones, tanto informacionales como tecnológicas, que oriente la inversión de recursos financieros, técnicos y humanos.

En términos de su preparación y como fase primera, se recomienda la designación consensual de un comité nacional, integrado por representantes de los sectores involucrados, esto es, profesionales de la información, miembros del sector académico vinculados a la información, miembros de las asociaciones profesionales, decisores activos en instituciones de servicios de información, ciencia y tecnología, y de manera imprescindible, técnicos en planificación provenientes de los organismos nacionales de planificación y desarrollo.

Como premisa teórica fundamental, y en razón de lo arriba expuesto, debe entenderse que las prioridades y el carácter de las soluciones específicas de orden informacional y tecnológico y de investigación y desarrollo deberán estar condicionadas por las prioridades y el contenido de los objetivos socioeconómicos y culturales establecidos en las distintas etapas de la estrategia nacional de desarrollo (Herrera et al. 1994).

De esta manera, entendemos que el diseño de una política de información y tecnología se inscribe dentro de un proceso dialógico que percibimos en una dole vertiente. Por una parte, la estrategia nacional contenida en los megaplanes de desarrollo determina—explícitamente o tácitamente—unas demandas específicas de información y tecnología, y de investigación y desarrollo. Por otra parte, y de ahí su carácter dialógico, la política y estrategia de información y tecnología que se adopte incidirá sobre la factibilidad de realización de las metas y objetivos propuestos en la estrategia de desarrollo nacional.

En definitiva la política que se diseñe debería tener la capacidad de dar respuestas a las demandas sociales y así establecer su necesaria conexión con el sistema productivo, social y cultural. Lo anteriormente dicho se inscribe en un enfoque de trabajo sistémico que tal y como lo expresa Pablo Bifani (1993:103) superaría "las limitaciones de los enfoques vigentes que se restringen a la selección de técnicas dentro de un universo dado, en el caso de la tecnología, y a una asignación presupuestaria de recursos en el caso de la ciencia". Bifani (1993:103) acertadamente apunta que

> es necesario superar el reduccionismo del proceso tradicional de selección tecnológica, definido por una tradición económica que insiste en ver ciencia y tecnología como factores externos, o como la resultante de un proceso decisional donde la variable tecnológica y sus impactos esperados son, en su mayor parte, ignorados.

Nosotros agregaríamos que en el caso de la información, es decir de su producción, organización, sistematización y diseminación, el problema es más grave aún, en tanto que ni siquiera se inscribe dentro de una lógica reduccionista como la que señala Pablo Bifani. En nuestras realidades, la información y su valor social, así como su carácter estratégico en el apoyo a la toma de decisiones y poder de negociación, han sido literalmente ignorados. En el caso específico de Venezuela, y a manera de ejemplo, se han diseñado nueve planes quinquenales de desarrollo y tres planes de ciencia y tecnología sin que explícitamente se la haya otorgado a la información un espacio propio y un peso específico. Nos atreveríamos a asegurar que el caso se repite, con mayor o menor proporción y con distintas variantes, en gran parte de los países latinoamericanos.

## Propuesta de contenido para una política nacional de información y tecnología: lineamientos generales

Lo que a continuación se expone, constituye una aproximación a las posibles áreas genéricas de contenido de una política de información y tecnología, para los ámbitos nacionales, subregionales y regionales.

El diseño de una presencia específica en las redes de comunicación electrónica, aunado al diseño de interconectividad telemática nacional y de provisión de servicios de información que se corresponda con las prioridades de acción detectadas, constituye un aspecto medular de una política de información y tecnología. Es también prioritario la definición de un enfoque dirigido a crear un balance equilibrado entre la tecnología y diseño de redes telemáticas bajo acciones coordinadas de inversión financiera, y el diseño de las aplicaciones informacionales: productos y servicios de información, estos son contenidos que den respuesta efectiva a las necesidades sociales de información. En general, se observa un exagerado sesgo tecnológico, en detrimento del diseño y elaboración de productos de información y servicios en las redes telemáticas.

El objetivo último ha de ser el garantizar las condiciones y capacidades que permitan y amplíen de manera sostenida la equidad y democratización del acceso a la información y a las tecnologías que hacen posible su organización y distribución. Así indica Yushkiavitshus (1994) de Unesco, que existe la necesidad de aproximarse al problema de una política nacional de información desde una perspectiva amplia y comprehensiva adoptando principios y directrices generales que garanticen que las actividades informacionales en el largo plazo contribuyan al desarrollo humano y al crecimiento económico (1994:19).

Las áreas de desarrollo de una política de información y tecnología según Yushkiavitshus (1994) y que aquí subscribimos, pueden clasificarse como sigue:

*1. Desarrollo infraestructural*

Las políticas específicas a ser diseñadas deberán estar dirigidas a incentivar, por una parte, una incorporación tecnológica, esto es desarrollo telemático de redes, coherente y articulado, que garantice una racionalización de la inversión de recursos financieros y aprovechamiento efectivo y eficaz de la tecnología. Así por ejemplo, se podría fomentar el desarrollo de redes conmutadas telemáticas constituyendo de esta manera ambientes de recursos compartidos para las instituciones/clientes, bajo un esquema de costo efectividad que favorezca tanto a los clientes/usuarios como a los proveedores (empresas de telecomunicaciones) de acceso.

De hecho, el diseño de redes telemáticas interconectadas bajo un esquema de alcance subregional y regional constituye una importante área funcional de cooperación cuya factibilidad técnica ya se ha planteado, y que se podría pensar en el marco de los distintos programas subregionales y regionales de cooperación. Sin embargo, su realización y concreción requiere de una voluntad política que haga realmente efectiva las posibilidades técnicas de interconexión e intercambio de información para los países de la región.

Por otra parte, deberán diseñarse políticas dirigidas a incentivar el desarrollo de recursos, productos y servicios de información que se correspondan orgánicamente con las prioridades y necesidades sociales de información. Asimismo, se deberán diseñar e instrumentar políticas y planes de fomento para la creación, sistematización, organización de la información, así como el fomento y desarrollo de una industria nacional de información.

*2. Desarrollo de recursos humanos calificados*

El área de formación de recursos humanos constituye uno de los aspectos medulares y de mayor importancia dentro de una política de información y tecnología. Se requiere de manera impostergable, definir perfiles de profesionalización para el sector de la información, dirigidos a desarrollar capacidades y habilidades para la creación de valor agregado a la información, esto es habilidades para detectar, analizar, sintetizar, interpretar y evaluar información y conocimiento con un pensamiento crítico, y desde una perspectiva inter y multidisciplinaria. Capacidades y habilidades técnicas que garanticen un uso eficiente y eficaz de las tecnologías; capacidades gerenciales que partan de principios de análisis, planificación, instrumentación, y control de calidad en el diseño de productos y servicios de información en ambientes integrados; y por último capacidades para la comprensión del entorno macrosocial, de las exigencias de la realidad nacional y regional en materia de información y diseño de servicios.

El desarrollo de capacitación de recursos humanos es quizás una de las áreas más factible a ser atendida como un proyecto funcional de cooperación dentro de los planes subregionales y regionales de integración en América Latina. Consideramos que estamos en una coyuntura que hace impostergable el diseño de un postgrado en estudios de la información y redes, de cobertura regional.

Por último, no podemos soslayar el hecho de que una estrategia nacional de información y tecnología debería fomentar políticas específicas que otorguen un justo valor salarial al profesional de la información.

*3. Desarrollo de mecanismos de diseminación, distribución y transferencia de información destinados a optimizar el uso de redes y sistemas de comunicación*

En esta área se requiere del diseño de políticas específicas que garanticen una transferencia adecuada de información intergubernamental, y de movilización de datos transfronteras que garanticen la seguridad y soberanía nacionales, así como políticas que fomenten una adecuada determinación de costos de producción de la información y comercialización de la misma.

*4. Definición de un marco de acción jurídico-legal relativo a la información*

Se trata de diseñar políticas específicas destinadas a garantizar la privacidad individual, la soberanía nacional, a regir la propiedad intelectual, a garantizar un adecuado enriquecimiento de la memoria y acervos documentales bibliográficos y no bibliográficos de las naciones: leyes de depósito legal, entre otras acciones. Corresponde a esta cuarta área de desarrollo el fomento de estándares, incentivos y regulaciones en el contexto de la relación del sector público con el sector privado para el desarrollo del sector de la información.

## A manera de epílogo

A la luz de todo lo expuesto en esta ponencia, creemos fehacientemente que el objetivo y fin último ha de ser el fortalecimiento de la relación horizontal Sur-Sur. Debemos ser agentes activos del cambio y concebir una visión clara de las sociedades que queremos construir (Herrera et al. 1994). En esta visión deberán basarse nuestras estrategias de información y tecnología, nuestra participación activa en el Internet, y—de manera insoslayable—el diseño de nuestras propias fuentes de información y el uso creativo y ventajoso que podamos darle a los recursos informacionales que provienen de otras regiones del mundo accesibles en el Internet, y en otras redes de redes; pero esto requiere un esfuerzo sistémico y sinérgico, sistemático y coherente que parta de lo nacional y devenga en "panhispánico" (Leañez Aristimuño 1996:5): un esfuerzo cuyos primeros pasos ya estamos dando, y que definitivamente coloque al sur de cara al sur.

Para finalizar, quisiéramos cerrar con Bernardo Kliksberg (1994) quien nos señala que progreso es lograr equilibrios macroeconómicos, aumentar la esperanza de vida, que los individuos incrementen el control sobre sus vidas, es darle acceso a los bienes culturales, y a un conjunto de elementos que hacen a la esencia del ser humano como entidad pensante, libre y participativa.

## REFERENCIAS

Avalos, Ignacio. 1991. "La política tecnológica venezolana: de la economía protegida a la economía abierta". *Espacio* 12 (2), 32–39.

Barbero, Jesús Martín. 1995. "La comunicación plural: paradojas y desafíos". *Nueva Sociedad* 140: 60–69.

Bifani, Pablo. 1993. "Cambio tecnológico y política científica y tecnológica". En Eduardo Martínez, ed., *Estrategias, planificación y gestión de ciencia y tecnología*, pp. 99–124. Caracas: Editorial Nueva Sociedad.

Edaz-Albertini, Javier. 1996. "Evaluación del impacto social de la Red Científica Peruana e Internet en el Perú 1991–1995". Ponencia presentada en el V Foro de Redes de América Latina y el Caribe. Lima, Perú del 13 al 20 de abril.

Ferrero Costa, Eduardo. 1994. "La integración en América Latina: situación actual y perspectivas". En Manfred Mols et al., eds., *Cambio de paradigmas en América Latina: nuevos impulsos, nuevos temores*, pp. 131–140. Caracas: Editorial Nueva Sociedad.

Herrera, Amilcar, et al. 1994. *Las nuevas tecnologías y el futuro de América Latina: riesgo y oportunidad*. México, D.F.: Siglo XXI Editores.

Kliksberg, Bernardo. 1994. "El rediseño del estado para el desarrollo socioeconómico y el cambio: una agenda estratégica para la discusión". *Reforma y Democracia. Revista del CLAD* 2:115–142.

Leañez Aristimuño, Carlos. 1996. "Auge o caída de española". *El Nacional,* 21 de abril, p. 5.

Sangmeister, Harmut. 1994. "El cambio de paradigmas: adios al desarrollismo y al cepalismo". En Manfred Mols et al., eds., *Cambio de paradigmas en América Latina: nuevos impulsos, nuevos temores*, pp. 179–190. Caracas: Editorial Nueva Sociedad.

Soriano de García Pelayo, Graciela. 1996. *El personalismo político hispanoamericano del siglo XIX: criterios y proposiciones metodológicas para su estudio*. Caracas: Monte Avila Editores Latinoamericana, C.A.

Yushkiavitshus, Henrikas. 1994. "Information Policies and Economics". En R. Alvarez-Ossorio y B. G. Goedegebuure, eds., *New Worlds in Information and Documentation*, pp. 17–21. Amsterdam: Elsevier.

# 23. More Programs, Fewer Voices: Caribbean Television in the Global Era

Elizabeth Mahan
Adolfo Vargas

In this paper we explore the cultural impact of the globalization of mass media programming, with particular emphasis on television in the Caribbean region. We do not present new findings on this topic, but rather review a number of old arguments and assess evidence presented by others in support of them in light of new thinking (if not always evidence) about how the production and consumption of mass media messages are implicated in the construction and evolution of cultural identity.

The Caribbean region provides an ideal arena for re-examining these themes. The sameness of the mass media "diet" offered to citizens of the Caribbean region points to a possible homogenization of aspects popular culture, while the apparent diversity of Caribbean cultures undermines the fears of those who see cultural destruction or homogenization as the inevitable outcome of the globalization of television and other forms of mass culture. At the same time, however, the persistence and renewal of distinctive cultural identities (the local in the global) can obscure unsettling political implications of increasing global economic integration.

## The Problem of Caribbean Culture

When scholars speak of Caribbean culture or identity, one suspects they are referring to an essence, something felt, perhaps, throughout the region. For Antonio Benítez Rojo (1992), the essence is rhythm, a pace and attitude that emanate from the African roots of Caribbean cultures, assuming new but related forms (repetitions) throughout the history of the *colonized* Caribbean. Like Sidney Mintz (1971), Benítez Rojo finds the basis of the common patterns among Caribbean cultures in the plantation and slavery, which explain greater degrees of Africanness within some Caribbean societies and the greater or lesser consolidation of a national identity within what came to be the independent nations of the region (Mintz 1971:32-35; Benítez Rojo 1992:33-81). The plantation and slavery gave rise to a particular experience of colonialism that created two-tier societies in which the dominant culture forbade or severely circumscribed overt expressions of subaltern—that is, slave or Afro-Caribbean—culture. When slavery ceased to be the basis of plantation labor, the two-tier structure remained, as did metropolitan cultural norms.[1]

Other scholars add the phenomenon of migration to the core experiences that have shaped, and continue to shape, Caribbean identity. The region owes its very existence as a sociocultural area to migration. But migration "... affects and alters both ... origins and destinations at the same time" (Richardson 1989: 223), suggesting that the processes that have been shaping Caribbean culture(s) also affect the metropolitan cultures that are the destinations of the migrants. From this perspective, manifestations of so-called American culture—McDonalds, Coca-Cola, blue jeans, tee shirts, rock music, and consumer products like twelve brands of shampoo and seven of toothpaste—may offer less evidence of cultural imperialism than of what Fernando Ortiz (1995) called transculturation and Néstor García Canclini (1990, 1992, 1993, 1994, and 1995) hybridization.

The plantation and slavery, the class structure bequeathed by colonialism, and migration have created a cultural mosaic: an arrangement of seemingly random bits and pieces that, viewed from a distance, reveals patterns and, perhaps, a whole, coherent picture. Caribbean peoples themselves experience this mosaic at the level of the pieces, although they often speak of Caribbean culture. This means that Jamaicans do not "feel" like Puerto Ricans; coastal Colombians and Venezuelans feel and, indeed, are different from Haitians, who in turn are culturally different from Dominicans; nevertheless, viewing the mosaic from afar, we can identify common elements and patterns, usually linked to African roots and, increasingly, to the availability and consumption of the kinds of consumer goods mentioned earlier. Far from exposing cultural homogenization, these manifestations of the age of globalization are the façade of an unbalanced, *interdependent* relationship between different nations and cultural complexes.

## The Global Communications Order

If the slave trade and plantation were the institutions responsible for the transculturation of African elements into Caribbean culture, the mass media—specifically commercial media—are their contemporary counterparts, bringing products, narratives, and images of one particular experience of modernity into the context of Caribbean modernity. These new pieces are incorporated into the mosaic—they do not replace it—to be experienced at the local level as elements of local culture, based on how the products, narratives, and images are used, which is, ultimately, the source of their meaning. From a distance, the mosaic will have changed, but at the level of local experience, the culture probably *feels* the same. Commercial mass media thus offer elements—advertisements as well as programs—that mingle with existing cultural patterns and practices to create new, hybridized cultures that remain distinct at the level of experience.

Nevertheless, something else occurs in the process of transculturation that affirms the uneasiness of those who, in the 1970s, feared the global spread of U.S. mass culture. To them, the transmission of media messages from the core to the periphery represented a new phase of imperialism—cultural imperialism—intended to re-colonize the Third World. Consumers of mass media messages were viewed as passive recipients of alien cultural norms.[2]

Research in anthropology and cultural studies since the late 1970s has cast doubt on the notion that traditional cultures were being or could be transformed into carbon copies of the United States. We have learned that cultural identity is not fixed or imposed by dominant powers or classes on subordinate peoples. It is created by all people out of the elements at hand, which include unequal social, political, and economic relations as well as whatever material resources may be available. Subaltern cultural identity and the practices that express it may oppose a dominant order, they may support it in contradictory ways, or they may impel changes in it. In reworking cultural identities, subaltern peoples create new ones, not mere derivatives of something better or more authentic from the past, or something borrowed from elites, but they do not change the underlying conditions of their subordination.

Like the critics of cultural imperialism, García Canclini places the production and consumption of mass media products and messages at the center of the problem of cultural identity. He argues, however, that the mass media have a simultaneous, dual effect, a tendency to integrate and to dissolve cultural identities. These tendencies do not move inexorably in the direction of acculturation (assimilation to the cultural norms of another group or society) or deculturation (the loss of one's own cultural identity); rather, they move toward the creation of new, hybrid cultures and new, hybridized identities (1990:268-269).

That these cultural transactions and transformations occur largely through market mechanisms does not mean that innovation and creativity are squelched. Indeed, the market demands these forces, which explains why traditional and so-called popular cultural expressions constantly reappear in new products. Although all that mass culture appropriates elements of popular culture and transforms them into mass media merchandise, these processes do not homogenize culture completely. The capacity to re-create, *to hybridize,* cultural differences is inevitable. Latin American and Caribbean societies are thus multidimensional, inherently multicultural.

Even so, the consolidation of mass media empires within nations and transnationally, which the critics of cultural imperialism viewed with such alarm, continued at a rapid pace during the 1980s. One vehicle of this arguably new order was conglomeration, the creation of media empires in Japan, Europe, and Latin America (in Brazil, Mexico, and Venezuela, in particular) that challenged the U.S. giants, some of which were themselves being incorporated into non–U.S. transnationals. Another instrument of the new order was co-production, which allowed U.S. producers and distributors to circumvent program quotas at the cost of permitting more open access to the U.S. domestic market. The reality underlying both these phenomena was (and is) transnationalization or globalization: the emergence of a single global market for cultural and other consumer products.[3]

What distinguished this reality from the vision feared by the critics of cultural imperialism was that the global cultural enterprises developed astute, segmented marketing strategies to sell the same product to culturally diverse audiences. According to one independent producer, programs ". . . can work in multiple global markets 'so long as the themes deal with primary human emotions'. . ." (Amdur 1993:17). Producers and distributors confirm that the global market they imagined in the early 1980s is in the process of formation, but they are aware, too, that they must maneuver carefully in this market. Some produce programs for regional markets, with segments that can be added or deleted to tailor the production to local audience taste. For example, *Sábado Gigante*, one of the most popular Spanish-language programs in the world, is produced both in Chile and Florida. Although the two programs were initially distinct, because of a belief that the tastes of the Chilean/Latin American audience differed from those of U.S. Latinos, elements of the show produced in each location are now added to the other version.[4] The show's longtime host, Don Francisco, goes one step further, acknowledging and advocating the power of television programs to mold audience tastes toward a pan-Latin culture, the foundation (and, at the same time, the superstructure) of an integrated Latin American market. According to Don Francisco, "Television production for Latin America ought to create a Latin American culture. Hispanic America must become like the European Community. That's the only way we can have a large enough market, the only way to be important" (Silva 1991:56).

To be competitive, producers must sell as few programs as possible to the widest audience possible. They believe, on the whole, that the global market can accommodate cultural difference because it is ". . . an increasingly fractionalized viewing environment in which marketing is king" (Tobenkin 1994:36.)[5] A by-product of this thinking is the proliferation of programs accompanied by a loss of program diversity. Thus, the global cultural market is the site of paradox: more programs and fewer voices speaking to larger and increasingly avid audiences.[6]

## Television in the Caribbean

New communications technologies have spurred the trend toward globalization because they are efficient and difficult to regulate. Consumers who can afford VCRs, satellite dishes, and computers buy them throughout Latin America and the Caribbean. The influx of these technologies represents a new, perhaps more intensive phase in the circular cultural processes of the Caribbean. Most of these devices enter the region with *return* migrants from the United States, or they are purchased with the help of remittances sent home by migrants. Not only located in upper- and upper-middle-class households, these new means for receiving foreign programs and films, coupled with a robust piracy industry, are also spreading throughout the Caribbean region. Whatever impact they have, however, is *in addition* to that of existing television systems and film-going options, which are already heavily dominated by programming from the United States, Venezuela, Brazil, Argentina, and Mexico.

If overwhelmingly commercial television, carrying mostly foreign programming and advertisements for transnational consumer products, does not offer much "authentic" visual culture to viewers, it does appear to integrate the entertainment and consumer markets throughout the Caribbean region into the global cultural industry in a permanently dependent position. This is a structural reality, but what does it tell us about how audiences understand the messages carried on Caribbean television systems?

To answer this question, we reviewed several studies on the production, distribution, and/or consumption of mass media in the Caribbean region, whose separate conclusions contradict each other but suggest what may be at stake in the globalization of cultural markets, if not of culture itself. It may be significant to note at the outset that none of the four studies we comment upon here either defines or describes Caribbean culture, although all use this concept.

Monica Payne's study of the reception of *The Cosby Show* in Barbados asked adults of different social classes to rate North American (i.e., U.S.) television programs as negative or positive influences on young people. She was particularly interested in the ". . . relevance and suitability of [*The Cosby Show*] for Caribbean viewers" (1994:241). Although her survey data revealed that adult viewers especially liked and enjoyed *The Cosby Show* and thought it presented "good" images of family life and gender roles, Payne's conclusions derive from the small percentage of viewers who felt the program might be inappropriate for Caribbean [*sic*] viewers, undercutting traditional values (such as male dominance). Most of the respondents expressing this view were non-manual workers, both male and female, concerned about the negative impact of *The Cosby Show* on manual workers, people who, they seemed to believe, could not hope to emulate the lifestyle portrayed (Payne 1994:242). Payne ignores the historical basis of the class tensions in Barbados that her findings reveal, pointing instead to the "possible influence of foreign media" in the elaboration of those class relations (p. 245).

In their study of the reception of cable and broadcast television in the Dominican Republic, Joseph Straubhaar and Gloria Viscasillas found that Dominican cable TV viewers watch more English-language programming than those whose options are limited to broadcast TV, in part because cable carries more English-language programs. They found that cable TV viewers *wanted* to view these programs as a way to learn English, which would help prepare them for jobs in tourism and multinational firms (Straubhaar and Viscasillas 1990:277-279). The authors hedge their conclusions about the impact of cable (i.e., foreign) programming on Dominicans, pointing instead to what may be the most significant impact of television globalized under the logic of the free market: the inculcation of consumption (and buying) habits.

Marlene Cuthbert and Stewart Hoover studied the use of VCRs in Barbados and Grenada. In both countries, VCR ownership is distributed throughout the population, with lower-class owners being the biggest customers for rented tapes. Both the technology and the tapes themselves are of foreign origin, especially the United States. The authors cite unspecified respondents' concerns about ". . . the erosion of traditional values, and the irrelevance of foreign video images to black Caribbean culture and values . . . [and] the erosion of the values of rural agricultural societies in which the extended family and village were the basic social units" (Cuthbert and Hoover 1990: 294).

Cuthbert and Hoover pass over this problematic assumption about the relationship of video to local culture, instead seeing cultural imperialism at work in the structure of the VCR market. They explain the lack of locally produced videos in shops in Barbados as the result of the negative repercussions of the Berne Convention on copyright, which would require local stations to pay royalties to local producers, thereby making the cost of running local productions prohibitive.

These observations about the negative side of copyright underline significant realities for TV and video producers in the Caribbean (or any other country or region where audiovisual production tends not to be profitable). First, the global information and communication order includes artists as well as media systems and audiences. Programs have to sell to be seen, and artists, too, expect to make money from their labors. Second, independent producers (like the Barbadian video artists) are excluded from the economies of scale afforded the transnational communications conglomerates. By implying that national artists should be more altruistic, Cuthbert and Hoover fail to acknowledge that the same economic system that brings a preponderance of foreign cultural content into the Caribbean also impels local artists to opt out of the local market. If independent artists want to distribute their productions *anywhere* and make money, they have to work through a transnational distributor. This means adjusting their artistic vision to the norms and standards of the global, commercial market, standards set by the U.S. film and video production industries (Folsie 1991: 42), but no longer necessarily foreign to Caribbean producers or audiences.[7]

In the final study we examined, Stuart Surlin attempts to determine the extent to which exposure to foreign media correlates with cultural attitudes (which presumably might become behaviors) favorable to that foreign culture. According to his survey, Montserratian college students watch more U.S.

television than Canadian, Jamaican, and even U.S. students, but they exhibit the highest level of "cultural consciousness," that is, a strong sense of unique cultural identity. Despite its limitations, Surlin's study offers an intriguing response to Cuthbert and Hoover and Payne, for it concludes that "the further apart mediated culture is from the viewer's culture, the less likely mediated culture can be used to disassociate from one's indigenous culture" (Surlin 1990:313). Surlin argues that viewers appear to have some degree of control over how they are influenced by television messages. On the one hand, if they value their own culture, foreign programs can be innocuous, merely entertaining. On the other hand, if viewers wish to learn new ways of being (for whatever reason), U.S. or other foreign programming might become a vehicle for this.

Though contradictory, the findings of these four studies bring the evaluation of cultural influence back to questions of political economy. The structure and dynamics of the global market limit the options for a truly free flow of cultural messages and productions, even as new technologies increase the volume of that flow. Options for production have expanded tremendously but profitable distribution networks are contracting. Entry into the global cultural market depends on the coherence between the vision of the artist and the so-called mass culture. Audiences apparently can consume vast quantities of "foreign" programming without losing a sense of their cultural identity.

## Conclusion: The Political Economy of Global Culture

Despite manifestations of globalized cultural consumption, no country can claim by and for itself an uncontested cultural superiority or hegemony (García Canclini 1992:30). New communications technologies increase opportunities to produce political and cultural statements and offer new means for receiving a hypothetical multitude of voices. Individuals and organizations have incredible possibilities to produce and disseminate their own versions of truth or reality. Still, most people's media and information "diet," in the industrialized countries and in sociocultural areas like the Caribbean, remains relatively sparse, a turn of events that leads García Canclini and his colleagues to argue that we have entered the age of the "simulacrum of information democracy" (1993:88; 1994).

The real impact of the ideas and versions of reality constructed by individuals and groups will be associated with the mix of possibilities presented by the media used to disseminate them, as much as by the ideas themselves. In Latin America and the Caribbean, these media are dominated by global cultural conglomerates, notably Globo in Brazil, Televisa in Mexico, and Venevisión in Venezuela, the latter two of which have formed joint ventures as partial owners of Univision, a U.S. Hispanic television network, to distribute their individually produced programming internationally. No producers—anywhere—can stay in business by addressing only a local audience (Amdur 1992:6).[8]

The growth of the three Latin American communications "empires"—Globo, Televisa, and Venevisión—did not change the political economy of cultural production for the rest of Latin America and the Caribbean. These conglomerates operate according to transnational media management criteria, which have allowed them to gain almost total control of their national markets and the regional Latin American–Caribbean market, and to expand into the international market, where they are subject to the same pressures as U.S., European, and Japanese competitors, with which they also have joint ventures. The Latin American "Big Three" compete *and* cooperate in the international market, and use as comparative advantage the existence of a huge Latin American, Caribbean, and Latino population as a primary target audience with wide possibilities for consumption. Their operations confirm the hegemonic tenacity of the "free flow" paradigm: they increase the volume of the commercial traffic in cultural goods, while limiting options for the distribution of alternative, minority, or noncommercial programming.

Concepts like transculturation and hybridization help us understand the resilience of cultural identity, but they also underscore the endurance of unequal power relations. Thus, while new communications technologies have widened dramatically the possibilities for individuals and groups to express their opinions, this flowering has been accompanied by a contraction in the number and types of distribution networks that can reach more than small, local audiences. The market still dictates that media programming garner large audiences to remain economically viable, which often means that controversial themes and topics as well as new voices are excluded or repackaged into seemingly neutral entertainment. To date, the so-called democratization of communications promised by the new technologies has yielded only some increases in viewing choices but little change in the options for placing alternative opinions or forms of expression within the easy reach of a large number of consumers. In the final analysis, the genius—good or evil—of the global communication order resides in its ability to create cultural markets in which to sell images of diversity, difference, and democracy, while concentrating the economic and political power of media in fewer and fewer hands.

## NOTES

1. This leads Mintz to argue that the Caribbean has always been a "westernized" socio-cultural area (1971:18).

2. See, for example, Luis Rammer Beltrán, "Alien Premises, Objects and Methods in Latin American Communication Research," in Everett M. Rogers, ed., *Communication and Development: Critical Perspectives* (Beverly Hills: Sage, 1976), pp. 15–42; Tapio Varis, "Global Traffic in Television," *Journal of Communication* 24 (Winter 1974), 103–109; and his follow-up study, "The International Flow of Television Programs," *Journal of Communication* (Winter 1984), 143–152. Varis found little change in the overall pattern of international TV program distribution after ten years of debate over the "free flow" of information. U.S. programming still dominated the global flow, although regional producers and distributors, especially in Latin America, were beginning to make inroads into the U.S. dominance.

3. See Noreene Janus, "Advertising and the Creation of Global Markets: The Role of New Technologies," in V. Mosco and J. Wasko, eds., *Critical Communications Review*, vol. 2 (Norwood, NJ: Ablex, 1984), pp. 57–70; and Noreene Janus, "Advertising and the Mass Media in the Era of the Global Corporation," in E. McAnany et al., eds., *Communication and Social Structure* (New York: Praeger, 1981), pp. 287–316.

4. *Sábado Gigante* follows the pattern of other international productions that offer options for customization according to perceptions of audience taste. See Amadur (1992:10).

5. The experience of Univision, the U.S. Spanish-language television network, seems to confirm this. The changes in ownership that gave the Mexican communications giant Televisa and its Venezuelan counterpart, Venevisión, each a 12.5 percent stake in Univision resulted in the elimination of some U.S.–produced shows and their substitution by Mexican programs, which were not initially popular with the audience. Before long, however, audiences accepted the new programming, and Univision's market share rose to about 70 percent (*Broadcasting*, February 14, 1994, p. 61). See also Rik Turner and Delinda Karle, "Shops See Unity of Latin America," *Advertising Age* 63 (April 27, 1992), pp. 14, 138. Elizabeth Mahan, "Culture Industries and Cultural Identities: Will NAFTA Make a Difference?," *Studies in Latin American Popular Culture* 14 (1995), 17–35, documents the segmented marketing of *tejano* music in the United States and Mexico.

6. See Gabriel Escobar and Anne Swardson, "From Monroe Doctrine to MTV Doctrine," *The Washington Post National Weekly Edition,* September 11–17, 1995, pp. 17–18.

7. Ingrid Sarti discusses the pressures on independent video producers in Brazil to conform to commercial models once they joined the Globo organization. See her "Between Memory and Illusion: Independent Video in Brazil," in Elizabeth Fox, ed., *Mass Media and Politics in Latin America* (London: Sage, 1989), pp. 157–163.

8. Joint ventures, like those of Venevisión and Televisa, are the mark of the current phase of the globalization of cultural markets. Joint ventures now link, or soon will, the U.S., Latin American, Caribbean, European, and Asian markets, not always under the dominant control of a U.S or European corporation.

Among the transnational joint ventures reported recently in the media trade press are the following: Venevisión with Spain's Tele-Cinco, which is owned by the Italian Berlusconi Group, to produce the *telenovela La Mujer Prohibida*, which is distributed throughout Latin America as well as in Spain and the United States; Spelling Entertainment (U.S.) with Multivisión (Mexico) for the cable channel Tele-Uno in Mexico; Tele-Communications Inc., the largest cable operator in the United States, with a 49 percent share in Televisa's Cablevisión SA; Sony Pictures Entertainment (Japan–U.S.) with HBO Ole, which is owned by HBO and Omnivision Latin American Entertainment, Inc.; Telemundo (U.S.), Reuters (Great Britain), Artear S.A. (Argentina), Antena 3

(Spain), and Productora y Comercializadora de Televisión S.A. de México to inaugurate a twenty-four-hour news service aimed at the global Spanish-speaking audience, which numbers some 380 million persons; Grupo Abril (Brazil) with HBO (U.S.) to provide HBO in Portuguese (with backing from Sony and Time-Warner); Venevisión International (Venezuelan, based in Miami) with Fremantle International (U.S.) to produce and market game shows in major Hispanic markets; GM Hughes (U.S.) with the Cisneros Group (Venezuela, owners of Venevisión), Televisão Abril (Brazil), and Multivisión de México for DirectTV, a direct-to-home satellite television service; and Alpha Lyracom Space Communications with Televisa for PanAmSat, a direct broadcast television system that will cover Latin America. See "Hispanic Cable Network Planned by Venevisión," *Broadcasting* 120 (June 17, 1992), p. 40; *Broadcasting* 122 (October 26, 1992), pp. 34, 67; Joe Flint, "Bart and Company Make a Run for the Border," *Broadcasting and Cable* 123 (July 31, 1993), p. 16; "Wheeling and Dealing in Miami Beach," *Broadcasting and Cable* 124 (January 31, 1994), p. 34; Steven Coe, "Sony Teams with HBO Ole," *Broadcasting and Cable* 124 (January 31, 1994), p. 35; Meredith Amdur and Nick Bell, "MIP TV Markets Rebounds," *Broadcasting and Cable* 124 (April 25, 1994), p. 36; Michael Connor/Reuters, March 9, 1995, distributed by C-reuters@clarinet.com; and "Gran alianza de gigantes de la comunicación," *El Diario/La Prensa*, November 22, 1995, p. 43.

## REFERENCES


Amdur, Meredith. 1992. "MIPCOM Lesson: No Country Is an Island." *Broadcasting* 122 (October 19), pp. 6, 10.

_______. 1993. "On the Table at Monte Carlo." *Broadcasting* 123 (February 15), pp. 16–17.

Benítez Rojo, Antonio. 1992. *The Repeating Island: The Caribbean and the Postmodern Perspective.* Trans. James E. Maraniss. Durham, NC: Duke University Press.

Cuthbert, Marlene, and Stewart Hoover. 1990. "Laissez-Faire Policies, VCRs and Caribbean Identity." In Stuart H. Surlin and Walter C. Soderlund, eds., *Mass Media and the Caribbean,* pp. 287–298. New York: Gordon and Breach

Folsie, Geoffrey. 1991. "International Television: A Flatter World?" *Broadcasting* 121 (October 7), p. 42.

García Canclini, Néstor. 1995. *Hybrid Cultures: Strategies for Entering and Leaving Modernity.* Trans. Christopher L. Chiappari and Silvia L. López. Minneapolis: University of Minnesota Press, 1995.

______. 1994. "Cultura popular: de la épica al simulacro." Paper presented at the Fourth Conference on Latin American Popular Culture, Providence, RI, October 27–29.

_______.1993. "The Hybrid: A Conversation with Margarita Zires, Raymundo Mier, and Mabel Piccini." In John Beverley and José Oviedo, eds., *The Postmodernism Debate in Latin America.* Trans. Michael Aronna. *Boundary 2: An International Journal of Literature and Culture* 20:3 (Fall), 77–92.

_______. 1992. "Cultural Reconversion." In George Yúdice, Juan Flores, and Jean Franco, eds., *On Edge: The Crisis of Contemporary Latin American Culture,* pp. 29–43. Minneapolis: University of Minnesota Press

_______. 1990. *Culturas híbridas: estrategias para entrar y salir de la modernidad.* México: Grijalbo.

Mintz, Sidney. 1971. "The Caribbean as a Socio-Cultural Area." In Michael Horowitz, ed., *Peoples and Cultures of the Caribbean: An Anthropological Reader,* pp. 17–46. Garden City, NY: Natural History Press.

Ortiz, Fernando. 1995. *Cuban Counterpoint: Tobacco and Sugar*. Trans. Harriet de Onís. Durham, NC: Duke University Press.

Payne, Monica A. 1994. "The 'Ideal' Black Family? A Caribbean View of 'The Cosby Show'." *Journal of Black Studies* 25 (December), 231–249.

Richardson, Bonhom C. 1989. "Caribbean Migrations, 1838–1985." In Franklin Knight and Colin A. Palmer, eds., *The Modern Caribbean,* pp. 203–228. Chapel Hill: University of North Carolina Press.

Silva, Samuel. 1991. "The Latin Superchannels." *World Press Review* (November), p. 56.

Straubhaar, Joseph, and Gloria Viscasillas. 1990. "Effects of Cable TV in the Dominican Republic." In Stuart H. Surlin and Walter C. Soderlund, eds., *Mass Media and the Caribbean,* pp. 273–286. New York: Gordon and Breach.

Surlin, Stuart H. 1990. "Caribbean Cultural Identification, Cultural Consciousness and Mass Media Imperialism." In Stuart H. Surlin and Walter C. Soderlund, eds., *Mass Media and the Caribbean,* pp. 299–317. New York: Gordon and Breach.

Tobenkin, David. 1994. "Marketing Is Rex in New Orleans." *Broadcasting and Cable* 124 (June 6), pp. 36–44.

# Contributors

JERRY W. CARLSON, City College, City University of New York

JESÚS CORTÉS, to come

PAUL CONWAY, Yale University

GEORGETTE M. DORN, Hispanic Division, Library of Congress

NELLY S. GONZÁLEZ, University of Illinois at Urban-Champaign

DEBORAH JAKUBS, Duke University

SARAH LANDERYOU, University of Denver

JESÚS LAU, Universidad Autónoma de Ciudad Juárez

ELIZABETH MAHAN, University of Connecticut

FILIBERTO F. MARTÍNEZ ARELLANO, State University of New York at Buffalo

DÉBORA MAZZA, Universidade Estadual Paulista

ROBERT W. MCCHESNEY, University of Wisconsin, Madison

MOLLY MOLLOY, New Mexico State University

MARKUS OBERT, Iberoamerikanisches Institut

LOUIS A. RACHOW, International Theater Institute of the United States

KAREN RANUCCI, International Media Resource Exchange

MICHELE M. REID, South Dakota State Library

KETTY RODRÍGUEZ, Texas Woman's University

LEILA MARIA FERREIRA SALLES, Universidade Estadual Paulista

SAADIA SÁNCHEZ VEGAS, Biblioteca Nacional de Venezuela

SUSAN SHAW, South Dakota State University

BARBARA STEWART, University of Massachusetts, Amherst

VÍCTOR F. TORRES-ORTIZ, Universidad de Puerto Rico

ADOLFO VARGAS, Universidad Simón Bolívar

EDUARDO VILLANUEVA MANSILLA, Pontífica Universidad Católica del Perú

LUIS M. VILLAR, Dartmouth College

GAYLE ANN WILLIAMS, University of Georgia

# Conference Program

**Monday, June 3, 1996**

| | |
|---|---|
| 9:00-10:00 A.M. | **Inaugural Session**<br>Eisner and Lubin Auditorium |
| Opening | *Peter Stern*<br>SALALM President<br>Rutgers University |
| Welcome | *Carlton Rochell*<br>Dean, Division of Libraries<br>New York University |
| | *Christopher Mitchell*<br>Director, Center for Latin American & Caribbean Studies<br>New York University |
| | *Douglas Chalmers*<br>Director, Institute of Latin American and Iberian Studies<br>Columbia University |
| José Torbio Medina Award | *Paula Covington*<br>Vanderbilt University |
| Welcome and Announcements | *Angela Carreño*<br>Local Arrangements<br>New York University |
| 10:00-10:30 A.M. | Book Exhibit Coffee Break |
| 10:30-11:30 A.M. | **Keynote Address** |
| | Rapporteur: *Thomas H. Marshall*<br>University of Arizona |
| | *Robert McChesney,* University of Wisconsin, Madison<br>"The Communications Revolution and the Assault on Democracy" |

| | |
|---|---|
| 11:30 A.M.-2:15 P.M. | **NYU International Visitor**<br>*José Soriano*: Red Científica Peruana<br>"El desarrollo de las redes en América Latina y el Caribe: El caso de la RCP" |
| 12:15-1:30 P.M. | Lunch |
| 1:30-2:15 P.M. | Travel to The New York Public Library |
| 2:30-2:45 P.M. | Celeste Bartos Forum, NYPL |
| Welcoming Remarks | *Paul LeClerc*<br>President, The New York Public Library<br><br>*Robert Marx*<br>Associate Director, Performing Arts Library for The New York Public Library |
| 2:30-4:30 P.M. | **Theme Panel I: "Song, Dance, Screen and State: Collecting in the Performing Arts"**<br><br>Moderator: *Denise Hibay*, The New York Public Library<br>Rapporteur: *Peter S. Bushnell*, University of Florida<br><br>*Peter Manuel,* John Jay College, CUNY<br>"Latin American Music: A Scholar's Perspective"<br><br>*Madeline Nichols*, Performing Arts Library, The New York Public Library<br>"Acts of Trust: The Americas Exchange Program for Dance"<br><br>*Jerry Carlson*, City College, CUNY<br>"The Boom Wasn't Just Novels: The Importance of Audiovisual Archives for Understanding Modern Latin American Culture"<br><br>*Louis Rachow*, International Theater Institute of the United States<br>"Collective Memory of a Continent: The Theater of Latin America Collection" |
| 4:30-6:00 P.M. | Opening Reception<br>Celeste Bartos Forum, NYPL |
| 7:00-8:30 P.M. | Meeting of the ARL Latin Americanist Research Resources Pilot Project Participants |

**Tuesday, June 4, 1996**

9:00-10:30 A.M. **Theme Panel II: "CD-ROMs and Multimedia in Latin America"**

Moderator: *Laurence Hallewell*, Columbia University
Rapporteur: *Cecila Puerto*, San Diego State University

*Cavan McCarthy*, Universidade Federal de Pernambuco
"Brazilian CD-ROMs as Informational and Reference Resources"

*Georgette M. Dorn*, Library of Congress
"The Archive of Hispanic Literature on Tape in the Cybernetic Age"

*Clayton Kirking,* Parsons School of Design
"20th Century Latin American Art Resources in Multimedia"

*Alvaro Risso,* Librería Linardi y Risso
"Narradores jóvenes de Uruguay en multimedia"

9:00-10:30 A.M. **Theme Panel III: "Bibliography: Access for the Library of the 21st Century"**

Moderator: *Luis Villar,* Dartmouth College
Rapporteur: *Víctor Torres*, Universidad de Puerto Rico

*Nelly González,* University of Illinois
"The Orthodox Method of Creation of the Gabriel García Márquez Bibliography, and Could It Be Done Electronically?

*Dolores Martin*, Library of Congress
"The Handbook of Latin American Studies Online"

*Luis M. Villar*, Dartmouth College
"Encoding Bibliographies for Machine-Readable Texts"

9:00-10:30 A.M. **Workshop I: "Digital Meets Analog: Electronic Resources and Print Publications"**

Moderator: *Joseph Holub*, University of Pennsylvania
Rapporteur: *Roma Arellano*, Latin America Data Base
Participants: *Peter T. Johnson,* Princeton University
*David Block*, Cornell University
*Dan Hazen*, Harvard University
*James Craig*, Micrographics, Inc.

10:30-11:00 A.M. Book Exhibit Coffee Break

11:00 A.M.-12:30 P.M. **Theme Panel IV: "New Resources and Access for Latin American Cinema and Video in the Second Centenary"**

Moderator: *Gayle Williams*, University of Georgia
Rapporteur: *Lynn Shirey*, Harvard University Law School

*Pedro Zurita*, Videoteca del Sur
"Videoteca del Sur: un modelo de distribución del mercado audiovisual latinoamericano"

*Karen Ranucci,* International Media Resource Exchange
"Making Connections: Using On-Line Databases to Link U.S. Educational Users to Latin American-Made Media Materials"

*Gayle Williams*, University of Georgia
"Latin American Cinema Resources on the Internet"

11:00 A.M.-12:30 P.M. **Theme Panel V: "Using the Web in Education and Library Services"**

Moderator: *Terry Peet*, Library of Congress
Rapporteur: *Tony A. Harvell*, University of San Diego

*Leila Maria Ferreira Salles*, Universidade Estadual Paulista
*Débora Mazza*, Universidade Estadual Paulista
"Communication Technologies and Education in Schools"

*Ketty Rodríguez*, Texas Woman's University
"Searching OCLC EPIC for Latin American Non-Print Materials"

*Barbara Stewart*, University of Massachusetts
"Latin American Web Sites for Catalogers and Technical Services"

*Filiberto F. Martínez Arellano*, State University of New York at Buffalo
"Internet Resources in Latin American Libraries"

12:30-2:00 P.M. Lunch Break

2:00-3:00 P.M. **Theme Panel VI: "Squatter Settlements Publications: Methods of Approach and Interpretation"**

Moderator: *Peter T. Johnson*, Princeton University
Rapporteur: *Sarah Landeryou*, University of Denver

*Robert Gay*, Connecticut College
"Brazilian Squatter Settlement Publications: Methods of Approach and Interpretation"

*Peter T. Johnson*, Princeton University
"Collecting and Organizing Brazilian Social Movement Ephemera"

2:00-3:00 P.M. **Presentation**

*Luis Villar*, Dartmouth College
"Electronic Scholarly Editing for the Library of the 21st Century"

2:00-3:00 P.M. **Workshop II: "Book and Serial Price Indexes"**

Rapporteur: *Cecilia Sercán*, Cornell University
*Dan Hazen*, Harvard University
*David Block*, Cornell University
*Scott Van Jacob*, University of Notre Dame

3:00-3:30 P.M. Book Exhibit Coffee Break

3:30-5:00 P.M. **Theme Panel VII: "The Virtual Library in Theory and Practice"**

Moderator: *David Block*, Cornell University
Rapporteur: *Marian Goslinga*, Florida International University

*Peter Graham*, Rutgers University
"Requirements for the Digital Research Library"

*Paul Conway*, Yale University
"The Open Book Project at Yale"

*Markus Obert*, Iberoamerikanisches Institut
"The Use of an Integrated Library System in the Iberoamerikanisches Institut and the Resumption of Cataloging Articles and Essays in Periodicals and Composite Works"

*David Magier,* Columbia University
"Digital Libraries: A View From the Third World"

3:30-5:00 P.M. **Theme Panel VIII: "Effective Bibliographic Instruction, Learning Theory, and Critical Thinking with Latin American Resources"**

Moderator: *Tony Harvell*, University of San Diego
Rapporteur: *Walter Brem*, University of California, Berkeley

*Norma Corral*, University of California, Los Angeles
"Latin American Studies BI: The Graduate Experience"

*Ree Dedonato*, Columbia University

*Theresa Maylone*, Long Island University
"Changing Times in Library Education: Conceptual and Theoretical Frameworks"

*Adán Griego*, University of California, Santa Barbara
"Latin American Studies BI: The Undergraduate Experience"

3:30-5:00 P.M. **Theme Panel IX: "The Impact of the Internet on Latin American Libraries and Scholarship"**

Moderator: *Ana-María Cobos*, Saddleback College
Rapporteur: *Rachel Barreto-Edensword*, Catholic University of America

*Eduardo Villanueva Mansilla*, Pontífica Universidad Católica del Perú
"Una aproximación al potencial de Internet como fuente de información desde América Latina"

*Jesús Lau*, Universidad Autónoma de Ciudad Juárez
"La divulgación del conocimiento en las universidades públicas mexicanas: la distribución de sus publicaciones"

*Saadia Sánchez Vegas*, Biblioteca Nacional de Venezuela
"Estrategias y políticas regionales de información y tecnología. América Latina en Internet: el futuro deseable"

5:30-8:30 P.M. Regional Latin American Cooperative Group Meetings:

LANE: Latin American Northeast Libraries Consortium
SALIFIA: California Cooperative Collection Development Group
LASER: Latin American Southeast Region

## Wednesday, June 5, 1996

9:00-10:30 A.M. **Theme Panel X: "Organizing, Protest, and Activism on the Web"**

Moderator: *Peter Stern*, Rutgers University
Rapporteur: *Sheila A. Milam*, University of Pittsburgh

*Douglas Chalmers*, Columbia University
"Rebuilding Civil Society Through the Net: Connecting NGO's Internationally"

*Molly Molloy*, New Mexico State University
"Internetworking as a Tool for Advocacy and Research: The Case of Chiapas News, 1994-Present"

*Sarah Landeryou*, University of Denver
"Providing Instruction on the Research Use of the Internet for Political Science and Human Rights Studies"

*Susan Shaw,* South Dakota State University
*Michele Reid*, South Dakota State Library
"Native Americans and Information Technology: Connection and Connectivity"

9:00-10:30 A.M. **Theme Panel XI: "Digitalization Projects in Latin American Research Materials"**

Moderator: *Scott Van Jacob,* University of Notre Dame
Rapporteur: *Nancy L. Hallock,* University of Pittsburgh

*Richard Phillips*, University of Florida
"Progress Report on the Digitization of Caribbean Newspapers Held at the University of Florida"

*Mark Grover*, Brigham Young University
"The ARL Latin Americanist Pilot Project and Cooperation: An Historical Perspective"

*Víctor Torres*, Universidad de Puerto Rico
"80 años de historia en imágenes: la digitización del periódico *El Mundo*"

*Scott Van Jacob,* University of Notre Dame
"Progress Report on the Digitization of Brazilian Government Documents"

10:30-11:30 A.M. **A Demo/Presentation by the Archivo General de Indias**

*Isabel Ceballos,* Jefe del Servicio de Descripción del Archivo de Indias, Seville
"El sistema informático del Archivo General de Indias: un ejemplo de informatización integral"

11:00 A.M.-12:30 P.M. **Theme Panel XII: "Media Trends: The Americas' Media in an Era of Globalization"**

Moderator: *Joseph Holub*, University of Pennsylvania
Rapporteur: *Susan H. Shaw*, South Dakota State University

*Silvio Waisbord*, Rutgers University
"Latin American Television and National Identities"

*Elizabeth Mahan*, University of Connecticut
"More Programs, Fewer Voices: Caribbean Television in the Global Era"

*William Solomon*, Rutgers University
"Press Coverage of Cuba: Divergent Views at Home and Abroad"

11:00 A.M.-12:30 P.M **Theme Panel XIII: "Widening the Net: Cooperative Approaches to Electronic Access"**

Moderator: *Deborah Jakubs*, Duke University
Rapporteur: *Sara M. Sánchez*, University of Miami

*Richard Ekman*, The Andrew W. Mellon Foundation
"Mellon Foundation Support for Expanded Access to Scholarly Resources in Latin American Studies"

*Hans Rütimann*, The Commission on Preservation and Access
"Initiatives of the Commission on Preservation and Access in Latin America"

*Deborah Jakubs*, Duke University
"The Latin Americanist Research Resources Library Project: The Challenges of a Distributed Model of Library Cooperation"

12:30-1:30 P.M. Lunch

1:30-2:15 P.M. Closing Session and Business Meeting of SALALM XLI

Rapporteur: Cecilia Sercán, Cornell University

2:30-4:00 P.M. Final Executive Board Meeting